The Fourth Synoptic Gospel

The Fourth Synoptic Gospel

John's Knowledge of Matthew, Mark, and Luke

Mark Goodacre

William B. Eerdmans Publishing Company
Grand Rapids, Michigan

Wm. B. Eerdmans Publishing Co.
2006 44th Street SE, Grand Rapids, MI 49508
www.eerdmans.com

© 2025 Mark Goodacre
All rights reserved
Published 2025
Printed in the United States of America

30 30 29 28 27 26 25   1 2 3 4 5 6 7

ISBN 978-0-8028-7513-6

Library of Congress Cataloging-in-Publication Data

Names: Goodacre, Mark S., author.
Title: The fourth synoptic gospel : John's knowledge of Matthew, Mark, and Luke / Mark Goodacre.
Description: Grand Rapids, Michigan : William B. Eerdmans Publishing Company, [2025] | Includes bibliographical references and index. | Summary: "The author argues that when John wrote his Gospel, he was familiar with and influenced by the Gospels of Matthew, Mark, and Luke"—Provided by publisher.
Identifiers: LCCN 2024053271 | ISBN 9780802875136 (paperback) | ISBN 9781467462716 (epub)
Subjects: LCSH: Bible. John—Criticism, interpretation, etc. | Bible. Gospels—Criticism, interpretation, etc. | Synoptic problem.
Classification: LCC BS2615.52 .G65 2025 | DDC 226.5/06—dc23/eng/20250610
LC record available at https://lccn.loc.gov/2024053271

For Lente

Contents

	Preface	ix
	List of Abbreviations	xii
1.	**First Impressions**	1
	"I Believe in Dodd"	2
	The Appeal of Oral Tradition	4
	Close Verbal Agreement	6
	How Much Agreement Should We Expect?	12
	Differences and Diagnostic Shards	14
	From Tradition to Gospel	17
2.	**When John Is Synoptic**	19
	The Gospels in Synopsis	20
	Parallel Orders	31
	"A Passion Narrative with an Extended Introduction"	36
	The Revelation of the Hidden Messiah	38
	What if John Is Synoptic?	43
3.	**John, from Mark, via Matthew and Luke**	45
	Matthean Redaction in John	46
	Lukan Redaction in John	56
	Oral Tradition or Literary Links?	71
4.	**John's Presupposition of Synoptic Narratives**	73
	Selectivity in the Synoptics	73
	Selectivity in John	74
	Presupposing Synoptic Narratives	76
	How Do We Know John Is Presupposing the Synoptic Gospels?	89
	Why Does It Matter?	91

CONTENTS

5.	**John's Dramatic Transformation of the Synoptics**	93
	From Synoptic Narration to Johannine Direct Speech	94
	Analogies from Matthew	98
	Analogies from the Protevangelium	100
	Altering Dramatis Personae	101
	Intertextual Dramatic Irony	102
	Dramatic Revision	104
	The Narrator's Presence in John	105
6.	**The Beloved Disciple for Readers of the Synoptics**	107
	One of the Twelve	108
	John Son of Zebedee	111
	Difficulties	113
	A Galilean Disciple	115
	From Readers of the Synoptics to the Authorship of John	131
7.	**John's Christological Transformation of the Synoptics**	134
	"The Messiah, the Son of God"	135
	Every Shared Title	137
	The "I Am" Sayings	140
	Why Synoptic Influence?	150
	"I Am"	152
	"The Father" and "the Son"	154
	The "Johannine Thunderbolt"	156
	Conclusion: The Fourth Gospel	161
	Works Cited	165
	Index of Authors	171
	Index of Subjects	173
	Index of Scripture and Other Ancient Texts	177

Preface

This book has a simple and straightforward thesis. It argues that the author of John's Gospel knew, used, presupposed, and transformed the Synoptics. The book began life as the Speaker's Lectures in Biblical Studies at the University of Oxford in May 2017, under the title "Did John Know the Synoptic Gospels?" The four lectures were early versions of chapters 1, 5, 6, and 7. I had already begun to develop the ideas featured here at the Martin Memorial Lectures, College of Emmanuel and Saint Chad, Saskatoon, in November 2016, and continued to work on them in the Carmichael-Walling Lectures, Abilene Christian University, in November 2017. I gave versions of chapters 6 and 7 at the E. J. and Amaretta Prevatte Biblical Studies Lecture Series, Campbell University Divinity School, in November 2023, and a version of chapter 2 as the Kennedy Wright Opening Lecture, at the University of Edinburgh School of Divinity, in September 2024. I am hugely grateful for these invitations and the wonderful and helpful feedback I received on each occasion.

I am also grateful to the members of the New Testament seminar in the Faculty of Divinity at the University of Cambridge, where I spoke in May 2020, giving a version of chapters 1 and 2, as well as in May 2024, where I gave a version of chapter 4. I am similarly grateful to the members of the New Testament seminar in the Faculty of Theology and Religion at the University of Oxford, where I gave an early version of chapter 3 in May 2020, and the University of Durham New Testament Seminar, in October 2021, where I gave a version of chapter 5. I also gave a lecture that summarized this book's thesis at ALT, the Akademi för Ledarskap och Teologi in Örebro, Sweden, in April 2024.

Although I would have finished this book several years ago if I had not been chair of the Department of Religious Studies at Duke University, I do want to thank my colleagues for their support and encouragement. I have also had the privilege of sharing several chapters of this book at our Graduate New Testament Seminar at Duke and in the Christianity in Antiquity (CIA) reading group at the University of North Carolina, Chapel Hill. I wish I had space to name the many friends and colleagues who have been so helpful. And it goes without saying that I could never have finished writing without the love and encouragement from my family and friends. They know who they are, and I hope they know how much they mean to me.

I mentioned above that this book began in a series of lectures, in 2017, at my alma mater, the University of Oxford, yet my interest in John's Gospel goes back much further than that. I took A-Level Religious Studies at Wulfric Comprehensive School in Burton-on-Trent in the 1980s. My mother, Janet Goodacre, was my teacher for the paper on John's Gospel, and my fascination with this gospel began there. She was an inspirational teacher, and I hope that this book offers some kind of inadequate and humble thank-you to her.

I wish that I were able to send a copy of this book to Ed Sanders and John Muddiman, both of whom were inspirational teachers and superb mentors when I was a student at the University of Oxford, and who died while I was writing this book. I wish, too, that I could send a copy to another beloved mentor from that time, John Ashton, who called me "his severest critic" in the preface to his *Understanding the Fourth Gospel*. I think he made the charge, which really amused him, because I was already, as a master's student, highly skeptical about reconstructing hypothetical sources and strongly in favor of John's knowledge of the Synoptics. John Ashton was a great teacher and friend, with an infectious intellectual curiosity. Even though he did not embrace questions of gospel relations, he was so encouraging that I know he would have loved to have heard my thoughts. I would never have imagined that I would end up writing a book on this topic, but as the years went by, I became ever more surprised that so many scholars thought John was independent of the Synoptics, and in the end, I could not resist the urge to write about it.

I like to joke that this book is the third part of a trilogy: *The Case Against Q* (2002) arguing that Luke knew Matthew and Mark, *Thomas and the Gospels* (2012) arguing that Thomas knew the Synoptics, and *The Fourth Synoptic Gospel* arguing that John also knew the Synoptics. What is common to all three is a skepticism about our ability, as scholars, to discover hypothetical sources, lost editions, and hidden layers, when that quest can lead us to miss extant sources that are right before our eyes.

I am so grateful to the fantastic team at Eerdmans, and especially to my editor, Trevor Thompson, whose patience and encouragement knows no bounds. I am afraid that I do not like to write long books, and to be frank, I can't say that I much like reading them either. I hope my readers will forgive me for avoiding the extended and dense footnoting that is now the norm in so much scholarly writing. This runs the risk of offending scholars whose works I have not acknowledged and of failing to show my working at every point, but I want this book to be as accessible as possible to students, as well as to those outside the academy who are interested in the topic. John has seven signs and seven "I am" sayings, and I have written seven chapters. I know that there are many other things that I could have said, but these are written to try to persuade you that John's Gospel knew and used the Synoptics, and that reflecting on this will provide new life for the discussion.

Abbreviations

Ant.	Josephus, *Jewish Antiquities*
BETL	Bibliotheca Ephemeridum Theologicarum Lovaniensium
BNTC	Black's New Testament Commentaries
CBQ	*Catholic Biblical Quarterly*
Epigr.	Theocritus, *Epigrams*
ETL	*Ephemerides Theologicae Lovanienses*
ExpTim	*Expository Times*
Gos. Pet.	Gospel of Peter
Gos. Phil.	Gospel of Philip
Gos. Thom.	Gospel of Thomas
ISBE	*International Standard Bible Encyclopedia.* Edited by Geoffrey W. Bromiley. 4 vols. Grand Rapids: Eerdmans, 1979–1988
JBL	*Journal of Biblical Literature*
JSHJ	*Journal for the Study of the Historical Jesus*
JSNT	*Journal for the Study of the New Testament*
JSNTSup	Journal for the Study of the New Testament Supplement Series
JTC	*Journal for Theology and the Church*
KJV	King James Version
LNTS	The Library of New Testament Studies
NAC	New American Commentary
NASB	New American Standard Bible
NET	New English Translation
NICNT	New International Commentary on the New Testament
NRSVue	New Revised Standard Version updated edition
NTS	*New Testament Studies*
NTTS	New Testament Tools and Studies
PCNT	Paideia Commentaries on the New Testament

Abbreviations

Prot. Jas.	Protevangelium of James
RB	*Revue biblique*
SBS	Stuttgarter Bibelstudien
SNTSMS	Society for New Testament Studies Monograph Series
SPNT	Studies on Personalities of the New Testament
SymS	Symposium Series
TLG	Thesaurus Linguae Graecae
WUNT	Wissenschaftliche Untersuchungen zum Neuen Testament

Numbers in the format 0/0/0/0+0 indicate the number of occurrences in Matthew/Mark/Luke/John+Acts.

An *R* after a reference indicates redactional modification, by Matthew or Luke, to Mark.

Chapter 1

First Impressions

The idea that the author of John's Gospel knew and used the Synoptics has an impressive historical pedigree. For most of Christian history, it has been the default position, from Clement to Calvin, continuing with the dawn of critical scholarship on the New Testament in the modern period. The view was still so widespread in the middle of the twentieth century that those arguing for John's independence saw themselves as swimming against the tide. Yet by the second half of the twentieth century, an alternative view had become popular. The idea that John was independent of the Synoptics was so successful that it almost achieved the status of a consensus.[1] What happened? Why did scholars fall out of love with an idea that was so widespread for so long?

There are several interlocking causes and contexts. The popularity of the two-source theory provided an essential backdrop. This theory, according to which Matthew and Luke used Mark and a hypothetical source Q independently of one another, was the primary operating model for exegesis of the Synoptic Gospels. If two literary works as similar in structure, content, and vocabulary as Matthew and Luke were independent of one another, how could John, with all its differences, have known either of them, or Mark? At the same time, scholars were studying the recently rediscovered Gospel of Thomas, and the view was

---

1. It is commonly claimed that a new consensus emerged in the second half of the twentieth century. See, e.g., Gail R. O'Day, "The Johannine Literature," in *The New Testament Today*, ed. Mark Allan Powell (Louisville: Westminster John Knox, 1999), 72–73. But the view can only be sustained by ignoring major players like C. K. Barrett, *The Gospel According to St. John: An Introduction with Commentary and Notes on the Greek Text*, 2nd ed. (Philadelphia: Westminster, 1978), W. G. Kümmel, *Introduction to the New Testament*, rev. ed. (Nashville: Abingdon, 1975), 200–204, and Frans Neirynck's multiple articles on the topic. A useful beginning point for the latter and for others in the Leuven school is found in A. Denaux, ed., *John and the Synoptics*, BETL 101 (Leuven: Peeters, 1992).

taking hold that Thomas was also independent of the Synoptics. Like Thomas, an independent John offered another route back to Jesus, at a moment when the quest for the historical Jesus was getting some new life. For many, the default position for the majority of extant early Christian works was independence—Luke was independent of Matthew, Q was independent of Mark, John was independent of the Synoptics, and Thomas was independent of everything.

"I Believe in Dodd"

The historical utility of this model was compounded by its theological value, and nothing is more important here than "realized eschatology," which used to be present everywhere. Under the influence of C. H. Dodd, the idea of the future as a reality in the here and now, the idea that Jesus had announced the arrival of the kingdom of God, became mainstream. Realized eschatology was not some narrowly Johannine, late development away from the primitive, futuristic eschatology of the historical Jesus, Paul, the first Christians, and the Synoptic evangelists. It was embedded in the tradition at every level. If the Synoptic parables might sometimes appear to have a futuristic eschatology, stripping away later, allegorical embellishments will reveal the underlying realized eschatology of Jesus's one-point parables. If Paul at first appears to have a naive eschatology of resurrection of the body, in which believers will one day meet Jesus in the air, the apostle's mind matures to the point where he imagines a simple transition to being with Christ.

Dodd's influence was felt not just in his academic homes at the Universities of Oxford, Cambridge, and Manchester but more broadly in English-speaking scholarship as a whole.[2] Moreover, his program was endorsed and developed in German-speaking scholarship by Joachim Jeremias, whose books on the parables of Jesus became hugely popular.[3] Although Jeremias attempted to nuance Dodd's view by speaking about eschatology "in a process of realization" and thus retaining the futuristic element that Dodd himself supported, the theology was the same. The earliest Christians did not believe in some kind of primitive,

---

2. See George B. Caird, "Charles Harold Dodd, 1884–1973," *Proceedings of the British Academy* 60 (1974): 497–510, for an appreciation. Caird's article gives a sense of the extent to which realized eschatology had become the default: "Like Columbus's Egg, realized eschatology is a discovery which is blindingly self-evident once someone has pointed it out" (501).

3. See especially Joachim Jeremias, *The Parables of Jesus*, rev. ed., trans. S. H. Hooke (London: SCM, 1963).

apocalyptic, dawning end of the world. They believed that the kingdom of God was already here.

Dodd's program was so successful that for many years it pervaded churches and schools all over Britain. C. H. Dodd was at the helm of the translation committee of the New English Bible, and generations of students and churchgoers heard at Mark 1:15, "The time *has come*; the kingdom of God *is upon you*." Although now almost entirely replaced by other translations that have had a greater pedigree, it is worth remembering that the New English Bible, first published in 1961, was for a generation hugely popular.[4]

The lynchpin of Dodd's project was the witness provided by John's Gospel. In some respects, John gave Dodd less work to do because no one, then or now, seriously denies the importance of realized eschatology as a major facet of John's theology. After all, the single most famous biblical verse, John 3:16, encapsulates it: "For God so loved the world that he gave his only Son so that everyone who believes in him will not die but have eternal life." There is no death for those who believe in God's Son. For them, eternal life is a present reality. "Whoever keeps my word will never taste death" (8:52). "I came that they may have life, and have it abundantly" (10:10). The examples could be multiplied.

There was, however, an obvious problem. While realized eschatology is undisputed in John, it could easily be argued—indeed often was argued—that this was a product of a developed Johannine theology, not in any way a witness to the earliest Christian tradition, let alone the historical Jesus. For Dodd, this was to underestimate the presence of historical tradition in John. First in *The Interpretation of the Fourth Gospel* and subsequently and more fully in *Historical Tradition in the Fourth Gospel*,[5] the scholar nicknamed "fifty bob Dodd" made a highly influential case for a historical nucleus in John's tradition, and not just narrative nuggets like the pool of Siloam or Solomon's portico but also Jesus's teaching.[6] John's eschatology was in continuity and not contrast with the beginnings of Christianity.

---

4. *The New English Bible: New Testament* (Oxford: Oxford University Press; Cambridge: Cambridge University Press, 1961).

5. C. H. Dodd, *The Interpretation of the Fourth Gospel* (Cambridge: Cambridge University Press, 1953). Note especially the appendix, "Some Considerations upon the Historical Aspect of the Fourth Gospel," 444–54; C. H. Dodd, *Historical Tradition in the Fourth Gospel* (Cambridge: Cambridge University Press, 1963).

6. G. L. Borchert, *John 1–11*, NAC 25A (Nashville: Broadman & Holman, 1996), 40, reports this oral tradition (but without a source). The name refers to the high price of Dodd's *Interpretation of the Fourth Gospel*. "Fifty bob" is fifty shillings, the equivalent of £2.50 in decimal currency. The first edition retailed at $8.00 in the United States in 1953.

CHAPTER 1

Although it is difficult to overestimate Dodd's influence, it is important not to misrepresent him. He was a gifted historian and exegete, and his work is a long way from apologetics. He recognized the extent of Johannine creativity and the contribution made by the imagination of the evangelist, and he thought of John "as being in its essential character a theological work, rather than history."[7] Nor did he ignore or sideline the futuristic elements in John's eschatology, noting that "the evangelist's own formula is ἔρχεται ὥρα καὶ νῦν ἐστιν" (referencing John 4:23; 5:25, "The hour is coming, and now is"; cf. 16:32, ἔρχεται ὥρα καὶ ἐλήλυθεν).[8] But his essential point was to balance Johannine creativity with the historical gold nuggets the evangelist was recasting in his own language. As an illustration, he concludes his discussion of future predictions in the following way: "In a word, I suggest that John is here reaching back to a very early form of tradition indeed, and making it the point of departure for his profound theological reinterpretation; and further, that the oracular sayings which he reports have good claim to represent authentically, in substance if not verbally, what Jesus actually said to his disciples—a better claim than the more elaborate and detailed predictions which the Synoptics offer."[9]

This means that for Dodd, understanding early Christian eschatology was a matter of appreciating the independence of John from the Synoptics, so that both the Synoptics and John could be seen as independently deriving from the similar early oral traditions. Although this became a common view in subsequent decades, and well beyond Dodd's death in 1973, it was at the time an unusual view. The tide was beginning to turn by the time he wrote *Historical Tradition* in 1963,[10] but his earlier work represents John's use of the Synoptics "almost as a dogma" held by "a majority of critics, for many years past."[11]

The Appeal of Oral Tradition

If Dodd is the person most responsible for this turning of the tide,[12] he is not the one usually credited with the first move against it. That honor goes to Percival Gardner-Smith, whose little book *Saint John and the Synoptics* argued

---

7. Dodd, *Interpretation*, 444.
8. Dodd, *Interpretation*, 7.
9. Dodd, *Historical Tradition*, 420.
10. "Recently there has been a certain trend away from this position" (Dodd, *Historical Tradition*, 8).
11. Dodd, *Interpretation*, 449.
12. See, e.g., D. Moody Smith, *John Among the Gospels*, 2nd ed. (Columbia: University of South Carolina Press, 2001), 53: "During the middle decades of the twentieth century,

that the Synoptic-John parallels are all better explained on the grounds of mutual dependence on oral tradition.[13] Gardner-Smith's book was influential, but it is weaker than Dodd's. It often begs the question, and it is full of sweeping statements and questionable judgments. Nevertheless, the fundamental explanation for similarities between the Synoptics and John is the same. Any kind of literary link is ruled out, and mutual dependence on oral traditions is the default position.

What Gardner-Smith and Dodd have in common, as well as Jesus College, Cambridge, where Gardner-Smith was dean and Dodd a fellow, is a reliance on oral tradition as the major factor in understanding the relationship between John and the Synoptics (or the lack of it). They were both writing in the heyday of form criticism, and oral tradition was all the rage. "It is now widely recognized," Dodd says in 1953, "that the main factor in perpetuating and propagating the Christian faith and the Gospel story was oral tradition in its various forms."[14]

The strength of the appeal to oral tradition is that it has the potential to explain every parallel at the same time as providing independent witnesses to the earliest Christian tradition and the historical Jesus. The similarities between John and the Synoptics are attributed to common traditions, and the differences diagnose literary independence. Since oral traditions are by their nature lost, except insofar as they are crystallized in texts, there is an innate plausibility in appealing to them. It is not like appealing to lost literary sources like Q or the signs source. And agnosticism about sources allows interpreters a certain freedom in their analysis and exegesis, as well as the opportunity to rescind from the kind of work that many scholars find tedious and best relegated to the introductory lectures.

There is a warning, though, in the imagery that scholars use when they appeal to oral tradition. It is a reservoir, a pool, a lake, or a river. It has channels and tributaries. It can be a stream or a living spring. This water imagery is endemic, and it has been used for decades. The imagery reveals a certain vagueness in what is being imagined. It is infinitely flexible. It is literally fluid. As a sole explanatory factor, then, it is allowed great malleability. There is nothing tangible, and the appeal of the lack of tangibility is the freedom it gives to the interpreter—unseen sources provide apparently untold explanatory power.

---

there was no more dominant and influential figure among English-speaking New Testament scholars than Dodd."

13. P. Gardner-Smith, *St. John and the Synoptic Gospels* (Cambridge: Cambridge University Press, 1938).

14. Dodd, *Interpretation*, 449.

CHAPTER 1

Given the faith that so many place in the explanatory power of oral tradition, however, it is worth remembering that on the two occasions when gospel authors mention specific oral traditions, it is to debunk them. In Matt 28:11–15, the evangelist tells his readers of a "story" about Jesus's resurrection that "has been widely circulated among the Judeans to this day," but which is false. The chief priests and the elders pay the soldiers to circulate a false story about the disciples having stolen Jesus's body. And John's Gospel itself ends with the story of a popular oral tradition, the report that the Beloved Disciple would not die, which the evangelist is keen to dispel. He knows the rumor "that this disciple would not die," but he contradicts it by explaining what Jesus actually said (John 21:22–23).

These stories do not, of course, mean that all oral tradition, and all appeals to oral tradition, should be considered problematic, but they are a reminder that even the ancients could treat oral tradition with caution. There is no difficulty in principle with including oral tradition in discussions of gospel interrelations, but the use of it as a default position at every step can mask evidence of literary links. The problem with the appeal to oral tradition is not what it affirms but what it denies. Of course, oral traditions were influential—it is difficult to imagine life without storytelling and the sharing of traditions. Any view of the origins of John must surely take this seriously. But the elevation of oral tradition as the sole means of explanation for John's links with the Synoptics, and so to question the influence of one gospel upon another, is unfortunate and unnecessary. We will make better sense of John if we return to the traditional view that John knew and used the Synoptic Gospels, and it is this thesis that is defended in this book.

CLOSE VERBAL AGREEMENT

For Gardner-Smith, and others influenced by his novel thesis, the reason for rejecting John's knowledge of the Synoptics is very simple: the agreements between John and the Synoptics are just not close enough. The differences are too great. In contrast to the close parallels between Matthew, Mark, and Luke, and their frequent close verbal agreement, John's parallels are more distant, and the verbal agreement very limited. But how true is this? Given the number of scholars who still affirm John's independence of the Synoptics, it is surprising to see how many close parallels there are. Let us take a look at a small sample, ahead of a fuller analysis in chapters 2 and 3. First, there is a striking agreement between Mark and John in their stories of a paralyzed man being healed (Mark 2:1–12; John 5:1–15):

MARK 2:9–12	JOHN 5:8–9
τί ἐστιν εὐκοπώτερον, εἰπεῖν τῷ παραλυ-τικῷ· Ἀφίενταί σου αἱ ἁμαρτίαι, ἢ εἰπεῖν· <u>Ἔγειρε</u> καὶ <u>ἆρον τὸν κράβαττόν σου καὶ περιπάτει</u>; ἵνα δὲ εἰδῆτε ὅτι ἐξουσίαν ἔχει ὁ υἱὸς τοῦ ἀνθρώπου ἐπὶ τῆς γῆς ἀφιέναι ἁμαρτίας <u>λέγει</u> τῷ παραλυτικῷ, Σοὶ λέγω, <u>ἔγειρε ἆρον τὸν κράβαττόν σου καὶ</u> ὕπαγε εἰς τὸν οἶκόν σου. καὶ ἠγέρθη <u>καὶ εὐθὺς</u> <u>ἄρας τὸν κράβαττον</u> ἐξῆλθεν ἔμπροσθεν πάντων.	<u>λέγει</u> αὐτῷ ὁ Ἰησοῦς· <u>Ἔγειρε ἆρον τὸν κράβαττόν σου καὶ περιπάτει.</u> <u>καὶ εὐθέως</u> ἐγένετο ὑγιὴς ὁ ἄνθρωπος καὶ ἦρε <u>τὸν κράβαττον</u> αὐτοῦ <u>καὶ περιεπάτει.</u>
"What is easier, to say to the paralyzed man, 'Your sins are forgiven,' or to say, '<u>Arise</u> and <u>take your pallet and walk</u>'? But in order that you might know that the Son of Man has authority upon the earth to forgive sins," he <u>says</u> to the paralyzed man, "I say to you, <u>Arise, take your pallet and</u> return to your home." <u>And immediately,</u> he <u>took his pallet</u>, and went out in front of them all.	Jesus <u>says</u> to him, <u>Arise, take your pallet and walk.</u> <u>And immediately</u>, the man became well and <u>took his pallet and</u> walked.[15]

The agreement between Mark and John here is worth noting. Seven of John's eleven words in verse 8 are found in Mark, six of them in a verbatim string, ἔγειρε ἆρον τὸν κράβαττόν σου καὶ . . . ("Arise, take your pallet and . . ."). John's use of περιπάτει ("walk"), paralleled in Mark 2:9, is appropriate in John because the man has been by the pool for thirty-eight years (John 5:5), so he can hardly be asked to return to his home (Mark 2:10). B. H. Streeter saw the use of the "out of the way phrase" τὸν κράβαττόν σου ("your pallet") as a strong indication that John was showing his knowledge of Mark here.[16] The fact that both Matthew and Luke lack the word in their parallels (Matt 9:1–8 // Luke 5:17–26) illustrates the point.

15. English translations here are mine.
16. B. H. Streeter, *The Four Gospels: A Study of Origins* (London: Macmillan, 1924), 397–98.

The difficulty, however, with examples like this is that the contexts in Mark and John are quite different. Mark's story is about a paralyzed man in Galilee who is let down through the roof of a house where Jesus is teaching, and John's story is about a paralyzed man in Judea who sits by the pool of Bethzatha. The striking parallel therefore gets overlooked given the different narrative context, and for those who think John did not know the Synoptics, the differences always receive more attention than the similarities. The differences effectively neutralize the striking similarities. Let us therefore take a look at an example where close agreement between Mark and John occurs in the same narrative context, the walking on the sea:[17]

MARK 6:50	JOHN 6:20
ὁ δὲ εὐθὺς ἐλάλησεν μετ' αὐτῶν, καὶ **λέγει αὐτοῖς**· Θαρσεῖτε, **ἐγώ εἰμι, μὴ φοβεῖσθε**.	ὁ δὲ **λέγει αὐτοῖς**· **ἐγώ εἰμι**· **μὴ φοβεῖσθε**.
But immediately he spoke with them, and **he says to them**: "Take heart, **I am, do not fear**!"	But **he says to them**: "**I am, do not fear**!"

Here, all of John's words are found in the Markan parallel. Moreover, John never elsewhere has this construction, ὁ δὲ + λέγει + αὐτοῖς ("but he is saying to them"), while it is at home in Mark (6:38; 6:50; 9:19; 10:24; cf. twice in Matthew—17:20 and 21:16; the figures are 2/4/0/1).[18] We will return to this passage below in chapter 7.

Examples like this recur in John. At the Last Supper, Jesus's solemn charge about the forthcoming betrayal features a nine-word verbatim string with both Mark and Matthew:

---

17. This passage is absent from Luke, and the wording is slightly different in Matt 14:22–33. English translations here are mine.

18. Numbers in this format, which will be used throughout this book, mean the number of occurrences in Matthew/Mark/Luke/John. Where there is a figure for Acts, too, that is added at the end, +0.

First Impressions

MATT 26:21	MARK 14:18	JOHN 13:21
καὶ ἐσθιόντων αὐτῶν εἶπεν· Ἀμὴν λέγω ὑμῖν ὅτι εἷς ἐξ ὑμῶν παραδώσει με.	καὶ ἀνακειμένων αὐτῶν καὶ ἐσθιόντων ὁ Ἰησοῦς εἶπεν· Ἀμὴν λέγω ὑμῖν ὅτι εἷς ἐξ ὑμῶν παραδώσει με ὁ ἐσθίων μετ' ἐμοῦ.	Ταῦτα εἰπὼν ὁ Ἰησοῦς ἐταράχθη τῷ πνεύματι καὶ ἐμαρτύρησεν καὶ εἶπεν· Ἀμὴν ἀμὴν λέγω ὑμῖν ὅτι εἷς ἐξ ὑμῶν παραδώσει με.
and while they were eating, he said, "Amen I say to you, one of you will betray me."	And when they had taken their places and were eating, Jesus said, "Amen I say to you, one of you will betray me, one who is eating with me."	After saying this Jesus was troubled in spirit, and said, "Amen, amen I say to you, one of you will betray me."[19]

This kind of agreement is telling. The words are in a specific narrative context, and only make sense in that context, in which Jesus is prophesying Judas's betrayal. This is not the kind of free-floating aphorism that could have been memorized in oral tradition. It requires this specific literary context for it to make sense. In other words, it is easier to imagine an early Christian sharing with another early Christian, "Love your enemies, and pray for your persecutors," or "Ask, and you will receive; knock, and the door will be opened to you," than it is to imagine someone saying, "Amen I say to you, one of you will betray me."

These three examples all feature Mark and John as common denominators, and these kinds of agreements are why some scholars see a literary link between these two gospels.[20] It would be a mistake, though, to think that all the best examples feature Mark. Sometimes, even in material that Mark and John share, Matthew or Luke will be closer to John. One example from Matthew is the soldiers giving Jesus the crown of thorns:

---

19. English translations here are mine.
20. See, e.g., Eve-Marie Becker, Helen Bond, and Catrin Williams, eds., *John's Transformation of Mark* (London: T&T Clark, 2021).

CHAPTER 1

MATT 27:28–29	MARK 15:17–18	JOHN 19:2–3
καὶ ἐκδύσαντες <u>αὐτὸν</u> χλαμύδα κοκκίνην περιέθηκαν αὐτῷ, καὶ <u>πλέξαντες στέφανον ἐξ ἀκανθῶν ἐπέθηκαν</u> ἐπὶ <u>τῆς κεφαλῆς αὐτοῦ</u> <u>καὶ</u> κάλαμον ἐν τῇ δεξιᾷ αὐτοῦ, καὶ γονυπετήσαντες ἔμπροσθεν αὐτοῦ ἐνέπαιξαν αὐτῷ λέγοντες· <u>Χαῖρε,</u> <u>βασιλεῦ τῶν Ἰουδαίων.</u>	καὶ ἐνδιδύσκουσιν <u>αὐτὸν</u> <u>πορφύραν</u> καὶ περιτιθέασιν αὐτῷ πλέξαντες ἀκάνθινον στέφανον· καὶ ἤρξαντο ἀσπάζεσθαι αὐτόν· <u>Χαῖρε,</u> <u>βασιλεῦ τῶν Ἰουδαίων·</u>	<u>πλέξαντες στέφανον ἐξ ἀκανθῶν ἐπέθηκαν</u> αὐτοῦ <u>τῇ κεφαλῇ</u>, <u>καὶ</u> ἱμάτιον <u>πορφυροῦν</u> περιέβαλον <u>αὐτόν</u>, καὶ ἤρχοντο πρὸς αὐτὸν καὶ ἔλεγον· <u>Χαῖρε,</u> ὁ <u>βασιλεὺς τῶν Ἰουδαίων·</u>
And they stripped <u>him</u> and put a scarlet robe on him. And <u>when they had twisted a crown from thorns, they placed it on</u> <u>his head</u>, and a reed in his right hand, and they bowed the knee before him, mocking him saying, "<u>Hail, King of the Judeans!</u>"	And they clothed <u>him</u> in a <u>purple cloak</u>, and when they had twisted some thorns into a crown, they put it on him. And they began saluting him, "<u>Hail, King of the Judeans!</u>"	<u>When they had twisted a crown from thorns, they placed it on his head</u>, and they clothed <u>him</u> in a <u>purple cloak</u>, and they came to him and said, "<u>Hail, the King of the Judeans!</u>"[21]

The wording is close, and this is a clear case of Matthew rewriting Mark in subtle ways. There is no new traditional material here, and most commentators would have no trouble simply attributing it to Matthew's redaction. It is just standard Matthean recasting in his own words, yet the Matthean rewording finds its way into John. We will look at several similar examples in chapter 3 below.

John also has close verbal parallels with Luke, one of the most striking of which is in the resurrection story, in a passage unique to the two:

---

21. The English translations here are mine.

First Impressions

LUKE 24:36, 40–41	JOHN 20:19–20
Ταῦτα δὲ αὐτῶν λαλούντων αὐτὸς ἔστη ἐν μέσῳ αὐτῶν καὶ λέγει αὐτοῖς· εἰρήνη ὑμῖν. ... καὶ τοῦτο εἰπὼν ἔδειξεν αὐτοῖς τὰς χεῖρας καὶ τοὺς πόδας. ἔτι δὲ ἀπιστούντων αὐτῶν ἀπὸ τῆς χαρᾶς καὶ θαυμαζόντων. ...	Οὔσης οὖν ὀψίας τῇ ἡμέρᾳ ἐκείνῃ τῇ μιᾷ σαββάτων, καὶ τῶν θυρῶν κεκλεισμένων ὅπου ἦσαν οἱ μαθηταὶ διὰ τὸν φόβον τῶν Ἰουδαίων, ἦλθεν ὁ Ἰησοῦς καὶ ἔστη εἰς τὸ μέσον, καὶ λέγει αὐτοῖς· Εἰρήνη ὑμῖν. καὶ τοῦτο εἰπὼν ἔδειξεν τὰς χεῖρας καὶ τὴν πλευρὰν αὐτοῖς. ἐχάρησαν οὖν οἱ μαθηταὶ ἰδόντες τὸν κύριον.
While they were talking about this, he[22] himself <u>stood among them and he says</u>[23] <u>to them,</u> "Peace be with you." ... And when he had said this, he showed them his hands and his feet. Yet for all their joy they were still disbelieving and wondering. ...	When it was evening on that day, the first day of the week, and the doors were locked where the disciples were, for fear of the Judeans,[24] Jesus came and <u>stood among them and he says to them,</u>[25] "Peace be with you." And when he had said this,[26] he showed them his hands and his side. Then the disciples rejoiced when they saw the Lord.

The links here between Luke and John are close. The sequence is the same—Jesus arrives and stands among them, he greets them in the same way, he shows them his body, and the disciples have joy; and it is narrated in similar language. We will take a look at a number of other Johannine parallels with Luke later in the book and will argue that the direction of influence goes from Luke to John, and not the other way round.

---

22. NRSVue, "Jesus."
23. NRSVue, "said," also in John.
24. NRSVue, "Jews."
25. NRSVue omits "to them," thus obscuring the parallel with Luke.
26. NRSVue, "After he said this," obscuring the parallel with Luke.

CHAPTER 1

How Much Agreement Should We Expect?

There is, however, a difficulty with discussions like this. How much agreement between similar works should we expect? Some scholars will put the bar higher than others. Part of the problem is that we are spoiled by the Synoptic Gospels themselves. The extraordinarily high degree of verbatim agreement between the Synoptics is actually very unusual in antiquity, when the norm was to paraphrase and to rewrite one's source material. Even though this fact is widely known, we still tend to read canonically, in the order in which the Gospels appear in the New Testament, and to read canonically is to read synoptically and to assume that the high degree of verbatim agreement we see between these three is normative.

There are, though, ways of testing how much verbatim agreement we ought to expect from John. In 1954, Charles Goodwin drew the analogy between John's use of the Old Testament and John's use of the Synoptics.[27] The advantage of this kind of study is obvious: no one doubts that John knew and used the Old Testament, and the gospel is explicit about it, mentioning Moses and Isaiah by name and frequently drawing attention to "what is written." Goodwin noted that unlike the Synoptics, John quotes freely and allusively. There are places where John has verbatim parallels with the Septuagint, and Goodwin drew attention to four—John 2:4 (1 Kgs 17:18), John 10:34 (Ps 82:6), John 12:38 (Isa 53:1), and John 19:24 (Ps 22:19)—but none of these are at all lengthy. In the first two examples, we are looking at only four words; in the second two, twelve.[28] The vast majority of John's scriptural quotations are loose, inexact, and at best paraphrasing the source material. On one occasion, John 7:37–38, it is difficult to work out what is even being quoted. In spite of the fact that Jesus says, "As the scripture has said . . ." (καθὼς εἶπεν ἡ γραφή . . . [7:38]), we can only guess at what the source is.[29] If John's Old Testament quotations are so free, Goodwin argued, it would be surprising if his rewriting of Synoptic materials conformed to a more rigid pattern.

There is another way of determining what degree of verbal agreement we should expect if John knew the Synoptics, one that is not normally noticed, a phenomenon that might be called "internal quotation variation."[30] The gospel is full of

---

27. Charles Goodwin, "How Did John Treat His Sources?," *JBL* 73 (1954): 61–75.
28. Goodwin, "How Did," 62.
29. Goodwin, "How Did," 72–73. For a thorough investigation of John's use of the Hebrew Bible, see Alicia D. Myers and Bruce G. Schuchard, eds., *Abiding Words: The Use of Scripture in the Gospel of John* (Atlanta: SBL Press, 2015), and the works cited there.
30. After writing this chapter in 2017, I was delighted to discover Jeffrey Tripp, *Direct Internal Quotation in the Gospel of John*, WUNT 493 (Tübingen: Mohr Siebeck, 2019), which has a detailed discussion of this phenomenon, though not to make the point that I am making here. See also Wendy E. S. North, *What John Knew and What John Wrote: A Study in John and*

self-quotations, self-quotations that show such variation that they should perhaps instead be called self-paraphrases. The point can be illustrated with a famous Johannine text, Jesus's conversation with Nicodemus about being born again:

> John 3:3: Ἀμὴν ἀμὴν λέγω σοι, ἐὰν μή τις <u>γεννηθῇ ἄνωθεν</u>, οὐ δύναται ἰδεῖν τὴν βασιλείαν τοῦ θεοῦ.
>
> John 3:7: μὴ θαυμάσῃς ὅτι εἶπόν σοι Δεῖ ὑμᾶς <u>γεννηθῆναι ἄνωθεν</u>.
>
> John 3:3: "Amen, amen, I say to you, unless someone is <u>born from above</u>, they are not able to see the kingdom of God."
>
> John 3:7: "Do not wonder that I said to you, 'It is necessary to be <u>born from above</u>.'"

When Jesus quotes himself, only moments after he has made the initial comment, he rewords what he just said. Only the words "born from above" are the same (γεννηθῇ/γεννηθῆναι ἄνωθεν). Another famous Johannine text features a similar self-paraphrase:

> John 8:31–33: Ἔλεγεν οὖν ὁ Ἰησοῦς πρὸς τοὺς πεπιστευκότας αὐτῷ Ἰουδαίους· Ἐὰν ὑμεῖς μείνητε ἐν τῷ λόγῳ τῷ ἐμῷ, ἀληθῶς μαθηταί μού ἐστε, <u>καὶ γνώσεσθε τὴν ἀλήθειαν, καὶ ἡ ἀλήθεια ἐλευθερώσει ὑμᾶς</u>. ἀπεκρίθησαν πρὸς αὐτόν· Σπέρμα Ἀβραάμ ἐσμεν καὶ οὐδενὶ δεδουλεύκαμεν πώποτε· πῶς σὺ λέγεις ὅτι <u>Ἐλεύθεροι γενήσεσθε</u>;
>
> John 8:31–33: Then Jesus said to the Judeans who had believed in him, "If you continue in my word, you are truly my disciples; <u>and you will know the truth, and the truth will make you free</u>." They answered him, "We are descendants of Abraham and have never been slaves to anyone. What do you mean by saying, '<u>You will be made free</u>'?"

A nine-word phrase has been rephrased into just two words, now with no reference to knowledge of the truth. Perhaps the most striking example of the phenomenon is in the conversation between Jesus and the Judeans in John 10:31–39, where Jesus says the following:

> John 10:36: ὑμεῖς λέγετε ὅτι <u>Βλασφημεῖς</u>, ὅτι εἶπον· <u>Υἱὸς τοῦ θεοῦ εἰμι</u>;
>
> John 10:36 "You are saying, '<u>You blaspheme</u>' because I said, '<u>I am the Son of God</u>.'"

---

the Synoptics (Lanham: Lexington, 2020), for a nuanced argument that observing John's use of his own material provides clues for how John used the Synoptics.

CHAPTER 1

But in fact they do not say, "You are blaspheming"; they say, "It is not for a good work that we are going to stone you, but for blasphemy" (10:33, Περὶ καλοῦ ἔργου οὐ λιθάζομέν σε ἀλλὰ περὶ βλασφημίας). And Jesus does not say, "I am the Son of God" but rather "I and the Father are one" (10:30, ἐγὼ καὶ ὁ πατὴρ ἕν ἐσμεν). The word "Son" is not even in the chapter.

There are many examples of the same phenomenon.[31] On one occasion, 14:28, ἠκούσατε ὅτι ἐγὼ εἶπον ὑμῖν· Ὑπάγω καὶ ἔρχομαι πρὸς ὑμᾶς ("You heard me say to you, 'I am going away, and I am coming to you'"), it is impossible to be sure when the disciples heard this. Is it 14:12, "Amen, amen, I say to you, the one who believes in me will also do the works that I do and, in fact, will do greater works than these, because I am going to the Father"? Perhaps, but it is hardly a direct quotation. Given the variation in John's internal quotations, it would hardly be surprising if his use of the Synoptics showed similar variation.

Differences and Diagnostic Shards

In spite of what we know about compositional conventions in antiquity and about the way that John's Gospel uses the Old Testament and even Jesus's voice, the independence model has a certain explanatory advantage. If John did not know the Synoptics, we have no access to his source material outside of the Old Testament. The model is able to explain everything because the oral tradition cannot be heard, and it is lost forever. Anything can be projected on to it. So when John agrees with Mark in speaking about "costly perfume made of pure nard" (Mark 14:3, ἀλάβαστρον μύρου νάρδου πιστικῆς πολυτελοῦς; John 12:3, λίτραν μύρου νάρδου πιστικῆς πολυτίμου), Leon Morris says that this is just the kind of "unusual expression" that "might well stick in the mind and be preserved in more than one line of oral tradition."[32] In other words, the rare and unusual expression is not allowed as evidence of a literary connection; it is a sign of oral tradition. So agreement between John and the Synoptics points to oral tradition, and absence of agreement points to oral tradition.

There is an important question of method here. The argument for John's independence leans heavily on the fact that there are many differences between the Synoptics and John. It was the repeated argument in Gardner-Smith's work.

31. John 1:15 // 1:30; 1:20 // 3:28 (etc.); 4:17–18 // 4:29 // 4:39; 4:50 // 4:53; 6:35 // 6:41 (etc.); 6:44 // 6:65; 8:51 // 8:52; 9:7 // 9:11; 9:21 // 9:23; 9:40 // 9:41; 13:10 // 13:11; 14:12? // 14:28; 16:14 // 16:15; 16:16–18 (etc.); 13:25 // 21:20.

32. Leon Morris, *The Gospel According to John*, rev. ed., NICNT (Grand Rapids: Eerdmans, 1995), 45.

First Impressions

He simply could not imagine that John could disagree so profoundly and so frequently with the Synoptics if he had known them. In more recent scholarship, Paul Anderson has argued that even if John's familiarity with Mark "cannot be ruled out," John's "dependence on Mark can." In spite of John's similarities with Mark, Anderson says, there are too many differences for the case to be made: "The problem with such a view, however, is that despite all these similarities, none of them is identical. Mark has 'green' grass; John has 'much' grass. While 'Holy One of God' is used as a title for Jesus in both Gospels, in Mark it is uttered by the demoniac (Mark 1:24), in John by Peter (John 6:69). In fact, of the forty-five similarities between John 6 and Mark 6 and 8, none of them is identical."[33]

Anderson is right to stress the differences between the Synoptics and John, but as well as underestimating the degrees of similarity, there is a danger in looking for absolute identity between a work and its sources. One of the similarities listed by Anderson, for example, is the note that "two hundred denarii" would not buy enough food for the five thousand (Mark 6:37 // John 6:7), an amount of money that is unique to Mark and John in ancient literature.[34] Sometimes even the shortest pieces of parallel wording can be "diagnostic shards," small pieces of evidence that diagnose literary contact.[35] The point can be made with respect to Anderson's own writings. When an author uses Anderson's neologism "interfluentiality," or his distinctive terminology of "bi-optic gospels," there is no question that that author's source is Paul Anderson, as a quick Google search will confirm.

One way to reflect on the issue is to ask how much agreement would convince us of literary contact. When setting out the strengths and weaknesses of the case, Anderson says, "Most devastatingly, Synoptic-dependence theories make no account of over 80 percent of John, which has no direct Synoptic parallels, and they fail to account for the fact that the most memorable of Synoptic passages are missing from John."[36] Given that John shares with the Synoptics passages like the feeding of the five thousand, the walking on the sea, the anointing, the triumphal entry, Peter's denial, Jesus's arrest, the crucifixion, burial, and resurrection, the point about John missing the most memorable Synoptic passages is probably overstated. But the "80 percent" figure is interesting because it

---

33. Paul N. Anderson, "Why This Study Is Needed, and Why It Is Needed Now," in *Critical Appraisals of Critical Views*, vol. 1 of *John, Jesus, and History*, ed. Paul N. Anderson, Felix Just, SJ, and Tom Thatcher, SymS (Atlanta: Society of Biblical Literature, 2007), 13–74, at 45.

34. See further pp. 28–29, below.

35. See further on "diagnostic shards" in Mark Goodacre, *Thomas and the Gospels: The Case for Thomas's Familiarity with the Synoptics* (Grand Rapids: Eerdmans, 2012), 49–65.

36. Paul N. Anderson, *The Riddles of the Fourth Gospel: An Introduction to John* (Minneapolis: Fortress, 2011), 112.

suggests that there is a percentage that would push us over the threshold. What should that percentage be? If in fact one-fifth of John's Gospel has significant parallels with the Synoptics, that might actually be telling, though it is, of course, always difficult to quantify things like this. A strong case can be made for the Protevangelium of James's knowledge of the Synoptics, and its presupposition of their narratives, but it has multiple passages that are not found in the Synoptics, and it omits multiple passages that are, including some that are quite surprising, like the shepherds in Luke's birth narrative.[37] Similar comments could be made about many other early Christian works, like the Gospel of Mary, the Dialogue of the Savior, and the Nature of the Rulers.

The argument from omission has been a major one in the case against John's knowledge of the Synoptics. Leon Morris expresses it by stating, "It is remarkable, if he knew them, that he has omitted so much that they contain and that he has worded what he has in just the way he has."[38] Since we do not have access to the oral traditions on which John is supposed to have drawn, it is impossible to see how much he "omitted" from those sources, but given the imagery in which the model is usually expressed, like lakes and rivers, it was presumably a huge amount of material, and far more material than was present in just the Synoptics. On any model, John omits lots of material. The difference is that the oral tradition is unseen and unheard, so we cannot know how much John has omitted from it, and the question can be avoided.

The argument from omission is even weaker for John than it is when the same type of argument is used in relation to material that Luke omitted from Matthew.[39] Authors, including the author of the Fourth Gospel, can be unpredictable, yet good reasons can usually be imagined for particular omissions. We would not have expected him to narrate the Gethsemane story (Matt 26:36–46 // Mark 14:32–42 // Luke 22:39–46) given Jesus's refusal to pray, "Father, save me from this hour!" (John 12:47). And given the relative serenity of Jesus's death in John, with the triumphant cry, "It is finished!" (John 19:30), it is not surprising that, like Luke, he omitted "My God! My God! Why have you forsaken me?" (Matt 27:46 // Mark 15:34).

Moreover, the book appears to have selected seven "signs" for special nar-

---

37. See Mark Goodacre, "The Protevangelium of James and the Creative Rewriting of Matthew and Luke," in *Connecting Gospels: Beyond the Canonical/Non-canonical Divide*, ed. Francis Watson and Sarah Parkhouse (Oxford: Oxford University Press, 2018), 57–76.

38. Leon Morris, "John, Gospel According to," *ISBE* 2:1104. The quotation from Morris is illustrative. The point is ubiquitous.

39. See Mark Goodacre, *The Case Against Q: Studies in Marcan Priority and the Synoptic Problem* (Harrisburg, PA: Trinity International, 2002), 49–59.

ration, so the author's omission of multiple other Synoptic miracles is unsurprising. The gospel is open and explicit about its selective nature. The closing verse makes a point of just how much has been omitted (John 21:25). For John, there were many other things that Jesus did. The world itself could not contain everything that could have been written, which is, I suppose, a strong indication of the weakness of the argument from omission. We will return to this issue in chapter 4 below.

FROM TRADITION TO GOSPEL

In this book, I will argue that there are significant literary parallels between the Synoptic Gospels and John, and that these are sufficient to establish that John was familiar with Matthew, Mark, and Luke. The author of the Fourth Gospel did not use Synoptic-like traditions but the Synoptic Gospels themselves.

It is important here to avoid prejudicing the discussion with the language of "dependence," which has plagued this debate as much as the related one on Thomas's use of the Synoptics.[40] Where the question is configured in terms of "dependence" rather than "knowledge," "use," or "familiarity," the discussion is always going to be problematic. A work like the Fourth Gospel, so different in so many ways from the Synoptics, is never going to be plausibly explained with a heavy concept of "dependence." If John knows the Synoptics, he has reworked them, he has reimagined them, and he has transformed them.

This draws our attention to a further difficulty with the way that the discussion is usually conceptualized. The standard way of comparing John to the Synoptics is in terms of "tradition." It is seen as a question of explaining parallel traditions, similar motifs. But by focusing too narrowly on microlevel similarities and differences in parallel traditions, we can miss the macrolevel conceptual parallels between John and the Synoptics, the intimate relationship between them at the level of concept and structure. When we compare John and the Synoptics, we should be looking not only at the minutiae but at the deep conceptual parallels between them. And this is not the kind of thing that is successfully conveyed via oral tradition. What is at issue is the way in which John, in parallel with the Synoptics, conceptualizes the Jesus story.

Chapter 2, "When John Is Synoptic," begins our closer look at John's commonalities with the Synoptic Gospels. I will argue that the degree of verbatim agree-

---

40. See Mark Goodacre, *Thomas and the Gospels: The Case for Thomas's Familiarity with the Synoptics* (Grand Rapids: Eerdmans, 2012), 5–7.

ment between John and the Synoptics is far greater than is usually appreciated, and that it is not only a question of verbatim agreement in individual passages; it is also a question of parallel passages, similar structures, and agreement with the fundamental literary conceit of the Synoptics.

Understanding the degree of similarity between John and the Synoptics presses the question about the direction of dependence. Chapter 3, "John, from Mark, via Matthew and Luke" argues that John features many telltale signs of knowledge of the Synoptics by repeating material that shows Matthew's and Luke's redactional fingerprints. The chapter highlights and illustrates ten examples of this phenomenon, five from Matthew and five from Luke. Even this, though, is not the full story. Several scholars have drawn attention to places where John appears to presuppose Synoptic accounts that he does not narrate. Chapter 4, "John's Presupposition of Synoptic Narratives," is the first to develop this insight into an argument for John's use of the Synoptics, highlighting and illustrating ten examples that show that it is not just the author but the target audience that knows the Synoptic Gospels.

Understanding how John has reworked and reimagined the Synoptic Gospels is, nevertheless, still a challenge. In chapter 5, "John's Dramatic Transformation of the Synoptics," I argue that John often takes Synoptic narration and turns it into direct discourse. This generally neglected phenomenon sheds light on John's compositional techniques, illustrating the dramatic mode of John's narrative. Seeing John as drama does, however, shed light on the gospel's greatest mystery. In chapter 6, "The Beloved Disciple for Readers of the Synoptics," I will argue that the mystery is solved when John is read against the background of the Synoptic Gospels, which is how readers have approached John since the beginning. John's first readers knew who the Beloved Disciple was because they also knew the Synoptic Gospels.

If the identity of the Beloved Disciple is the Fourth Gospel's greatest mystery, its most important subject is the identity of Jesus. In chapter 7, "John's Christological Transformation of the Synoptics," I will argue that there is significant continuity between the Christologies of the Synoptics and John. Like the Synoptics, this is a gospel of Jesus, the Messiah and the Son of God, and even the most distinctive elements of John's Christology, the "I am" sayings, and John's "Father" and "Son" language, find their source in the Synoptic Gospels, especially Matthew.

Chapter 2

When John Is Synoptic

Everyone who has done academic work on the New Testament knows that there are three Synoptic Gospels, Matthew, Mark, and Luke. And then there is John. John is different. John is on its own. Students learn to erect a firewall between the moment when the Synoptic Jesus departs from the disciples at the end of Luke 24 and the Johannine Word made flesh moves onto the cosmic stage on the next page, in John 1. It is a complete reset, not even to the start of the New Testament, with Mark's Isaianic prophecy, or Matthew's Abrahamic genealogy, or Luke's temple epiphany, but to the very opening of the Old Testament, before the Genesis narrative—"In the beginning."

The Johannine firewall is there because students need to know just how similar the Synoptics are to one another and just how different John is from all three. John has no baptism of Jesus, no transfiguration, no Gethsemane, no parables, no exorcisms, and no Eucharist. Unknown characters like Nathanael, Nicodemus, Lazarus, the blind man, and the Samaritan woman roam the pages of the Fourth Gospel, and Jesus is larger than life, with an unambiguous confidence about his own identity. The kingdom of God was at hand in the Synoptics; eternal life is now present in John.

For much of the time, John tells different stories—longer, richer narratives with more dialogue, in a work that is structured differently, with a lot more time spent in Jerusalem than in Galilee. Where there are similar stories, they are told in different language. The call of Simon Peter is mediated through his brother Andrew. The "centurion" in Capernaum becomes a "royal official" in Cana. In the feeding of the five thousand, even the words for "bread" and "fish" are different.

All of these things, and more like them, we have learned, and we have taught. The clear differences between John and the other canonicals demonstrate one essential insight: that John is not Synoptic. Matthew, Mark, and Luke are Synoptic because they are not John. John is not Synoptic because it is not Matthew, Mark, and Luke. We have echoed it in books, articles, blog posts, podcasts, and videos to the point where it is a received truth, the best kind of well-known fact. We have repeated it so many times that we never think to question it. If our students grasp the point, we congratulate ourselves that we have laid a successful foundation and can move on to the next step.

And yet, it is not true, and I would like to explain why.

The Gospels in Synopsis

In spite of what we tell our students, the Synoptic Gospels are not labeled differently from John because they are "just so different." It is true, of course, that there are many differences from John, in structure, language, vocabulary, content, character, personnel, theology, eschatology, and Christology. But difference is a question of degree. Luke has parallels with Mark that Matthew lacks, and Matthew has parallels with Mark that Luke lacks. Matthew and Luke have material in common that Mark lacks, and all three have seriously different takes on who Jesus was and how he talked. Difference and degrees of difference are already embedded in the discussion of Matthew, Mark, and Luke. To that extent, John is like the Synoptics. There are degrees of difference.

But the reason given in the textbooks for John not being Synoptic is that it cannot be laid side by side in a synopsis in the way that Matthew, Mark, and Luke can be. The Synoptic Gospels are literally "Synoptic" because they can be "seen together" in a gospel synopsis, the etymology often helpfully explained as *syn-* (with) and *-optic* (seen). And therein lies the problem, this specifically synoptic problem, because in fact John frequently can be laid side by side with Matthew, Mark, and Luke in a synopsis.

We have already seen some examples of this in chapter 1, in passages like the walking on the sea, where John is close to Mark, or the Last Supper, where Matthew, Mark, and John share a nine-word verbatim string of agreement. But the agreement between John and the Synoptics is there from the outset. There is no difficulty, for example, in placing John's preaching about Jesus in a four-column synopsis like this:

MATT 3:11	MARK 1:7–8	LUKE 3:16	JOHN 1:26–27
	καὶ ἐκήρυσσεν λέγων·	ἀπεκρίνατο λέγων πᾶσιν ὁ Ἰωάννης·	ἀπεκρίθη αὐτοῖς ὁ Ἰωάννης λέγων·
Ἐγὼ μὲν ὑμᾶς βαπτίζω ἐν ὕδατι εἰς μετάνοιαν·	Ἔρχεται ὁ ἰσχυρότερός μου	Ἐγὼ μὲν ὕδατι βαπτίζω ὑμᾶς· ἔρχεται δὲ ὁ ἰσχυρότερός μου,	Ἐγὼ βαπτίζω ἐν ὕδατι· μέσος ὑμῶν ἕστηκεν ὃν ὑμεῖς οὐκ οἴδατε,
ὁ δὲ ὀπίσω μου ἐρχόμενος ἰσχυρότερός μού ἐστιν, οὗ οὐκ εἰμὶ ἱκανὸς τὰ ὑποδήματα βαστάσαι·	ὀπίσω μου, οὗ οὐκ εἰμὶ ἱκανὸς κύψας λῦσαι τὸν ἱμάντα τῶν ὑποδημάτων αὐτοῦ· ἐγὼ ἐβάπτισα ὑμᾶς ὕδατι, αὐτὸς δὲ	οὗ οὐκ εἰμὶ ἱκανὸς λῦσαι τὸν ἱμάντα τῶν ὑποδημάτων αὐτοῦ·	ὁ ὀπίσω μου ἐρχόμενος, οὗ οὐκ εἰμὶ ἄξιος ἵνα λύσω αὐτοῦ τὸν ἱμάντα τοῦ ὑποδήματος.
αὐτὸς ὑμᾶς βαπτίσει ἐν πνεύματι ἁγίῳ καὶ πυρί·	βαπτίσει ὑμᾶς ἐν πνεύματι ἁγίῳ.	αὐτὸς ὑμᾶς βαπτίσει ἐν πνεύματι ἁγίῳ καὶ πυρί·	
"I baptize you with water for repentance, but	He proclaimed,	John answered all of them by saying, "I baptize you with water, but	John answered them, saying[1] "I baptize with water. Among you stands one whom you do not know,
the one who is coming after me is more powerful than I, and	"The one who is more powerful than I is coming after me;	one who is more powerful than I is coming;	the one who is coming after me;

---

1. NRSVue lacks "saying," thus hiding this Mark and John agreement.

CHAPTER 2

MATT 3:11	MARK 1:7–8	LUKE 3:16	JOHN 1:26–27
I am not worthy to carry his sandals.	I am not worthy to stoop down and untie the strap of his sandals. I have baptized you with water, but he will baptize you with the Holy Spirit."	I am not worthy to untie the strap of his sandals.	I am not worthy to untie the strap of his sandal."
He will baptize you with the Holy Spirit and fire."		He will baptize you with the Holy Spirit and fire."	

The underlined words in this synopsis are John's agreements with one or more of the other three. Of the thirty-one words here in John, twenty of them are paralleled in the Synoptics, including the unique expression "to loose [λῦσαι/λύσω] the strap of his sandal(s) [αὐτοῦ τὸν ἱμάντα τοῦ ὑποδήματος]." John shares several words with all three others, several with just Matthew and Luke, several with Matthew alone, and several with Luke alone. Scholars do not hesitate to see the links here between Matthew, Mark, and Luke as pointing to literary connections, even if they disagree about the nature of the connections. Matthew and Luke are widely held to be using Mark here, and there are important agreements between Matthew and Luke that suggest a direct link between them too.[2] But here, John is just as Synoptic as the Synoptics, and the synopsis shows us these parallels without any wiggly lines or jiggery-pokery. Somewhat remarkably, Percival Gardner-Smith stated that "there is nothing here that implies literary connexion," but he set the bar too high, and by focusing only on John's parallels with Mark, he hides the evidence of John's parallels with Matthew and Luke.[3]

There are similar examples. When the high priest's slave's ear is cut off, each gospel has fascinating divergences while telling the same story similarly:

---

2. For the difficulties with the idea that this is a "Mark-Q overlap," see my "Taking Our Leave of Mark-Q Overlaps: Major Agreements and the Farrer Theory," in *Gospel Interpretation and the Q Hypothesis*, ed. Mogens Müller and Heike Omerzu, LNTS 573 (London: Bloomsbury, 2018), 201–22.

3. P. Gardner-Smith, *St. John and the Synoptic Gospels* (Cambridge: Cambridge University Press, 1938), 3.

MATT 26:51–52	MARK 14:47	LUKE 22:49–51	JOHN 18:10–11
καὶ ἰδοὺ εἷς τῶν μετὰ Ἰησοῦ ἐκτείνας τὴν χεῖρα ἀπέσπασεν τὴν μάχαιραν αὐτοῦ	εἷς δέ τις τῶν παρεστηκότων σπασάμενος τὴν μάχαιραν	ἰδόντες δὲ οἱ περὶ αὐτὸν τὸ ἐσόμενον εἶπαν· Κύριε, εἰ πατάξομεν ἐν μαχαίρῃ;	Σίμων οὖν Πέτρος ἔχων μάχαιραν εἵλκυσεν αὐτὴν
καὶ πατάξας	ἔπαισεν	καὶ ἐπάταξεν εἷς τις ἐξ αὐτῶν	καὶ ἔπαισεν
τὸν δοῦλον τοῦ ἀρχιερέως ἀφεῖλεν αὐτοῦ τὸ ὠτίον.	τὸν δοῦλον τοῦ ἀρχιερέως καὶ ἀφεῖλεν αὐτοῦ τὸ ὠτάριον.	τοῦ ἀρχιερέως τὸν δοῦλον καὶ ἀφεῖλεν τὸ οὖς αὐτοῦ τὸ δεξιόν.	τὸν τοῦ ἀρχιερέως δοῦλον καὶ ἀπέκοψεν αὐτοῦ τὸ ὠτάριον τὸ δεξιόν· ἦν δὲ ὄνομα τῷ δούλῳ Μάλχος.
τότε λέγει αὐτῷ ὁ Ἰησοῦς· Ἀπόστρεψον τὴν μάχαιράν σου εἰς τὸν τόπον αὐτῆς, πάντες γὰρ οἱ λαβόντες μάχαιραν ἐν μαχαίρῃ ἀπολοῦνται·		ἀποκριθεὶς δὲ ὁ Ἰησοῦς εἶπεν· Ἐᾶτε ἕως τούτου·	εἶπεν οὖν ὁ Ἰησοῦς τῷ Πέτρῳ· Βάλε τὴν μάχαιραν εἰς τὴν θήκην·
		καὶ ἁψάμενος τοῦ ὠτίου ἰάσατο αὐτόν.	
			τὸ ποτήριον ὃ δέδωκέν μοι ὁ πατὴρ οὐ μὴ πίω αὐτό;

CHAPTER 2

MATT 26:51–52	MARK 14:47	LUKE 22:49–51	JOHN 18:10–11
		When those who were around him saw what was coming, they asked, "Lord,	
Suddenly one of those with Jesus	But one of those who was standing near		Therefore Simon Peter, who had
put his hand on his <u>sword</u>, <u>drew it</u>,	drew his <u>sword</u>	should we strike with the <u>sword</u>?" And one of them	a <u>sword</u>, <u>drew it</u>
and struck <u>the slave of the high priest</u>, cutting <u>off his</u> ear.	and hit <u>the slave of the high priest</u> <u>and</u> cut <u>off his</u> <u>ear</u>.	struck <u>the slave of the high priest</u> <u>and</u> cut off <u>his</u> right ear.	and hit[4] <u>the slave of the high priest, and</u> cut <u>off his</u> right <u>ear</u>. And the name of the slave was Malchus.
Then <u>Jesus says</u>[5] <u>to</u> him, "Put your <u>sword</u> back <u>into</u> its place, for all who take the sword will die by the sword.		But <u>Jesus said</u>, "No more of this!"	<u>Jesus said</u> <u>to</u> Peter, "Put your <u>sword</u> back <u>into</u> its sheath.
		And he touched his ear and healed him.	
			Am I not to drink the cup that the Father has given me?"[6]

---

4. NRSVue is problematic here. It has "struck" for all four canonical Gospels, whereas in the Greek, Matthew and Luke agree with one another against Mark and John—πατάσσω in Matthew and Luke against παίω in Mark and John. I have adjusted in the English translation to "struck" for πατάσσω and "hit" for παίω.

5. NRSVue, "said," here adjusted to show the contrast with Luke and John.

6. There is also a structural parallel between Matt 26:53 and John 18:11b, but I have left this out of the synopsis for ease of viewing.

This is a great example of the similarities and differences among these four gospels in synopsis, and one that works well in classes on gospel interrelations and redaction criticism. All four gospels have "the slave of the high priest" being struck by a sword and his ear getting severed. John agrees with Luke in specifying that it was his "right" ear (see further on this below, pp. 60–61) and with Matthew in having Jesus commanding the offender to put away the sword. Only Matthew has the typically poetic "All who take the sword will die by the sword" (a Matthean "machaeric" rhythm; see further below), and only Luke has Jesus healing the slave's ear. Only John names the protagonists as Malchus and Peter, just as he names the protagonists in the anointing story as Mary and Judas (see below), the disciples in the feeding of the five thousand (Matt 14:13–21 // Mark 6:30–44 // Luke 9:10–17) as Andrew and Philip (John 6:5–9), and the doubting disciples at the resurrection (Matt 28:17 // Luke 24:38) as Thomas (John 20:24–29). It is a good example of John in synopsis with Matthew, Mark, and Luke, with clear agreements alongside characteristic disagreements.

Sometimes entire passages are structured and worded similarly. The best example of this is the anointing of Jesus (Matt 26:6–13 // Mark 14:3–9 // John 12:1–8; cf. Luke 7:36–50). Here, John is close to both Mark and Matthew. Indeed, he is far closer to Mark and Matthew in this pericope than is Luke in his very different version of the anointing (Luke 7:36–50), a version with which John also has parallels.[7] John shares with Mark and Matthew a cluster of motifs in a passage that is structured in the same way in all three:

1. The incident takes place in Bethany,
2. just before Passover,
3. at a dinner where a woman has a jar of very expensive perfume,
4. which she uses to anoint Jesus;
5. there are complaints about the costliness of the perfume, which could have been given to the poor;
6. Jesus says "Leave her.... The poor you will always have with you.... But you will not always have me."
7. Jesus interprets the anointing in connection with his burial (Matt 26:12 // Mark 14:8; John 12:7).

---

7. See below, pp. 56–58, for discussion of John's knowledge of Luke's version of the anointing. Although John's knowledge of Luke helps to explain his divergences here from Mark and Matthew, it is easiest to take the different parallels in turn.

CHAPTER 2

Looking at a gospel synopsis for this passage shows how close Matthew, Mark, and John are here. For ease of illustration, I have restricted the synopsis to the elements that show the closest relations, but the reader should note that in spite of the common setting in Bethany (Matt 26:6 // Mark 14:3 // John 12:1), the verbal correspondences at the beginning of the pericopes are relatively few, with Matthew and Mark locating the scene in the house of a previously unknown character called "Simon, the man with leprosy," and John locating it in the house of his now familiar characters, Mary, Martha, and Lazarus.

MATT 26:7–11	MARK 14:3–7	JOHN 12:3–8
προσῆλθεν αὐτῷ γυνὴ	ἦλθεν γυνὴ	ἡ οὖν Μαριὰμ
ἔχουσα ἀλάβαστρον	ἔχουσα ἀλάβαστρον	λαβοῦσα
μύρου βαρυτίμου	μύρου	λίτραν μύρου
	νάρδου πιστικῆς	νάρδου πιστικῆς
	πολυτελοῦς·	πολυτίμου ἤλειψεν τοὺς
	συντρίψασα τὴν	πόδας τοῦ Ἰησοῦ καὶ
καὶ κατέχεεν	ἀλάβαστρον κατέχεεν	ἐξέμαξεν ταῖς θριξὶν
ἐπὶ τῆς κεφαλῆς αὐτοῦ	αὐτοῦ τῆς κεφαλῆς.	αὐτῆς τοὺς πόδας αὐτοῦ·
ἀνακειμένου.		ἡ δὲ οἰκία ἐπληρώθη ἐκ
		τῆς ὀσμῆς τοῦ μύρου.
ἰδόντες δὲ	ἦσαν δέ τινες	λέγει δὲ Ἰούδας ὁ Ἰσκαριώ-
		της εἷς
οἱ μαθηταὶ ἠγανάκτησαν	ἀγανακτοῦντες πρὸς	τῶν μαθητῶν αὐτοῦ, ὁ μέλ-
λέγοντες·	ἑαυτούς·	λων αὐτὸν παραδιδόναι·
Εἰς τί	Εἰς τί	Διὰ τί
ἡ ἀπώλεια αὕτη;	ἡ ἀπώλεια αὕτη τοῦ μύρου	
ἐδύνατο γὰρ	γέγονεν;	
τοῦτο	ἠδύνατο γὰρ τοῦτο τὸ μύρον	τοῦτο τὸ μύρον
πραθῆναι	πραθῆναι ἐπάνω	οὐκ ἐπράθη
πολλοῦ καὶ	δηναρίων τριακοσίων καὶ	τριακοσίων δηναρίων καὶ
δοθῆναι πτωχοῖς.	δοθῆναι τοῖς πτωχοῖς·	ἐδόθη πτωχοῖς; εἶπεν
	καὶ ἐνεβριμῶντο αὐτῇ.	δὲ τοῦτο οὐχ ὅτι περὶ τῶν
		πτωχῶν ἔμελεν αὐτῷ, ἀλλ'
		ὅτι κλέπτης ἦν καὶ τὸ γλωσ-
		σόκομον ἔχων τὰ βαλλόμενα
γνοὺς		βάσταζεν.

When John Is Synoptic

MATT 26:7–11	MARK 14:3–7	JOHN 12:3–8
δὲ ὁ Ἰησοῦς <u>εἶπεν</u> αὐτοῖς· Τί κόπους παρέχετε τῇ γυναικί; ἔργον γὰρ καλὸν ἠργάσατο εἰς ἐμέ· <u>πάντοτε γὰρ τοὺς πτωχοὺς ἔχετε μεθ' ἑαυτῶν,</u> <u>ἐμὲ δὲ οὐ πάντοτε ἔχετε·</u>	ὁ δὲ Ἰησοῦς <u>εἶπεν·</u> Ἄφετε <u>αὐτήν·</u> τί αὐτῇ κόπους παρέχετε; καλὸν ἔργον ἠργάσατο ἐν ἐμοί. <u>πάντοτε γὰρ τοὺς πτωχοὺς ἔχετε μεθ' ἑαυτῶν,</u> καὶ ὅταν θέλητε δύνασθε αὐτοῖς εὖ ποιῆσαι, <u>ἐμὲ δὲ οὐ πάντοτε ἔχετε·</u>	<u>εἶπεν</u> οὖν ὁ Ἰησοῦς· Ἄφες <u>αὐτήν,</u> ἵνα εἰς τὴν ἡμέραν τοῦ ἐνταφιασμοῦ μου τηρήσῃ αὐτό· <u>τοὺς πτωχοὺς</u> γὰρ <u>πάντοτε ἔχετε μεθ' ἑαυτῶν,</u> <u>ἐμὲ δὲ οὐ πάντοτε ἔχετε.</u>
a woman came to him with an alabaster jar of very costly <u>perfume</u>,[8] and she poured it on his head as he sat at the table. But when the <u>disciples</u> saw it, they were angry and said, "<u>Why</u> this waste? For <u>this</u>[12] could have been <u>sold for</u>	a woman came with an alabaster jar of very costly <u>perfume of pure nard</u>,[9] and she broke open the jar and poured the perfume on his head. But some were there who said to one another in anger, "<u>Why</u> was the perfume wasted in this way? For <u>this perfume</u> could have been <u>sold for</u> more than	Mary took a pound of very costly[10] <u>perfume of</u>[11] <u>pure nard</u>, anointed Jesus's feet, and wiped them with her hair. The house was filled with the fragrance of the perfume. <u>But</u> Judas Iscariot, one of his <u>disciples</u> (the one who was about to betray him), says,[13] "<u>Why</u> was this perfume not <u>sold for</u>

---

8. NRSVue, "ointment," thus hiding the agreement with John. Also in Matt 26:9, 12; Mark 14:3, 4, 5.
9. NRSVue, "very costly ointment of nard," thus hiding some of the agreement with John.
10. NRSVue, "costly" (no "very").
11. NRSVue, "made of."
12. NRSVue, "this perfume."
13. NRSVue, "said."

MATT 26:7–11	MARK 14:3–7	JOHN 12:3–8
a large sum <u>and the money given to the poor.</u>"	<u>three hundred denarii and the money given to the poor.</u>" And they scolded her.	<u>three hundred denarii and the money given to the poor</u>?" (He said this not because he cared about the poor but because he was a thief; he kept the common purse and used to steal what was put into it.)
But <u>Jesus</u>, aware of this, <u>said</u> to them, "Why do you trouble the woman? She has performed a good service for me.	But <u>Jesus said</u>, "<u>Leave her alone</u>;[14] why do you trouble her? She has performed a good service for me.	<u>Jesus said</u>, "<u>Leave her alone</u>. She bought it so that she might keep it for the day of my burial.
<u>For you always have the poor with you,</u>	<u>For you always have the poor with you,</u> and you can show kindness to them whenever you wish,	<u>For</u>[15] <u>you always have the poor with you,</u>
<u>but you will not always have me."</u>	<u>but you will not always have me."</u>	<u>but you will not</u>[16] <u>always have me."</u>

As well as the structural parallels across these three gospels, which themselves suggest a literary link, there are some close verbal connections. Mark and John share the remarkably specific reference to "three hundred denarii," and Matthew and John share an eight-word verbatim string, ἔχετε μεθ' ἑαυτῶν, ἐμὲ δὲ οὐ πάντοτε ἔχετε ("you have with you, but you will not always have me"). This is longer than any of the verbatim strings between Matthew and Mark in this passage.

The reason that the similarities are striking is that they could indicate that there is literary contact between the gospels, so it is worth asking whether links like these do indeed diagnose a literary relationship. Is it possible that the links could in fact be explained on the classic model of shared oral tradition? I don't think so. The verbatim agreements are as telling as the structural agreements,

---

14. NRSVue, "let her alone," thus obscuring the agreement with John.
15. NRSVue omits "for," thus obscuring the agreement with Matthew and Mark.
16. NRSVue, "do not," thus obscuring the agreement with Matthew and Mark.

and moreover, this is one of only two occasions when denarii amounts feature in Mark. The other is in Mark 6:37, when "two hundred denarii" will not buy enough food for the five thousand. There is only one other denarii amount in John too, and it is exactly the same amount in exactly the same context, "two hundred denarii" for the five thousand (John 6:7). If Mark and John picked up both of these details from oral tradition, the coincidence would be remarkable. Were these the only occasions when Jesus's followers mentioned denarii? Were these the only denarii amounts in the supposedly vast ocean of oral tradition? The stories can clearly be told without these denarii amounts, as Matthew's and Luke's parallels show.[17] The amounts become all the more striking when we remember that denarii are not found in great numbers in Galilee or Judea, where these stories are set.[18] Moreover, a TLG search will confirm that these are the first occurrences anywhere in extant Greek literature of "two hundred denarii" and "three hundred denarii," so it seems unlikely that these were standard amounts in the culture to mean "a lot of money."

In this passage, and others like it, scholars do not hesitate to say that Matthew is in a direct literary relationship with Mark. If we want to avoid the double standard, we should see John as in a direct literary relationship with Matthew and Mark. This does not, of course, establish the direction of contact. Could this be a question of Matthew's or Mark's familiarity with John rather than the reverse? It would be a difficult case to make. The secondary nature of John's account seems clear from the curious anatomy of John's anointing, whereby Mary anoints Jesus's feet and wipes them with her hair, which apparently draws in a key element from the Lukan anointing (Luke 7:36–50), and this does not make sense in the new context. In Luke, the anonymous woman is in Simon the Pharisee's house (Luke 7:36) and has done all the things that Simon, as host, has failed to do (Luke 7:44–45). In that context, it makes sense for her to wipe Jesus's feet with her hair. It is not her house. In John, they are in the house of Martha, Mary, and Lazarus, with Martha serving (John 12:1–2). In her own house, she would presumably have had access to towels and would not have needed to use her hair. When John is writing on his own, he does have Jesus use a towel

---

17. It is interesting to note that Luke does have denarii amounts in his anointing story (Luke 7:36–50), in the parable of the two debtors (Luke 7:41–43). Perhaps Luke added Mark's "three hundred denarii" and "two hundred denarii" to get his "five hundred denarii," but more likely, this is just a coincidence.

18. Mark Chancey, *Greco-Roman Culture and the Galilee of Jesus*, SNTSMS 134 (Cambridge: Cambridge University Press, 2011), 175, "The denarius, for example, is mentioned numerous times [in the Gospels]—this, despite the fact that the coin, produced at distant mints, appears to have had only limited circulation in Palestine at the time of Jesus. References to it might reflect the dating and provenance of the gospels more than the historical setting of Jesus."

(λέντιον) twice (John 13:4–5). Moreover, this foreign element in the Johannine story leads to the unfortunate result that the perfume is now in Mary's hair and not on Jesus's feet (see further on this in chapter 3 below).

John's secondary nature may also be apparent in a seldom-noticed feature. In both Mark and John, Jesus says, "Leave her alone" ("Ἄφετε αὐτήν, Mark 14:6; Ἄφες αὐτήν, John 12:7). In Mark, the rebuke makes sense because the people have just "scolded her" (καὶ ἐνεβριμῶντο αὐτῇ, Mark 14:5), but in John it does not work so well because it is not preceded by the note about the scolding. It looks like the author, having adjusted the personnel from Mark's anonymous bystanders to Judas, and having added his parenthesis on Judas's motivations (John 12:6), has then inadvertently dropped the scolding that necessitates Jesus's rebuke. It might be said that the scolding is implied in the question about the three hundred denarii, but it is not clear that this question is directed to Mary.

The stage directions in Mark are easy to follow. The anonymous bystanders in Mark make the angry comment to one another (Mark 14:4), then they scold the woman (Mark 14:5), and then Jesus rebukes them (Mark 14:6). In John, it is not clear whom Judas is addressing with the question (λέγει δὲ Ἰούδας ὁ Ἰσκαριώτης), there is no note about scolding, yet Jesus still says, "Leave her alone." This is the kind of inadvertent slip that is common when one writer is using another's work and is analogous to the phenomenon of "editorial fatigue" found in Matthew's use of Mark, Luke's use of Matthew and Mark, the Protevangelium of James's use of Matthew and Luke, as well as other works from antiquity.[19]

In some ways, though, this is to get ahead of ourselves. In chapter 3, we will look at ten examples of where John, in synopsis, shows knowledge of Matthew's redaction of Mark and Luke's redaction of Mark. But before taking that more detailed journey into the evidence for John's literary knowledge of the Synoptics, it is worth pausing to take in the point that John's Gospel is itself often Synoptic, that there are places where it is straightforward to line up the Fourth Gospel with one or more of the other three gospels and to see clear literary parallels.

I am aware, of course, that these synopses are all my own constructions, in which I am attempting to draw attention to John's literary parallels with the Synoptics, concentrating on those pericopes, and those parts of pericopes, where John is closest to the others, underlining the points of agreement, and so on. Perhaps the reader will think that this is some kind of sleight of hand. Perhaps

19. Cf. Mark Goodacre, "Fatigue in the Synoptics," *NTS* 44 (1998): 45–58.

the author who thinks he can conjure away Q is engaging in the kind of misdirection that manipulates John to appear in synopsis. If John can indeed be Synoptic, why does no one else ever point this out? Why does John not appear in the published gospel synopses that we all use from day to day? It does. While writing this book, I consulted Aland's synopsis every day,[20] not just to check on intra-Synoptic parallels but to check on Synoptic-John parallels. This is the standard gospel synopsis used by all scholars in the field, a basic purchase for every graduate student of the New Testament. In passage after passage, there is a column present for John. It's even in the title: *Synopsis Quattuor Evangeliorum*. In case the Latin masks the reality, this means *Synopsis of the Four Gospels*.

PARALLEL ORDERS

If it is clear, though, that the Fourth Gospel can often be laid side by side in individual passages with the other three, there is a further important issue that needs to be addressed. The identity of the Synoptic Gospels is not solely a matter of language and degrees of verbal agreement. There is also the question of order. One of the reasons that scholars treat the Synoptic Gospels together, and see a literary relationship between them, is that they have so many similarities in the order of passages. And John is so different. It is well known, for example, that the cleansing of the temple occurs in a radically different position, right at the beginning of the gospel (John 2:13-25) rather than toward the end (Matt 21:12-13 // Mark 11:15-17 // Luke 19:45-46). Or to take another celebrated example, the miraculous catch of fish happens early on in Luke (Luke 5:1-11), so early, in fact, that it is the moment when Peter decides to follow Jesus. By contrast, it is right at the end of John's Gospel (John 21:1-14), so late that it is part of the story of Jesus's resurrection, in what many scholars see as an epilogue to the gospel. Examples like these surely demonstrate that John's order differs radically from the order of the Synoptics?

Not really. These are actually exceptions to the rule. John usually has parallel passages in the same relative order as the Synoptics. Let us take a closer look. The following table is not exhaustive, but it lists the major parallel passages.

---

20. Kurt Aland, *Synopsis Quattuor Evangeliorum*, 15th rev. ed. (Stuttgart: Deutsche Bibelgesellschaft, 1996). See also K. Aland, ed., *Synopsis of the Four Gospels—Greek/English*, 10th ed. (Stuttgart: Deutsche Bibelgesellschaft, 1994), and K. Aland, ed., *Synopsis of the Four Gospels—English* (Revised printing, Stuttgart: Deutsche Bibelgesellschaft, 1985).

CHAPTER 2

JOHANNINE PASSAGE	SYNOPTIC PARALLELS
John 1:19–23: John in the wilderness	Matt 3:1–6 // Mark 1:2–6 // Luke 3:1–6
John 1:24–28: John on Jesus's identity	Matt 3:11–12 // Mark 1:7–8 // Luke 3:15–18
John 1:29–34: Dove descends on Jesus	Matt 3:13–17 // Mark 1:9–11 // Luke 3:21–22
John 1:35–42: Call of Simon and Andrew	Matt 4:18–22 // Mark 1:16–20 // Luke 5:1–11
John 2:13–22: Cleansing of the temple	Matt 21:12–13 // Mark 11:15–17 // Luke 19:45–46
John 4:46–54: Officer's son healed	Matt 8:5–13 // Luke 7:1–10
John 6:1–15: Feeding of the five thousand	Matt 14:13–21 // Mark 6:32–44 // Luke 9:10–17
John 6:16–21: Walking on the sea	Matt 14:22–33 // Mark 6:45–52
John 6:67–71: Peter's confession	Matt 16:13–20 // Mark 8:27–30 // Luke 9:18–21
John 12:1–8: Anointing	Matt 26:6–13 // Mark 14:3–9 // Luke 7:36–50
John 12:12–19: Triumphal entry	Matt 21:1–9 // Mark 11:1–10 // Luke 19:28–40
John 13:21–30: Prophecy of betrayal	Matt 26:21–25 // Mark 14:18–21 // Luke 22:21–23
John 13:36–38: Prophecy of denial	Matt 26:30–35 // Mark 14:26–31 // Luke 22:31–34
John 18:1–12: Arrest	Matt 26:47–56 // Mark 14:43–52 // Luke 22:47–53
John 18:13–24: Annas and Caiaphas; denial	Matt 26:57–68 // Mark 14:53–65 // Luke 22:54–71
John 18:25–27: Peter's denial (continued)	Matt 26:69–75 // Mark 14:66–72 // Luke 22:54–62

JOHANNINE PASSAGE	SYNOPTIC PARALLELS
John 18:28–19:16a: Jesus before Pilate	Matt 27:1–2, 11–26 // Mark 15:1–15 // Luke 23:1–5, 13–25
John 19:16b–37: Crucifixion	Matt 27:32–56 // Mark 15:21–41 // Luke 23:26–49
John 19:38–42: Burial	Matt 27:57–61 // Mark 15:42–47 // Luke 23:50–56
John 20:1–10: Vacated tomb	Matt 28:1–8 // Mark 16:1–8 // Luke 24:1–12
John 20:11–18: Appearance to Mary Magdalene	Matt 28:9–10
John 20:19–29: Appearance to disciples	Matt 28:16–20, Luke 24:36–49
John 21:1–14: Miraculous catch of fish	Luke 5:1–11

Out of these twenty-three passages, only three are found in a different sequence in John, the temple incident, the triumphal entry, and the miraculous catch of fish. Other than the two textbook examples of John's different order, the only other passage that is in a different order is the triumphal entry, which precedes the anointing in Mark and Matthew but comes after it in John. Even here, it is worth noting that John's contrast is only with Matthew and Mark; Luke's anointing comes at a far earlier point in the narrative, while Jesus is still in Galilee (Luke 7:36–50). Moreover John's triumphal entry appears at a very similar point proportionally to Mark's triumphal entry, as we will see below.

Parallels in order are important because they suggest a literary link rather than a link deriving from oral tradition. This is a question of parallel literary arrangement. The walking on the sea, for example, does not have to follow the feeding of the five thousand, as it does in Matthew, Mark, and John. This feeding story can be told without being paired with the walking on the sea. That is how the feeding is narrated in Luke, who omits the walking on the sea. Nor do Matthew's and Mark's very similar feeding of the four thousand (Matt 15:32–39 // Mark 8:1–10) have a paired walking on the sea narrative. Some scholars will, of course, suggest that "the sequence was already in the source used by Mark,"[21] but this kind of recursion does not help because it still requires John to know Mark's

---

21. J. Painter, "The Johannine Literature," in *Handbook to Exegesis of the New Testament*, ed. Stanley E. Porter, NTTS 25 (Leiden: Brill, 1997), 555–90, at 577.

imagined source, or for John's imagined source to know Mark's imagined source, and so on. And the source, in the nature of the case, has to resemble Mark enough for the link to work. As C. K. Barrett once said in this context, "The fact is that there crops up repeatedly in John evidence that suggests that the evangelist knew a body of traditional material that either was Mark, or was something much like Mark; and any one who after an interval of nineteen centuries feels himself in a position to distinguish nicely between 'Mark' and 'something much like Mark,' is at liberty to do so. The simpler hypothesis, which does not involve the postulation of otherwise unknown entities, is not without attractiveness."[22] Moreover, this is just one pair of passages from the longer list of parallels above. If this were the only parallel sequence between John and the Synoptics, it might be easier to imagine coincidence or prior hypothetical entities, but John's departures from the Synoptic order are actually infrequent.

There is, of course, some narrative logic in the parallel sequences. The call of the disciples has to occur toward the beginning of each narrative, and Jesus's arrest is narrated before his trial, which precedes Jesus's death, which precedes his resurrection, and so on. But to lean on this point would be to confuse story and discourse and to ignore the fact that there are intra-Synoptic variations in the way that these events are narrated. It is worth noticing distinctive elements in the literary framing even of the passion narrative.

To take Peter's denial, for example, both Mark and John situate Peter in "the courtyard of the high priest" (εἰς τὴν αὐλὴν τοῦ ἀρχιερέως, Mark 14:54 // John 18:15) where he "warms himself" (θερμαινόμενος, Mark 14:54 // John 18:18) at a fire, before they narrate the story of Jesus facing high priest and council (Mark 14:55–65 // John 18:19–24). They then pick up the story about Peter's denial afterward (Mark 14:66–72 // John 18:25–27). It is true that there are differences between the two. John adds "another disciple," and the first of Peter's denials is narrated straight away, but the literary framing in each is the same. The point here is that the story does not need to be told in this way. Matthew and Luke do not tell it in this way. Matthew narrates the trial in front of Caiaphas (Matt 26:57–68) before narrating Peter's denial (Matt 26:69–75), and Luke does the reverse, narrating first Peter's denial (Luke 22:54–62) and then the story of Jesus before the council (Luke 22:66–71). The parallel literary framing in Mark and John is noticeable.

Moreover, this kind of sandwich structure, or intercalation, is a well-known feature of Mark's style. There are at least six occasions in Mark when a story

---

22. C. Kingsley Barrett, "John and the Synoptic Gospels," *ExpTim* 85 (1974): 228–33, at 232. As a succinct critique of Gardner-Smith, Barrett's article is unequalled.

begins, only to be interrupted by another, before the narrative returns to the original story again:[23]

MARKAN PASSAGE	STORY BEGINS	STORY INTERRUPTED	STORY RESUMES
3:20–35	3:20–21: Jesus's family approaches	3:22–30: Beelzebub controversy	3:31–35: Jesus's true family
5:21–43	5:21–24: Jairus approaches	5:25–34: Woman with hemorrhage	5:35–43: Jairus's daughter raised
6:6b–32	6:6b–13: Mission of the twelve	6:14–29: John the Baptist executed	6:30–32: Return of the twelve
11:12–25	11:12–14: Jesus curses the fig tree	11:15–19: Cleansing of the temple	11:20–25: The fig tree has withered
14:1–11	14:1–2: Plot to arrest Jesus	14:3–9: Anointing	14:10–11: Arrest planned with Judas
14:53–72	14:53–54: Peter in the courtyard	14:55–65: Trial before high priest	14:66–72: Peter denies Jesus

Matthew and Luke retain some of these intercalations but not all of them. Where they do retain this literary structure, as, for example, where Luke 8:40–56 has the story of Jairus's daughter sandwiching the story of the woman with a hemorrhage, this is generally seen as an example of Luke's use of Mark—Luke is retaining the way that Mark has crafted the narrative. This is why John's parallel (John 18:15–27) to the last of Mark's intercalations (Mark 14:53–72), introducing the story of Peter's denial, interrupting it with the trial before the high priest and council, then returning to it, is so striking. It looks like John is familiar with this characteristic Markan literary structure.[24]

---

23. See especially Tom Shepherd, "The Narrative Function of Marcan Intercalation," *NTS* 41 (1995): 522–40. These six are a minimal list; some scholars see more examples.
24. For this as an example of a Markan characteristic feature that is taken over more sparsely by Matthew, Luke, and John, see John Dominic Crossan, *The Birth of Christianity: Discovering What Happened in the Years Immediately After the Execution of Jesus* (San Francisco: HarperSanFrancisco, 1998), 106–7, 113–14.

CHAPTER 2

"A Passion Narrative with an Extended Introduction"

So far in this chapter, we have seen examples of John appearing alongside Matthew, Mark, and Luke in synopsis, in parallel passages, and we have also seen parallel sequences between those three gospels and John. But there is something still more fundamental about the way that John's Gospel is structured. In spite of the fact that Martin Kähler's description of "a passion narrative with an extended introduction" is usually applied to Mark, it is equally applicable to John. Kähler himself was talking about all four canonical Gospels.[25] If anything, John out-Marks Mark by devoting the whole of the last half of the gospel to the last week of Jesus's life, much of it to the one momentous evening (John 13–17), so that Jesus's teaching is thoroughly immersed in a precrucifixion context.

Moreover, just as Mark early on signals the coming conflict (Mark 2:1–3:6), so too John foreshadows the passion from the beginning, in a move that would explain one of his few differences from the Synoptic order (see chart above). When Jesus appears in Jerusalem at Passover, immediately after the narration of the first sign (John 2:1–12), John does not just prefigure the conflict to come in the second half of the gospel. He actually draws forward an aspect of that conflict to this early moment and narrates his version of the temple incident (John 2:13–22). There are, of course, those who argue for the historicity of the Johannine placement of the incident, but to dwell on a debatable point about historicity would be to miss the certain point about the narrative function of the story in John, which is explicitly to foreshadow the passion story and evoke Jesus's death and resurrection (John 2:19–22). We will return to this below.

The structural similarities between Mark and John are in fact much closer than is commonly perceived. It is possible to quantify, roughly, the extent of the "extended introduction" in each work, and on the assumption that the triumphal entry begins the passion narrative proper, it is striking to see how similar its position is in each gospel:

Mark 1:1–10:52	John 1:1–12:11
422 verses[26]	534 verses
63.8 percent	61.7 percent

25. Martin Kähler, *The So-Called Historical Jesus and the Historic Biblical Christ*, trans. Carl E. Braaten (Philadelphia: Fortress, 1964), 80 n. 11.

26. The figures here are based on Mark having 661 verses, omitting Mark 7:16; 9:44, 46; 11:26; 15:28; 16:9–20, and John having 866 verses, omitting John 5:4; 7:53–8:11. These figures are slightly adjusted from Mark Goodacre, "Parallel Traditions or Parallel Gospels? John's Gospel as a Re-imagining of Mark," in *John's Transformation of Mark*, ed. Eve-Marie Becker, Helen

Mark 11:1–11: Triumphal entry	John 12:12–19: Triumphal entry
Mark 11:1–16:8 239 verses 36.2 percent	John 12:12–21:25 332 verses 38.3 percent

In other words, the "extended introduction" in both of the gospels occupies just over 60 percent of the whole, and the passion narrative begins at a very similar moment. If the passion narrative proper is thought to begin later, with Jesus's arrest, the same point can still be made:

Mark 1:1–14:43 577 verses 87.3 percent	John 1:1–17:26 728 verses 84.1 percent
Mark 14:43–52: Arrest	John 18:1–14: Arrest
Mark 14:43–16:8 84 verses 12.7 percent	John 18:1–21:25 138 verses 15.9 percent

We should not imagine, of course, that the evangelist has precisely measured his Markan scroll, with a view to introducing his own passion narrative in a similar position. The point is to notice the broad similarities in the way that the two gospels are structured. It looks like Mark's Gospel could have inspired the way that John's Gospel tells its similar and often parallel story. Could this be coincidence? Of course. Is it likely to be coincidence? I doubt it, but every scholar and every student sets their own bar for where coincidence ends and direct contact begins. Given the continuum of parallels between the Synoptics and John, some will find it less stressful to draw a straight line of influence than to think that the links are the result of oral traditions, crisscross contacts, and coincidence.

The issue can be illustrated not only with respect to the passion narrative but also with respect to the beginning of all four canonical Gospels—the outset of that "extended introduction." Both Mark and John begin their narratives with John the Baptist and his proclamation of the identity of Jesus (Mark 1:1–8; John 1:6–8, 15, 19–36). Although they have prologues about birth and infancy (Matt 1–2; Luke 1–2), Matthew and Luke do the same (Matt 3:1–17; Luke 3:1–20), and Luke adds a

---

Bond, and Catrin Williams (London: T&T Clark, 2021), 85, because I had forgotten there to omit the textually uncertain individual verses.

birth story for John the Baptist too (Luke 1:5–25, 39–80). All four gospels appear to agree that the appropriate point at which to begin the story of Jesus is with John the Baptist. Why is this? Who told John, if his gospel was independent of the Synoptics, that this is where the story should begin? If John is independent of them, why does he begin in the same way, with John the Baptist's testimony to Jesus, followed by the dove descending on Jesus, followed by the calling of the disciples, and so on? This is not a question of individual traditions but of narrative direction and overall literary structure. The generic constraints of writing a *bios* ("biography") do not account for this specific way of configuring the Jesus story.

There were surely other ways that the story could be told. We know of several. Paul begins his story by focusing on Jesus as the seed of David (Rom 1:3), and the Gospel of Thomas begins by taking the "living Jesus" as the one whose enigmatic sayings need to be interpreted (Gospel of Thomas incipit and saying 1). Neither appears to treat John the Baptist as the necessary and inevitable beginning of the gospel message.[27] Our inability to see the peculiarity of this way of telling the Christian story may be due to the models of Christian origins we have worked with for so long, where Luke is independent from Matthew, and John from all three Synoptics. On these models, Mark's way of configuring the narrative is not trend setting but normative. It is a master narrative that was there from the beginning, independently accessed by Q, Mark, John, and other sources now lost to us.

Perhaps, too, our failure to find the similarities striking may say more about our innate canonical bias than anything else. Our presumption of the normativity of telling the story in this way not only ignores the countless other non-canonical ways of telling Jesus's story, but it assumes that there is something inevitable, something preordained, about the Synoptic and Johannine constructions. In this way of thinking, the similarities are down to independent witnesses to the shared master narrative, instead of witnessing to worldviews that are derived from literary contact.

The Revelation of the Hidden Messiah

So far we have seen many similarities between the four canonical Gospels, beginning with words and sentences, continuing to entire passages, and extending to the structure and proportions of whole gospels.[28] There is, however, something

---

27. For other examples, see Francis Watson and Sarah Parkhouse, eds., *Telling the Christian Story Differently: Counter-narratives from Nag Hammadi and Beyond* (London: T&T Clark, 2020).

28. One of the strengths of Andrew Lincoln, *The Gospel According to St. John*, BNTC (London: Continuum, 2005), is that as well as word, verse, and pericope level compari-

still more fundamental. John shares with the Synoptics the same literary conceit, that the story is one in which Jesus's identity is hidden, only to be retrospectively understood in the light of the resurrection. Just as Kähler's "passion narrative with an extended introduction" gets forgotten when it comes to John, so too William Wrede's *Messianic Secret* is usually remembered as a study of Mark's Gospel alone.[29] In some ways, this is unsurprising given the boldness of Jesus's public pronouncements in John, which we rightly stress in our introductory lectures in a bid to make sure that our students have grasped the differences between the Synoptics and John. But once again we are in danger of taking our own propaganda too seriously. In spite of the apparently public revelations in John, the evangelist repeatedly depicts Jesus as a hidden Messiah, whose identity is clear only to insiders who will go on to witness the resurrection. There are three elements to the way that John configures this: (1) There are insiders who understand and outsiders who do not; (2) Jesus hides himself from the crowds; and these are resolved by (3) the hermeneutical key of the resurrection. Let us take each in turn.

Insiders and Outsiders

John divides Jesus's audience into two. There are those who believe, who understand who Jesus is, for whom Jesus's speeches make sense, and there are others who are hostile to Jesus and who fail to understand his speeches, thinking him either blasphemous or incomprehensible. Examples are manifold, but John 10:24–27 illustrates the two groups effectively:

> John 10:24–27: So the Judeans[30] gathered around him and said to him, "How long will you keep us in suspense? If you are the Messiah, tell us plainly." Jesus

---

sons, he looks at larger motifs; see, e.g., his summary comment, "While there are some instances of similarities with Synoptic material, where an equally strong case for John's use of Synoptic-like independent tradition might be made, this commentary argues that the much stronger case is that John knows the Synoptic Gospels themselves. The case becomes even stronger when not simply isolated pericopes are compared, as is frequently done, but when whole units of material or whole motifs are also taken into account, as will be indicated below" (32).

29. William Wrede, *The Messianic Secret* (Cambridge: Clarke, 1971); trans. of *Das Messiasgeheimnis in den Evangelien: Zugleich ein Beitrag zum Verständnis des Markusevangeliums* (Göttingen: Vandenhoeck & Ruprecht, 1901). But for exceptions, see John Ashton, *Understanding the Fourth Gospel*, 2nd ed. (Oxford: Oxford University Press, 2007), 207–11, Troels Engberg-Pedersen, *John and Philosophy: A New Reading of the Fourth Gospel* (Oxford: Oxford University Press, 2017), 315–20, and works cited in notes 31 and 33 below. Wrede himself did not, of course, see the messianic secret motif as Mark's literary creation (*Messiasgeheimnis*, 145).

30. NRSVue, "Jews."

answered, "I have told you, and you do not believe. The works that I do in my Father's name testify to me; but you do not believe, because you do not belong to my sheep. My sheep hear my voice. I know them, and they follow me."

In other words, in spite of Jesus's bold and unequivocal declarations, many simply cannot hear what he is saying. To them, they sound like riddles, and Jesus is not speaking plainly. This functions in a way similar to the parable secret in Mark 4:10–12 (parr. Matt 13:10–17 // Luke 8:9–10). There are "those around him with the twelve," to whom "has been given the secret of the kingdom of God," and there are "those outside," for whom "everything comes in parables." Like Matthew (13:13–15), Mark (4:12), and Luke (8:10), John explains the phenomenon by appealing to Isa 6:9–10. There are those whose eyes have been blinded (John 9:39; 12:40) and whose hearts have been hardened (John 12:40). The allusion to Isaiah occurs in all three Synoptics (Matt 13:13–15; Mark 4:12; Luke 8:10), but John here shares with Matthew the fuller quotation of Isaiah (Matt 13:14–16), which Luke saves for the end of Acts (Acts 28:25–27).

It could be argued that John's Gospel not only uses but also improves on the way that Mark configures the secrecy theme. The difficulty with Mark's presentation is that the inner group, the twelve, appear to remain ignorant, and it is not just the outsiders whose hearts are hardened but the twelve themselves (Mark 6:52 and 8:17; cf. 9:32). They all flee (Mark 14:27, 50–52), and they are still absent at the end of the gospel. They famously fail to grasp who Jesus is and how he must suffer. Even the faithful female disciples flee in fear and say nothing as the curtain falls (Mark 16:8). By contrast, the disciples in John ultimately do understand who Jesus is. They are the friends (John 15:13–15), children (13:33; 14:18) who are chosen (13:18) and loved (13:1; 15:9, 12–13) by Jesus, and although most of them are absent at the cross, the Beloved Disciple remains faithful, along with Mary Magdalene, the mother of Jesus, and Mary wife of Clopas (John 19:25–27), before all of them (absent Judas) see and believe (John 20:8, 18, 20, 25, 28–29). The motif of insiders and outsiders parallels but ultimately improves on Mark's by properly contrasting the understanding disciples with the confused outsiders.

The Hidden Messiah

Just as Jesus often withdraws himself in Mark (Mark 1:35; 4:10; 6:46; 7:24; cf. 3:7, 13; 4:34, 36; 6:31–32; 7:33; 8:13, 23; 9:2; 11:19; 13:3; 14:32–33), so too Jesus frequently hides himself in John:[31]

---

31. On the hidden Messiah motif, see especially Susan Miller, "'Among You Stands One

John 7:10–11: But after his brothers had gone to the festival, then he also went, not publicly but as it were in secret. The Judeans were looking for him at the festival and saying, "Where is he?"

John 8:59: So they picked up stones to throw at him, but Jesus hid himself and went out of the temple.

John 11:54: Jesus therefore no longer walked about openly among the Judeans[32] but went from there to a town called Ephraim in the region near the wilderness, and he remained there with the disciples.

John 12:36b–37: After Jesus had said this, he departed and hid from them. Although he had performed so many signs in their presence, they did not believe in him.

In the latter case, the passage combines the hidden-Messiah motif with the insiders-outsiders motif—Jesus hides himself (12:36), and while hidden, the narrator steps on to the stage to expound Isa 53:1 alongside Isa 6:10 (12:37–43), the heart-hardening passage that John shares with the Synoptics (see above). In other words, these are aspects of the same phenomenon, according to which Jesus's identity is revealed only to those he chooses, and only when the time is right.[33] The narrator explains that the scriptural insight is reliable in that Isaiah had the key revelation: "Isaiah said this because he saw his glory and spoke about him" (John 12:41). Seeing his glory is the guarantee that the revelation is true, just as the narrator underlined that "we have seen his glory" in John 1:14. We will return to this in chapter 6 below, but it is worth noting at this point that these claims to having witnessed his glory function to reveal Jesus's true identity, the one that is known only to insiders, and that finally becomes clear in Jesus's resurrection, which brings us to the next point.

Whom You Do Not Know' (John 1:26): The Use of the Tradition of the Hidden Messiah in John's Gospel," in *The Ways That Often Parted: Essays in Honor of Joel Marcus*, ed. Lori Baron, Jill Hicks-Keeton, and Matthew Thiessen (Atlanta: SBL Press, 2018), 243–63, and literature cited there. Although the feature is occasionally noted in Johannine scholarship, it is rarely seen as deriving from Mark's redactional presentation of the motif. See also note 36 below.

32. NRSVue, "Jews."

33. Cf. M. W. G. Stibbe, "The Elusive Christ: A New Reading of the Fourth Gospel," *JSNT* 44 (1991): 19–37, especially 25, "The constant emphasis in Johannine scholarship on Jesus the revealer needs challenging precisely for this reason. The Jesus of John's story is just as much the concealer as the revealer; just as much the one who conceals truth as the one who discloses it." Stibbe hints that John's "elusive Christ" may have been influenced by Mark's characterization of Jesus (32–33).

CHAPTER 2

The Resurrection as the Hermeneutical Key

In John, just as in the Synoptics, the resurrection marks the turning point for the full revelation of Jesus's identity, the hermeneutical key to the gospel, which the readers already possess, without which the characters in the drama are doomed to confusion. The key passage in Mark famously occurs at the conclusion of the transfiguration story, where resurrection is defined as the turning point:

> Mark 9:9–10: As they were coming down the mountain, he ordered them to tell no one about what they had seen, until after the Son of Man had risen from the dead. So they kept the matter to themselves, questioning what this rising from the dead could mean.

In spite of its importance, there is a problem with the way that Mark expresses the idea. The resurrection is pivotal, but there is no indication in the narrative that the disciples ever did get the crucial revelation. Luke makes good on Mark's lack and develops the insight by adding the element of remembering. And it is this element that is also important in John:

> Luke 24:5–8: "Why are you looking for the living among the dead? He is not here, but has been raised! <u>Remember [μνήσθητε]</u> how he told you, while he was still in Galilee, that the Son of Man must be delivered[34] into the hands of sinners, and be crucified, and on the third day rise again?" <u>Then they remembered [ἐμνήσθησαν] his words</u>.

> John 2:22: After he was raised from the dead, <u>his disciples remembered [ἐμνήσθησαν]</u> that he had said this; and they believed the scripture and the word that Jesus had spoken.

> John 12:16: His disciples did not understand these things at first; but when Jesus was glorified, <u>then they remembered [ἐμνήσθησαν]</u> that these things had been written of him and had been done to him.

Like Luke, John makes the Markan motif more coherent, with disciples who ultimately succeed in understanding Jesus's identity and mission, as they interpret his words, in the light of the Scriptures, through a remembering that is triggered by the resurrection.

---

34. NRSVue, "handed over," which creates an awkward and unnecessary repetition with the "hands of sinners."

Hans Conzelmann once said that the messianic secret was the "hermeneutical presupposition of the gospel genre."[35] Regardless of whether one accepts the idea that there is a unique "gospel genre," his insight makes sense of the essence of the Synoptics and John. These gospels are obsessed with Jesus's death at the same time as explaining his life as one that was hidden to outsiders, a mystery to those he had not made his own. Jesus's identity was understood only by insiders who, after the resurrection, understood the mystery and narrated it from the insiders' perspective. It is a brilliant literary trope, and it is arguable that John perfects what he shares with the other canonical Gospels.[36]

WHAT IF JOHN IS SYNOPTIC?

I am not suggesting that we change the time-honored nomenclature that separates "the Synoptic Gospels" from John. Well, I am not suggesting it seriously, unless someone would like to talk me into it. The differences are obvious, undoubtable, and important. John really is sufficiently different from the other three for us to treat it a little differently and to ask questions about why it is so different. Nevertheless, there is a serious point beyond any attempt to be provocative. By pounding away at the language of "the Synoptic Gospels," "the Synoptic problem," and "the gospel synopsis," we give ourselves the excuse to treat John not just as a different work but as a different kind of work, one that is not Synoptic, that cannot be lined up with others in a synopsis, and that therefore cannot be in any kind of literary relationship with them.

The reality, however, is that in spite of the Fourth Gospel's multiple divergences from Matthew, Mark, and Luke, it is frequently Synoptic. It can be—and often is—placed alongside one or more of the others in a gospel synopsis, sometimes to draw attention to parallel phrases and sentences, sometimes to show parallels with whole paragraphs, and sometimes to make clear that entire passages are structured in the same way. Moreover, the Fourth Gospel's parallels with the Synoptics extend beyond the kinds of similarities that can be explained

---

35. Hans Conzelmann, "Present and Future in the Synoptic Tradition," *JTC* 5 (1968): 26–44, at 43.

36. Cf. Engberg-Pederson, *John as Philosophy*, 319, "If one believes (as one should) that John must have taken over (and developed) from Mark the whole genre of the gospel narrative as this had been created by the latter, one must surely also agree that John has taken over and developed the much more specific theme of the Messianic secret that constitutes the 'inner form' in Mark of the genre of the gospel narrative, the theme that drives the story to its conclusion."

by oral traditions. In spite of the fact that John is often thought to have a radically different order from the Synoptics, there is a surprisingly similar parallel sequence of passages. Like Mark, John is a "passion narrative with an extended introduction," and like Mark, the passion narrative begins at a similar point.

I have argued in this chapter that the similarities between John and the Synoptics are on a spectrum from words, to phrases, to sentences, to paragraphs, to passages, to gospel structures, but the most striking thing of all is that the Synoptics and John share the same fundamental literary conceit, of the hidden Messiah who is only truly understood by insiders whom he has called, who only retrospectively understand the whole because they have witnessed the resurrection. It is, of course, possible that John could have landed independently on so similar a literary conceit to the Synoptics, but to have done so at the same time as having so many parallels to the Synoptics across the spectrum will be, for some, a big ask.

Is John Synoptic? Frequently. Did John know the Synoptics? Yes, but the case requires more than simply drawing attention to places where John is Synoptic. The questions about oral traditions, coincidences, and other unknowns will always provide potential alternatives to John's knowledge of the Synoptics, so it will be worth taking a closer look at places where John shows knowledge of how Matthew reworked Mark, and how Luke reworked Mark. This is the topic of chapter 3.

Chapter 3

John, from Mark, via Matthew and Luke

Given the recent renewal of interest in the idea of John's transformation of Mark,[1] it is easy to forget that John's knowledge of Mark may often have been mediated through Matthew and Luke. The attraction of comparing John with Mark is clear: both gospels leapfrog any birth or infancy stories and begin with John the Baptist; both invest heavily in the idea of a hidden Messiah; and both are loved for their enigmatic, theological richness. Yet many of the most striking parallels between John and the Synoptics are found in Matthew and Luke, and not only in their double tradition and special material but also in material that they themselves derive from Mark.[2] And if it turns out that John, after all, shows knowledge of the ways that Matthew and Luke redacted and reframed their Markan material, the case for John's knowledge of the Synoptics would appear to be settled. In this chapter, I would like to present several examples of places where John shows knowledge of Matthew's redaction of Mark and of Luke's redaction of Mark.[3] Given the evidence that this provides for John's knowledge of the Synoptics, I will then offer some suggestions about why some scholars have missed or resisted this conclusion.

---

1. See especially Eve-Marie Becker, Helen Bond, and Catrin Williams, eds., *John's Transformation of Mark* (London: T&T Clark, 2021).

2. I am here assuming Markan priority, for which I have argued in several publications, including chapter 2 of *The Case Against Q: Studies in Marcan Priority and the Synoptic Problem* (Harrisburg, PA: Trinity International, 2002); and most recently in "The Farrer Hypothesis," in *The Synoptic Problem: Four Views*, ed. Stanley E. Porter and Bryan R. Dyer (Grand Rapids: Baker, 2016), 47–66.

3. The method of looking for the presence of redactional material from a source is so well established in the field that it does not require an extended discussion. See James W. Barker, *John's Use of Matthew* (Minneapolis: Fortress, 2015), 16–27, for a recent summary discussion.

CHAPTER 3

Matthean Redaction in John

Matthew is sometimes thought to be unpromising territory in the search for Johannine parallels.[4] B. H. Streeter was convinced of John's knowledge of Mark and Luke, but he sat lightly toward Matthew.[5] So too C. K. Barrett.[6] Yet there are several places where Matthew's changes to Mark appear in parallel material in John, suggesting that John knew Matthew's Gospel. I would like to draw attention to five examples, one from John 4, and the others from the passion and resurrection narratives.[7]

"The Fever Left Him/Her" (Matt 8:15 // John 4:52)

MATT 8:15	MARK 1:31	JOHN 4:52
καὶ ἥψατο τῆς χειρὸς αὐτῆς, καὶ <u>ἀφῆκεν αὐτὴν ὁ πυρετός</u>, καὶ ἠγέρθη καὶ διηκόνει αὐτῷ.	καὶ προσελθὼν ἤγειρεν αὐτὴν κρατήσας τῆς χειρός· καὶ <u>ἀφῆκεν αὐτὴν ὁ πυρετός</u>, καὶ διηκόνει αὐτοῖς.	ἐπύθετο οὖν τὴν ὥραν παρ' αὐτῶν ἐν ᾗ κομψότερον ἔσχεν· εἶπαν οὖν αὐτῷ ὅτι Ἐχθὲς ὥραν ἑβδόμην <u>ἀφῆκεν αὐτὸν ὁ πυρετός</u>.
And he touched her hand, and <u>the fever left her</u>, and she got up and began to serve him.	He came and took her by the hand and lifted her up. Then <u>the fever left her</u>, and she began to serve them.	So he asked them the hour when he began to recover, and they said to him, "Yesterday at one in the afternoon <u>the fever left him</u>."[8]

---

4. But see Barker, *John's Use of Matthew*.
5. B. H. Streeter, *The Four Gospels: A Study of Origins* (London: Macmillan, 1924), 396.
6. C. K. Barrett, *The Gospel According to St. John: An Introduction with Commentary and Notes on the Greek Text*, 2nd ed. (Philadelphia: Westminster, 1978), 15–16.
7. I will also argue in chapter 7 that John's Christology is strongly influenced by Matthew's.
8. Luke 4:39 has similar phrasing, too, καὶ ἐπιστὰς ἐπάνω αὐτῆς ἐπετίμησεν τῷ πυρετῷ, καὶ ἀφῆκεν αὐτήν ("Then he stood over her and rebuked the fever, and it left her").

John, from Mark, via Matthew and Luke

The reader might at first balk at this example given that the relevant expression, ἀφῆκεν αὐτὴν ὁ πυρετός ("the fever left her"), is identical in both Matthew and Mark. Moreover, in John the expression comes in a different incident, the healing of the royal official's son (John 4:45–54), rather than the healing of Peter's mother-in-law (Matt 8:14–15 // Mark 1:29–31 // Luke 4:38–39). This kind of thing happens elsewhere in John, as we saw above (Mark 2:10–12 // John 5:8–9) and will see again (Luke 22:53 // John 7:30, below), but what is particularly striking here is that this story in Matthew is adjacent to the healing of the centurion's boy (Matt 8:5–13), which closely parallels the healing of the officer's son in John. It looks like John has his eye on his Matthew scroll, where these stories uniquely stand side by side:

MATTHEW	MARKAN PARALLEL	JOHANNINE PARALLEL
4:18–22: Call of the first disciples	1:16–20	1:35–42
4:23–25: Jesus ministers to crowds	1:39; 3:7–8	
5–7: Sermon on the Mount		
8:1–4: Man with leprosy	1:40–45	
8:5–13: Centurion's boy		4:45–54: Officer's boy
8:14–15: Peter's mother-in-law	1:29–31	
"The fever left her"	"The fever left her"	"The fever left him"

John has told his version of the centurion's boy story, and an expression from the adjacent story, found only in this position in Matthew, has caught his eye, his mind's eye, or his ear.[9]

It might be objected that the expression in question, "The fever left him/her," sounds pretty generic. Perhaps it was simply an everyday expression of the kind that might pop into John's head by coincidence or from shared oral tradition? We might have thought so, but in fact it is not. The expression occurs in only these three places, Matt 8:15, Mark 1:31, and John 4:52, in the whole of the New Testament. Moreover, the expression never, to our knowledge,[10] features in

---

9. John Muddiman, "John's Use of Matthew: A British Exponent of the Theory," *ETL* 59 (1983): 333–37, at 337, makes this suggestion in his reflections on a letter from Austin Farrer. He is followed by F. Neirynck, "John 4,46–54: Signs Source and/or Synoptic Gospels," *ETL* 60 (1984): 367–75, at 373; see also Michael D. Goulder, *Luke: A New Paradigm*, JSNTSup 20 (Sheffield: Sheffield Academic, 1989), 380, and Andrew Lincoln, *The Gospel According to St. John*, BNTC (London: Continuum, 2005), 36, "John, then, almost certainly has to be familiar with Matthew's editorial arrangement."

10. Which is, in this context, a TLG search.

CHAPTER 3

Greek literature until this point. And the word πυρετός ("fever") is itself much rarer than we might have thought, and it occurs on only two further occasions in the New Testament, Luke 4:39 (the Lukan parallel) and Acts 28:8.

The Crown of Thorns (Matt 27:27–29 // Mark 15:16–18 // John 19:1–3)

MATT 27:27–29	MARK 15:16–18	JOHN 19:1–3
<u>Τότε</u>		<u>Τότε</u> οὖν ἔλαβεν ὁ Πιλᾶτος τὸν Ἰησοῦν καὶ ἐμαστίγωσεν. καὶ
οἱ στρατιῶται τοῦ ἡγεμόνος παραλαβόντες τὸν Ἰησοῦν εἰς τὸ πραιτώριον συνήγαγον ἐπ᾽ αὐτὸν ὅλην τὴν σπεῖραν. καὶ ἐκδύσαντες αὐτὸν χλαμύδα κοκκίνην περιέθηκαν	Οἱ δὲ στρατιῶται ἀπήγαγον αὐτὸν ἔσω τῆς αὐλῆς, ὅ ἐστιν πραιτώριον, καὶ συγκαλοῦσιν ὅλην τὴν σπεῖραν. καὶ ἐνδιδύσκουσιν αὐτὸν πορφύραν καὶ περιτιθέασιν	οἱ στρατιῶται
αὐτῷ, καὶ <u>πλέξαντες στέφανον ἐξ ἀκανθῶν ἐπέθηκαν</u> ἐπὶ <u>τῆς κεφαλῆς αὐτοῦ καὶ</u> κάλαμον ἐν τῇ δεξιᾷ αὐτοῦ, καὶ γονυπετήσαντες ἔμπροσθεν αὐτοῦ ἐνέπαιξαν αὐτῷ λέγοντες· Χαῖρε, βασιλεῦ τῶν Ἰουδαίων.	αὐτῷ πλέξαντες ἀκάνθινον στέφανον· καὶ ἤρξαντο ἀσπάζεσθαι αὐτόν· Χαῖρε, βασιλεῦ τῶν Ἰουδαίων·	<u>πλέξαντες στέφανον ἐξ ἀκανθῶν ἐπέθηκαν</u> <u>αὐτοῦ τῇ κεφαλῇ</u>, καὶ ἱμάτιον πορφυροῦν περιέβαλον αὐτόν, καὶ ἤρχοντο πρὸς αὐτὸν καὶ ἔλεγον· Χαῖρε, ὁ βασιλεὺς τῶν Ἰουδαίων·

John, from Mark, via Matthew and Luke

MATT 27:27–29	MARK 15:16–18	JOHN 19:1–3
Then		Then Pilate took Jesus and had him flogged.
the soldiers of the governor took Jesus into the governor's headquarters, and they gathered the whole cohort around him. They stripped him and put a scarlet robe on him, and	And[11] the soldiers led him into the courtyard of the palace (that is, the governor's headquarters); and they called together the whole cohort. And they clothed him in a purple cloak; and they put	And the soldiers,
after twisting a crown from thorns,[12] they put it on his head. They put a reed in his right hand and knelt before him and mocked him, saying, "Hail, King of the Jews!"	on him a crown twisted from thorns.[13] And they began saluting him, "Hail, King of the Jews!"	after twisting a crown from thorns, put it on his head,[14] and they dressed him in a purple robe. They kept coming up to him, saying, "Hail, King of the Jews!"

This is another case of John being a fourth Synoptic gospel. There are no difficulties in representing the similarities and differences straightforwardly in a synopsis. There are twenty-seven words in John 19:2–3a, and fifteen of them are parallel with Matthew. This is the kind of evidence that convinces scholars of a literary relationship of some kind between the Synoptics. Πλέκω is found only here in the Gospels and Acts (1/1/0/1+0), and ἄκανθα is found only in this context in John (19:2, 5), while it is common in the Synoptics. But while this vocabulary is shared by Matthew, Mark, and John, the syntax in Matthew and John agrees against Mark. Matthew and John both have πλέξαντες στέφανον ἐξ ἀκανθῶν ἐπέθηκαν ("having twisted a crown from thorns, they put. . . .") whereas

11. NRSVue, "Then," creating an agreement with Matthew where it does not exist.
12. NRSVue has "and after twisting some thorns into a crown," which adjusts Matthew's wording to Mark's; see note 13.
13. NRSVue, "after twisting some thorns into a crown they put it on him."
14. NRSVue, "wove a crown of thorns and put it on his head," which masks some of the parallel wording with Matthew.

Mark has περιτιθέασιν αὐτῷ πλέξαντες ἀκάνθινον στέφανον ("they put on him a crown twisted from thorns").

Moreover, both Matthew and John have the same redundancy, where the crown of thorns is placed "upon his head" (αὐτοῦ τῇ κεφαλῇ).[15] One might, of course, respond, "Where else would you place a crown?" But that is actually the point. It is not necessary to specify "the head." Mark's account makes sense without it.[16] Matthew has a similar redundant clarificatory addition to Mark 7:14–15 involving a part of the body when he talks about words that proceed from "the mouth" (Matt 15:10–11).[17] Similarly, Jesus "opened his mouth" (ἀνοίξας τὸ στόμα αὐτοῦ) to begin teaching the Sermon on the Mount (Matt 5:2).[18] The disciples in 17:8 do not simply "look up" at Jesus. They "raised their eyes" (ἐπάραντες δὲ τοὺς ὀφθαλμοὺς αὐτῶν; contrast Mark 9:8) and saw only him.[19] Where in Mark 10:51 Bartimaeus "wants to see," the two blind men in Matt 20:33 ask "that our eyes may be opened" (ἀνοιγῶσιν οἱ ὀφθαλμοὶ ἡμῶν). And in Matt 26:51, the person who strikes the high priest's slave first "put his hand on his sword," uniquely among the four gospel accounts of this incident (Mark 15:47 // Luke 22:50 // John 18:10).

It looks like Matthew has made minor adjustments in rewording his Markan narrative source, and these minor adjustments have found their way into John. Appeals to oral tradition do not help here. There is no new substance in Matthew or John. There is only an agreement in how to word the same content. This is literary borrowing.

---

15. Robert H. Stein, "The Matthew-Luke Agreements Against Mark: Insight from John," *CBQ* 54 (1992): 482–502, at 490 n. 27, asks, "Is this due to an independent logical assumption? (Where else would they put a crown?) More likely is the view that another tradition, with which John was familiar, specified this." This kind of recursion—not Matthew but Matthew's source—is endemic among those who maintain John's independence. It is not clear why it is preferable to project agreements onto hypothetical prior sources.

16. Mark does mention that Jesus is struck on the head (Mark 15:19 // Matt 27:30), but here "the head" is not redundant because there are other places on the body where Jesus could be assaulted.

17. On this example, see further Mark Goodacre, *Thomas and the Gospels: The Case for Thomas's Familiarity with the Synoptics* (Grand Rapids: Eerdmans, 2012), 70–71.

18. The redundancy is well illustrated here by the fact that translations like the New International Version do not mention his mouth, with "he began to teach them."

19. The redundancy is again well captured by the New International Version's translation, "When they looked up."

Joseph of Arimathea (Matt 27:57–58a // Mark 15:42–43 // John 19:38)

MATT 27:57–58	MARK 15:42–43	JOHN 19:38
Ὀψίας δὲ γενομένης	Καὶ ἤδη ὀψίας γενομένης, ἐπεὶ ἦν παρασκευὴ ὅ ἐστιν	Μετὰ δὲ ταῦτα ἠρώτησεν τὸν Πιλᾶτον
ἦλθεν	προσάββατον, ἐλθὼν	
ἄνθρωπος πλούσιος	Ἰωσὴφ [ὁ]	Ἰωσὴφ [ὁ]
ἀπὸ Ἀριμαθαίας, τοὔνομα	ἀπὸ Ἀριμαθαίας εὐσχήμων	ἀπὸ Ἀριμαθαίας,
Ἰωσήφ, ὃς καὶ αὐτὸς	βουλευτής, ὃς καὶ αὐτὸς ἦν	ὢν
ἐμαθητεύθη τῷ Ἰησοῦ·	προσδεχόμενος τὴν βασιλείαν τοῦ θεοῦ,	μαθητὴς τοῦ Ἰησοῦ κεκρυμμένος δὲ διὰ τὸν
οὗτος προσελθὼν	τολμήσας εἰσῆλθεν πρὸς	φόβον τῶν Ἰουδαίων,
τῷ Πιλάτῳ ᾐτήσατο	τὸν Πιλᾶτον καὶ ᾐτήσατο	ἵνα ἄρῃ
τὸ σῶμα τοῦ Ἰησοῦ.	τὸ σῶμα τοῦ Ἰησοῦ.	τὸ σῶμα τοῦ Ἰησοῦ·
As evening approached, there came a rich man	When evening had come, and since it was the day of Preparation, that is,	After these things,
from Arimathea, named Joseph,	the day before the Sabbath, Joseph of Arimathea, a respected member of the council,	Joseph of Arimathea,
who also himself was <u>discipled to Jesus</u>.	who was also himself waiting expectantly for the kingdom of God,	who was <u>a disciple of Jesus</u>, though a secret one because of his fear of the Judeans,
Going to Pilate, he asked for the body of Jesus, and Pilate ordered that it be given to him.	went boldly to Pilate and asked for the body of Jesus.	asked Pilate to let him take away the body of Jesus.

Mark's note that Joseph of Arimathea was a "counselor" (βουλευτής) who was "seeking the kingdom of God" (ἦν προσδεχόμενος τὴν βασιλείαν τοῦ θεοῦ) is revised by Matthew to make him "discipled to Jesus" (ἐμαθητεύθη τῷ Ἰησοῦ). Matthew's redaction is clearly mirrored by John, who calls him a "disciple of Jesus" (μαθητὴς τοῦ Ἰησοῦ), with the added note that the discipleship was "secret because of fear of the Judeans" (κεκρυμμένος δὲ διὰ τὸν φόβον τῶν Ἰουδαίων). The latter note is, of course, characteristically Johannine, but the idea that Joseph was a disciple is shared with Matthew, who appears to have inferred the detail from Mark's more neutral statement.

Mark's story makes better historical sense. Joseph is a sympathetic Judean counselor who has the status to approach Pilate and ask for Jesus's body. That he is not a disciple of Jesus is clear from the statement that Mary Magdalene and Mary of Joses "see where he was laid" (Mark 15:47). They are observing the action, and the narrative assumes that they are not in any sense collaborating with Joseph. In Matthew's redaction, Joseph becomes a disciple, but now the logic for the women's noninvolvement in the burial (Matt 27:61) has gone. Matthew's secondary revision of Mark has been taken over by John, who develops it further by introducing Nicodemus (John 19:39–42), and their preparation of Jesus's body for burial displaces any role for the women, who then reappear somewhat awkwardly in John 20:2. The evidence for John's familiarity with Matthew's redaction of Mark continues in the next verse.

Jesus's Tomb (Matt 27:59–60 // Mark 15:46 // John 19:41)

MATT 27:59–60	MARK 15:46	JOHN 19:41
καὶ λαβὼν τὸ σῶμα ὁ Ἰωσὴφ ἐνετύλιξεν αὐτὸ σινδόνι καθαρᾷ, καὶ ἔθηκεν αὐτὸ ἐν τῷ καινῷ αὐτοῦ μνημείῳ ὃ ἐλατόμησεν ἐν τῇ πέτρᾳ.	καὶ ἀγοράσας σινδόνα καθελὼν αὐτὸν ἐνείλησεν τῇ σινδόνι καὶ ἔθηκεν αὐτὸν ἐν μνημείῳ ὃ ἦν λελατομημένον ἐκ πέτρας.	ἦν δὲ ἐν τῷ τόπῳ ὅπου ἐσταυρώθη κῆπος, καὶ ἐν τῷ κήπῳ μνημεῖον καινόν, ἐν ᾧ οὐδέπω οὐδεὶς ἦν τεθειμένος
And having taken the body, Joseph wrapped it in a clean linen cloth and laid it in his own new tomb, which he had hewn in the rock.[20]	And having bought a linen cloth, and having taken him down, he wrapped him in the linen cloth, and laid him in a tomb that had been hewn out of the rock.	Now there was a garden in the place where he was crucified, and in the garden there was a new tomb in which no one had ever been laid.

20. These are my translations of Matthew and Mark, and in the next synopsis also Luke. John is as it appears in the NRSVue.

Matthew makes a minor but important addition to Mark, noting that the tomb in which Jesus was placed was "his own new tomb" (ἐν τῷ καινῷ αὐτοῦ μνημείῳ). The note is shared with John, who also makes it a "new tomb" (μνημεῖον καινόν), one in which no one had been laid. The idea that it was a "new tomb" is likely to have proceeded from Matthew's apologetic concerns about Jesus's tomb. The story of the guard at the tomb works to dispel the rumor that the disciples might have stolen the body (Matt 27:62–66; 28:11–15), and the notion that the tomb was new, and so empty, guards against the possibility that there could have been any confusion about Jesus's body. First-century tombs in Jerusalem of the kind imagined in the Synoptics and John were all multiperson tombs, and the anxiety about correctly identifying Jesus's body is a major element in all four of these stories.[21]

One of the reasons that this example of Matthean redaction appearing in John is often missed is that the same element is also a minor agreement with Luke:

MATT 27:59–60	LUKE 23:53	JOHN 19:41
καὶ λαβὼν τὸ σῶμα ὁ Ἰωσὴφ ἐνετύλιξεν αὐτὸ σινδόνι καθαρᾷ, καὶ ἔθηκεν αὐτὸ ἐν τῷ **καινῷ** αὐτοῦ μνημείῳ ὃ ἐλατόμησεν ἐν τῇ πέτρᾳ.	καὶ καθελὼν ἐνετύλιξεν αὐτὸ σινδόνι, καὶ ἔθηκεν αὐτὸν ἐν μνήματι λαξευτῷ <u>οὗ οὐκ ἦν οὐδεὶς οὔπω κείμενος</u>.	ἦν δὲ ἐν τῷ τόπῳ ὅπου ἐσταυρώθη κῆπος, καὶ ἐν τῷ κήπῳ μνημεῖον **καινόν**, ἐν ᾧ <u>οὐδέπω οὐδεὶς ἦν τεθειμένος</u>
And having taken the body, Joseph wrapped it in a clean linen cloth and laid it in his own *new* tomb, which he had hewn in the rock.	And having taken it down, he wrapped it in a linen cloth, and laid it in a rock-hewn tomb <u>in which no one had ever been laid.</u>	Now there was a garden in the place where he was crucified, and in the garden there was a *new* tomb <u>in which no one had ever been laid.</u>

The difficulty with Matthew's word "new" (καινός) is that even a new tomb could contain bodies other than Jesus's, and the more recently they had died, the more likely it is that there could have been some confusion about which body was which. Luke, then, closes this possibility down, clarifying that this was in fact a tomb "in which no one had ever been laid" (οὗ οὐκ ἦν οὐδεὶς οὔπω κείμενος, Luke 23:53), and it is a sign of John's secondary relationship here that he includes both Matthew's "new" and Luke's "in which no one had ever been

---

21. See further Goodacre, "How Empty Was the Tomb?," *JSNT* 44 (2021): 134–48, at 139–43.

laid" (ἐν ᾧ οὐδέπω οὐδεὶς ἦν τεθειμένος). In other words, John has included not only Matthew's addition to Mark but also Luke's.

The difficulty with this, however, is that there are many scholars who think that Luke did not know Matthew, which means that Luke could not have derived his "in which no one had ever been laid" from an interpretation of Matthew's "new tomb." It is, instead, a coincidence or a shared tradition. On this model, John compounds the problem given his parallels with the wording of both Matthew and Luke. This then becomes a second and a third coincidence, for those who also see John as independent of the Synoptics. On occasions like this, the independence models begin to creak, whereas Luke's knowledge of Matthew, and John's knowledge of both, tells a coherent and plausible story.

"Go and Tell My Brothers" (Matt 28:10 // John 20:17)

MATT 28:9–10	JOHN 20:17–18
καὶ ἰδοὺ Ἰησοῦς ὑπήντησεν αὐταῖς λέγων· Χαίρετε. αἱ δὲ προσελθοῦσαι ἐκράτησαν αὐτοῦ τοὺς πόδας καὶ προσεκύνησαν αὐτῷ. τότε λέγει αὐταῖς ὁ Ἰησοῦς· Μὴ φοβεῖσθε· ὑπάγετε ἀπαγγείλατε τοῖς ἀδελφοῖς μου ἵνα ἀπέλθωσιν εἰς τὴν Γαλιλαίαν, κἀκεῖ με ὄψονται.	λέγει αὐτῇ Ἰησοῦς· Μή μου ἅπτου, οὔπω γὰρ ἀναβέβηκα πρὸς τὸν πατέρα· πορεύου δὲ πρὸς τοὺς ἀδελφούς μου καὶ εἰπὲ αὐτοῖς· Ἀναβαίνω πρὸς τὸν πατέρα μου καὶ πατέρα ὑμῶν καὶ θεόν μου καὶ θεὸν ὑμῶν. ἔρχεται Μαριὰμ ἡ Μαγδαληνὴ ἀγγέλλουσα τοῖς μαθηταῖς ὅτι Ἑώρακα τὸν κύριον καὶ ταῦτα εἶπεν αὐτῇ.
And behold Jesus met them, saying, "Greetings!" And they came to him, took hold of his feet, and worshiped him. Then Jesus says to them, "Do not be afraid; go and announce to my brothers[22] to go to Galilee; there they will see me."	Jesus says to her, "Do not touch me, because I have not yet ascended to the Father. But go to my brothers and say to them, 'I am ascending to my Father and your Father, to my God and your God.'" Mary Magdalene went and announced to the disciples, "I have seen the Lord," and she told them that he had said these things to her.

---

22. NRSVue has "brothers and sisters" for ἀδελφοί. The gender inclusive translation is usu-

Mark's resurrection story ends abruptly, with Mary Magdalene, Mary of James, and Salome not telling anyone what has happened because they are afraid (Mark 16:8). By contrast, Matthew's story continues so that Mary Magdalene and "the other Mary" set off to tell the disciples, they meet Jesus en route, they take hold of his feet, and they are instructed now by Jesus to go and tell the disciples, who are characterized as "my brothers." Although John, typically, has significant differences here, like Mary Magdalene appearing alone,[23] it is striking that the disciples are "my brothers," in agreement with Matthew.

This way of characterizing the disciples is much more at home in Matthew than it is in John. On multiple occasions, Matthew's Gospel uses ἀδελφός in a metaphorical sense to refer to those we might otherwise characterize as disciples or other followers of Jesus.[24] The foundation for this idea is a story, found in all three Synoptics, of Jesus's true family (Matt 12:46–50 // Mark 3:31–35 // Luke 8:19–21), where those doing God's will (Matthew and Mark) or hearing God's word and doing it (Luke) replace Jesus's biological family and become mother, brothers, and sisters.

Although found in Mark and Luke, too, the usage is especially characteristic of Matthew, where it comes seventeen times (Matt 5:22 [twice], 23, 24, 47; 7:3, 4, 5; 12:48, 49; 18:15 [twice], 21, 35; 23:8; 25:40, and here).[25] In John, this kind of metaphorical family relationship has not featured until now. It appears to be presupposed from the Synoptics, here under influence from Matthew, yet it is the first time that we have heard it. The disciples are characterized differently in John's Gospel. They are Jesus's children, who would be "orphans" (ὀρφανοί) if Jesus left them (John 14:18),[26] or they are Jesus's "friends" (φίλοι) for whom Jesus

---

ally preferable, but here there does seem to be a gender contrast, with the "women" (γυναῖκες, 28:5) contrasted with the "brothers." For more on the gender dynamics here, see my "Mary, Mary, and Another Mother: How Matthew Read Women in Mark's Gospel," forthcoming. The NRSVue is inconsistent here and uses "brothers" for ἀδελφοί in John 20:17, thereby partially masking the parallel.

23. But see pp. 88–89 on 21:2, which presupposes the plural women of the Synoptic narratives.

24. New Testament scholars often borrow the anthropologists' term "fictive kinship" for this kind of metaphorical usage, but the term is problematic because "fictive" can imply "not real" or "fictional," when the very point of the terminology in the gospels is that Jesus's true relatives are the nonblood relatives (especially Matt 12:46–50 // Mark 3:31–35 // Luke 8:19–21). The term is now often seen as problematic in anthropological and ethnographic studies, and it should be dropped in New Testament scholarship too.

25. The overall gospel figures are, by my count, 17/3/7/2 (Mark 3:33, 34; 10:30; Luke 6:41, 42 [three times]; 8:21; 17:3; 22:32; John 20:17; 21:23). Overall figures for all usages of ἀδελφός are 39/20/24/14.

26. Cf. John 21:5, when Jesus addresses the disciples present as Παιδία ("children").

CHAPTER 3

lays down his life (John 15:13), "friends" (φίλοι) if they do what Jesus commands (John 15:14), and "friends" (φίλοι) to whom Jesus has given his knowledge of the Father (John 15:15). They become Jesus's brothers only when John is writing in parallel with Matthew. The evangelist's usual way of characterizing the disciples has given way to the Matthean way of doing it. It is true that it is appropriate here in John 20:17, given the language of a shared Father, "my Father and your Father," so we are not looking at a case of Johannine fatigue with Matthew but nevertheless, "Father" language has appeared before in John adjacent to "friends" language (John 15:13-15), and it looks like it is the Matthean usage that is here drawing John into the less familiar metaphorical territory.

It is worth noting that four of these five examples are clustered in two adjacent passages. Although it is possible that John is accessing Matthew from memory, the proximity of these examples may show that the author has his scroll of Matthew open as he composes his burial and resurrection story, and his eye is catching certain interesting Matthean expressions.

Lukan Redaction in John

The question of John's knowledge of Luke is often explored through the intriguing parallels between Luke's special material and John, parallels that at the very least suggest contact between Lukan and Johannine materials. Most impressively, John and Luke alone feature the sisters Martha and Mary (Luke 10:38-42; John 11-12); and the name Lazarus is found only in a Lukan parable about resurrection (Luke 16:19-31) and a Johannine story about resurrection (John 11). Moreover, the cluster of links here between John 11-12 and Luke extend to some interesting verbatim agreement with Luke's anointing story (Luke 7:36-50), most strikingly the description of the woman's actions with her hair:

LUKE 7:37-38	JOHN 11:2	JOHN 12:3
καὶ ἰδοὺ γυνὴ ἥτις ἦν ἐν τῇ πόλει ἁμαρτωλός, καὶ ἐπιγνοῦσα ὅτι κατάκειται ἐν τῇ οἰκίᾳ τοῦ Φαρισαίου, κομίσασα ἀλάβαστρον μύρου καὶ στᾶσα ὀπίσω παρὰ τοὺς πόδας αὐτοῦ κλαίουσα, τοῖς δάκρυσιν	ἦν δὲ Μαριὰμ ἡ ἀλείψασα τὸν κύριον μύρῳ καὶ	ἡ οὖν Μαριὰμ λαβοῦσα λίτραν μύρου νάρδου πιστικῆς πολυτίμου

LUKE 7:37–38	JOHN 11:2	JOHN 12:3
ἤρξατο βρέχειν <u>τοὺς πόδας</u> <u>αὐτοῦ</u> <u>καὶ</u> <u>ταῖς θριξὶν</u> τῆς κεφαλῆς <u>αὐτῆς</u> <u>ἐξέμασσεν</u>, καὶ κατεφίλει <u>τοὺς πόδας</u> <u>αὐτοῦ</u> καὶ <u>ἤλειφεν</u> τῷ <u>μύρῳ</u>.	<u>ἐκμάξασα</u> <u>τοὺς πόδας</u> <u>αὐτοῦ</u> <u>ταῖς θριξὶν</u> <u>αὐτῆς</u>, ἧς ὁ ἀδελφὸς Λάζαρος ἠσθένει.	<u>ἤλειψεν</u> <u>τοὺς πόδας</u> τοῦ Ἰησοῦ <u>καὶ</u> <u>ἐξέμαξεν</u> <u>ταῖς θριξὶν αὐτῆς</u> <u>τοὺς πόδας αὐτοῦ</u>· ἡ δὲ οἰκία ἐπληρώθη ἐκ τῆς ὀσμῆς <u>τοῦ</u> <u>μύρου</u>.
And a woman in the city who was a sinner, having learned that he was eating in the Pharisee's house, brought an alabaster jar of <u>perfume</u>.[27] She stood behind him at <u>his feet</u>, weeping, and began to bathe <u>his feet</u> with her tears and <u>she wiped</u>[28] <u>them</u> <u>with</u> the <u>hair</u> of <u>her</u> head,[29] and she kissed her feet and <u>anointed</u>[30] them with <u>the perfume</u>.	Mary was the one who <u>anointed</u> the Lord <u>with</u> <u>perfume</u> <u>and</u> <u>wiped his</u> <u>feet</u> <u>with</u> <u>her</u> <u>hair</u>; her brother Lazarus was ill.	Mary took a pound of costly <u>perfume</u> made of pure nard, <u>anointed</u> Jesus's <u>feet</u>, <u>and</u> <u>wiped</u> <u>them</u> <u>with</u> <u>her</u> <u>hair</u>. The house was filled with the fragrance of <u>the</u> <u>perfume</u>.

We noted above (pp. 29–30) that John's condensing of these details, from the Lukan crying-wiping-anointing to the Johannine anointing-wiping, has led to the unfortunate result that the expensive perfume is now on Mary's hair and not on Jesus's feet, but what is also striking here is the cluster of parallel vocabulary, ἀλείφω ("anoint"), ἐκμάσσω ("wipe"), πόδες ("feet"), and θρίξ ("hair"). These words are all found in

27. NRSVue translates μύρον here as "ointment" but in the Johannine parallels as "perfume." I have adjusted here to "perfume" to make the translations consistent. NRSVue also translates it "ointment" in the Matthean and Markan parallels (Matt 26:7, 9, 12; Mark 14:3, 4, 5). The word occurs only in these four parallel contexts in the Synoptics and John (cf. Rev 18:13).

28. NRSVue has "to dry," but as with the different translations of μύρον (see previous note), this masks the parallel with John's "she wiped" (ἐκμάσσω in both).

29. NRSVue here omits "of her head."

30. NRSVue, "kissing and anointing," adjusted to show the parallel in John.

CHAPTER 3

Luke's and John's anointing stories but are absent from Mark's and Matthew's, while ἐκμάσσω ("wipe") is found in only these two contexts in the New Testament.[31]

Although many scholars have found such parallels diagnostic of Johannine familiarity with Luke, the difficulty is that the extent of Lukan creativity here is disputed. While a good case can be made for Luke 7:36–50 as Luke's creative reworking of Mark's and Matthew's anointing stories (Matt 26:6–13 // Mark 14:3–9),[32] some see the differences between Luke and Mark (// Matthew) as so great that there must be other, oral tradition sources involved. And where there are oral traditions lurking, these could have found their way to John, and so John's links with Luke would not be signs of literary influence but of shared oral tradition.

What we need, then, are cases where the Fourth Gospel shows knowledge of Luke's literary reworking of Mark, cases where small, redactional flourishes in Luke find their way into John. We have already seen several cases of Matthean redactional reworkings of Mark showing up in John. The same is also true for Luke. As with Matthew, let us take five examples of John's knowledge of Lukan redaction of Mark.[33]

Satan Enters Judas (Mark 14:10–11 // Luke 22:3–6 // John 13:26b–27)

MARK 14:10–11	LUKE 22:3–6	JOHN 13:26B–27
Καὶ	<u>Εἰσῆλθεν</u> δὲ <u>Σατανᾶς εἰς</u>	βάψας οὖν τὸ ψωμίον
Ἰούδας	Ἰούδαν τὸν καλούμενον	δίδωσιν Ἰούδᾳ Σίμωνος
Ἰσκαριὼθ ὁ εἷς	Ἰσκαριώτην, ὄντα ἐκ τοῦ	Ἰσκαριώτου. καὶ μετὰ τὸ
τῶν δώδεκα	ἀριθμοῦ τῶν δώδεκα· καὶ	ψωμίον τότε <u>εἰσῆλθεν εἰς</u>
ἀπῆλθεν πρὸς τοὺς	ἀπελθὼν συνελάλησεν τοῖς	ἐκεῖνον ὁ <u>Σατανᾶς</u>. λέγει
ἀρχιερεῖς ἵνα αὐτὸν	ἀρχιερεῦσιν καὶ στρατηγοῖς	οὖν αὐτῷ ὁ Ἰησοῦς· Ὃ ποι-
παραδοῖ αὐτοῖς.	τὸ πῶς αὐτοῖς παραδῷ	εῖς ποίησον τάχιον.
οἱ δὲ ἀκούσαντες	αὐτόν. καὶ	
ἐχάρησαν καὶ	ἐχάρησαν καὶ	
ἐπηγγείλαντο αὐτῷ	συνέθεντο αὐτῷ	
ἀργύριον δοῦναι.	ἀργύριον δοῦναι. καὶ	

---

31. Cf. Barrett, *Gospel*, 390, on John 11:2, "John points forward to the incident which he describes in 12:1–8; but it seems clear that he is able to presuppose that his readers were already familiar with it; this implies that they were Christians, and knew the synoptic tradition (or a tradition closely akin to it). The words used in this allusion—μύρον, ἀλείφειν, ἐκμάσσειν, πόδες, θρίξ—are all used again in 12:3. All of them are found in the Lucan anointing story, only μύρον in the Marcan."

32. See, e.g., Goulder, *Luke*, 397–406.

33. With Luke, the point is complicated slightly for those, like me, who also see Luke as using Matthew, but to keep the presentation straightforward, and to be as inclusive as possible, I will focus here on Luke's use of Mark.

John, from Mark, via Matthew and Luke

MARK 14:10–11	LUKE 22:3–6	JOHN 13:26B–27
καὶ ἐζήτει πῶς αὐτὸν εὐκαίρως παραδοῖ.	ἐξωμολόγησεν, καὶ ἐζήτει εὐκαιρίαν τοῦ παραδοῦναι αὐτὸν ἄτερ ὄχλου αὐτοῖς.	
And Judas Iscariot, who was one of the twelve, went to the chief priests in order to hand him over to them. And when they heard it, they were greatly pleased, and promised to give him money. So he sought an opportunity to hand him over.	And Satan entered into Judas, the one called Iscariot, who was of the number of the twelve; and he went away and conferred with the chief priests and officers about how he might hand him over to them. And they were greatly pleased and agreed to give him money. And he consented and sought an opportunity to hand him over to them when no crowd was present.	So when he had dipped the piece of bread, he gave it to Judas son of Simon Iscariot. After he received the piece of bread, Satan entered into him. Jesus said to him, "Do quickly what you are going to do."

Luke's account of Judas planning his betrayal follows Mark's closely,[34] with one substantive addition, the note that "Satan" (Σατανᾶς) "entered into" (εἰσῆλθεν εἰς) him. John's use of the term Σατανᾶς ("Satan") is striking given his preference for the term διάβολος ("devil") in 6:70, 8:44, and 13:2, and two of these also deal with Judas (6:70 and 13:2). This is the only time that John uses the term Σατανᾶς ("Satan"), in contrast to Luke, who uses it five times in all, including once in the same context, when Jesus says, in the lead up to the prediction of Peter's denial, that "Satan has asked to sift all of you like wheat" (ἰδοὺ ὁ Σατανᾶς ἐξῃτήσατο ὑμᾶς τοῦ σινιάσαι ὡς τὸν σῖτον, Luke 22:31).[35] The fact that this is an unseen cosmic

---

34. Although the spelling of Ἰσκαριώτης is the same here in Luke and John, against Ἰσκαριώθ in Mark, it probably does not help with the source question. Luke has Ἰσκαριώθ in 6:16, paralleling Mark 3:19 (contrast Matt 10:4, Ἰσκαριώτης), and Ἰσκαριώτης here, paralleling Matt 26:14. John, like Matthew, always has Ἰσκαριώτης (6:71; 12:4; 13:2, 26; 14:22). Only John calls him "son of Simon Iscariot."

35. Figures for Σατανᾶς ("Satan") are 3/5/5/1+2.

CHAPTER 3

event that is effectively interpreting and providing motivation for Judas's actions makes it all the more likely that this detail has entered the narrative at the authorial level and is not an independent oral tradition shared by Luke and John. Luke's editorial modification of Mark has found its way into John.

The Right Ear (Mark 14:47 // Luke 22:50 // Luke 18:10)

MARK 14:47	LUKE 22:50	JOHN 18:10
εἷς δέ [τις] τῶν παρεστηκότων σπασάμενος τὴν μάχαιραν ἔπαισεν τὸν δοῦλον τοῦ ἀρχιερέως καὶ ἀφεῖλεν αὐτοῦ τὸ ὠτάριον.	καὶ ἐπάταξεν εἷς τις ἐξ αὐτῶν τοῦ ἀρχιερέως τὸν δοῦλον καὶ ἀφεῖλεν τὸ οὖς αὐτοῦ τὸ δεξιόν.	Σίμων οὖν Πέτρος ἔχων μάχαιραν εἵλκυσεν αὐτὴν καὶ ἔπαισεν τὸν τοῦ ἀρχιερέως δοῦλον καὶ ἀπέκοψεν αὐτοῦ τὸ ὠτάριον τὸ δεξιόν· ἦν δὲ ὄνομα τῷ δούλῳ Μάλχος.
But one of those who was standing near drew his sword and struck the slave of the high priest and cut off his ear.	And one of them hit the slave of the high priest and cut off his <u>right</u> ear.	Therefore Simon Peter, who had a sword, drew it and struck the slave of the high priest, and cut off his <u>right</u> ear. And the name of the slave was Malchus.

We looked at this across all four canonicals above (pp. 22–25), noting the Synoptic similarities as well as the interesting differences, one of which is relevant here. Luke's account of Jesus's arrest follows Mark's closely, with only minor changes like this one. Luke specifies that it was the high priest's slave's "right" ear (τὸ οὖς αὐτοῦ τὸ δεξιόν) that was severed. The evangelist may, of course, have had an alternative source of tradition for this, but it seems more likely that it is a piece of Lukan editorial activity. He does something similar in Luke 6:6, when he specifies, in the healing of the man with the withered hand, that it was his "right" hand (καὶ ἦν ἄνθρωπος ἐκεῖ καὶ ἡ χεὶρ αὐτοῦ ἡ δεξιὰ ἦν ξηρά; contrast Mark 3:1). Similarly, in Acts 3:7, Peter takes the man "by the right hand and raised him up" (πιάσας αὐτὸν τῆς δεξιᾶς χειρὸς ἤγειρεν αὐτόν). Although most scholars have now dropped the idea of "Luke the physician," it was details like these—interest in the human anatomy, reference to body parts, and precision about these body parts—that gave the idea a certain romance.[36] As we saw above, Matthew, too, shows a real interest in specifying body parts, to the point of redundancy,[37] so this is clearly not the exclusive preserve of Luke. Nevertheless, it is much less common for John to specify body parts, still less "right" and "left" hands, feet, or ears, so it is interesting that he here shares Luke's precision, paralleling Luke's redaction of Mark.

Laying a Hand on Him and the Hour (Mark 14:49 // Luke 22:53 // John 7:30)

MARK 14:48–49	LUKE 22:52–53	JOHN 7:30
Ὡς ἐπὶ λῃστὴν ἐξήλθατε μετὰ μαχαιρῶν καὶ ξύλων συλλαβεῖν με; καθ' ἡμέραν ἤμην πρὸς ὑμᾶς ἐν τῷ ἱερῷ διδάσκων καὶ οὐκ ἐκρατήσατέ με·	Ὡς ἐπὶ λῃστὴν ἐξήλθατε μετὰ μαχαιρῶν καὶ ξύλων; καθ' ἡμέραν ὄντος μου μεθ' ὑμῶν ἐν τῷ ἱερῷ οὐκ ἐξετείνατε <u>τὰς χεῖρας ἐπ'</u> ἐμέ· ἀλλ' αὕτη ἐστὶν ὑμῶν <u>ἡ ὥρα</u> καὶ ἡ ἐξουσία τοῦ σκότους.	ἐζήτουν οὖν αὐτὸν πιάσαι, καὶ οὐδεὶς ἐπέβαλεν <u>ἐπ'</u> αὐτὸν <u>τὴν χεῖρα</u>, ὅτι οὔπω ἐληλύθει <u>ἡ ὥρα</u> αὐτοῦ.
"Have you come out with swords and clubs to seize me, as though I were a rebel? Every day I was with you, teaching in the temple courts, and you did not arrest me. But the scriptures must be fulfilled."	"Have you come out with swords and clubs as though I were a rebel? Every day I was with you in the temple, and you did not <u>lay hands on me</u>. But this is your <u>hour</u> and the power of darkness!"	Then they tried to arrest him, but no one <u>laid a hand</u>[38] <u>on him</u> because his <u>hour</u> had not yet come.

---

36. The classic studies were William K. Hobart, *The Medical Language of St. Luke* (Grand Rapids: Baker, 1954), and Adolf von Harnack, *Luke the Physician: The Author of the Third Gospel and the Acts of the Apostles* (London: Williams & Norgate, 1907), refuted in H. J. Cadbury, *The Style and Literary Method of Luke* (Cambridge: Harvard University Press, 1920), 39–72; but Hobart missed the Johannine parallel here, and Cadbury (*Style*, 48) focuses on Harnack, *Luke*, 185.

37. See also "right eye" (Matt 5:29), the "right hand" (Matt 5:30; contrast Mark 9:43), the "right cheek" (Matt 5:39; contrast Luke 6:29), and the "right" and "left" hands (Matt 6:3).

38. NRSVue, "hands."

CHAPTER 3

Luke's dependence on Mark for the arrest scene is clear—he has several words in verbatim agreement with Mark, as the above synopsis illustrates. But Luke makes two interesting additions. Jesus tells those arresting him that they did not lay their hands upon him (οὐκ ἐξετείνατε τὰς χεῖρας ἐπ' ἐμέ),[39] and he says that it is "your hour" (ὑμῶν ἡ ὥρα). In a different context of John, the tabernacles discourse (John 7), certain unnamed people attempt to arrest Jesus, and it is striking to see the same two elements that are found in the Lukan arrest scene. They are not able to lay a hand on Jesus (οὐδεὶς ἐπέβαλεν ἐπ' αὐτὸν τὴν χεῖρα) because it is not yet his hour (ὅτι οὔπω ἐληλύθει ἡ ὥρα αὐτοῦ). The scene seems to presuppose the very thing that Luke goes on to narrate, that there will be a moment when the hour comes, when they will be able to lay hands on Jesus.

This link between John and Luke's redaction of Mark is often missed,[40] perhaps because of its different narrative context in John, but the pairing of "hand" (or "hands") and "hour" is clear and striking, and it occurs in a literary addition that Luke makes to Mark. Although the literary contexts are different, they are nevertheless related because both deal directly with Jesus's arrest. In Luke, the hour has come, and they can lay hands on Jesus. In John, the hour has not yet come, and they cannot yet lay a hand on him. This is one of only two times that anyone attempts to lay a hand (or hands) on Jesus in John, and the second is later in the same discourse (7:44, ἀλλ' οὐδεὶς ἐπέβαλεν ἐπ' αὐτὸν τὰς χεῖρας). The expression is found in all three Synoptics, but it is particularly characteristic of Luke. The one occurrence in Mark is at Jesus's arrest, where they lay hands on Jesus and seize him (Mark 14:46, οἱ δὲ ἐπέβαλαν τὰς χεῖρας αὐτῷ καὶ ἐκράτησαν αὐτόν; similarly worded in Matt 26:50), but Luke has the expression redactionally not only here in 22:53 but twice more, once in 21:12, in prophecies of future persecution (Πρὸ δὲ τούτων πάντων ἐπιβαλοῦσιν ἐφ' ὑμᾶς τὰς χεῖρας αὐτῶν καὶ διώξουσιν; contrast Matt 24:17 // Mark 14:9), and once in 20:19, where it is again combined with the word ὥρα ("hour"):

---

39. The motif of laying hands on Jesus does, however, occur several verses earlier, in Mark 14:46; see below.

40. Harold W. Attridge, "John and Other Gospels," in *The Oxford Handbook of Johannine Studies*, ed. Judith M. Lieu and Martinus C. de Boer (Oxford: Oxford University Press, 2018), 44–62, at 50, is an honorable exception.

John, from Mark, via Matthew and Luke

MATT 21:46	MARK 12:12	LUKE 20:19
καὶ ζητοῦντες αὐτὸν κρατῆσαι	Καὶ ἐζήτουν αὐτὸν κρατῆσαι,	καὶ ἐζήτησαν οἱ γραμματεῖς καὶ οἱ ἀρχιερεῖς ἐπιβαλεῖν ἐπ' αὐτὸν τὰς χεῖρας ἐν αὐτῇ τῇ ὥρᾳ, καὶ
ἐφοβήθησαν τοὺς ὄχλους, ἐπεὶ εἰς προφήτην αὐτὸν εἶχον.	καὶ ἐφοβήθησαν τὸν ὄχλον, ἔγνωσαν γὰρ ὅτι πρὸς αὐτοὺς τὴν παραβολὴν εἶπεν. καὶ ἀφέντες αὐτὸν ἀπῆλθον.	ἐφοβήθησαν τὸν λαόν, ἔγνωσαν γὰρ ὅτι πρὸς αὐτοὺς εἶπεν τὴν παραβολὴν ταύτην.
They wanted to arrest him,	When they realized that he had told this parable against them, they wanted to arrest him,	When the scribes and chief priests realized that he had told this parable against them, they wanted <u>to lay hands on him at that very hour</u>, but
but they feared the crowds, because they regarded him as a prophet.	but they feared the crowd. So they left him and went away.	they feared the people.

It is worth adding that the same locution, of violent hands being laid on Jesus's followers, as a way of describing an arrest, is a regular feature in Acts:

Acts 4:3: καὶ <u>ἐπέβαλον αὐτοῖς τὰς χεῖρας</u> καὶ ἔθεντο εἰς τήρησιν εἰς τὴν αὔριον.

<u>So they laid hands on</u>[41] them and put them in custody until the next day.

Acts 5:18: καὶ <u>ἐπέβαλον τὰς χεῖρας ἐπὶ τοὺς ἀποστόλους</u> καὶ ἔθεντο αὐτοὺς ἐν τηρήσει δημοσίᾳ.

<u>And they laid hands upon</u>[42] the apostles and put them in the public prison.

Acts 12:1: Κατ' ἐκεῖνον δὲ τὸν καιρὸν <u>ἐπέβαλεν Ἡρῴδης ὁ βασιλεὺς τὰς χεῖρας</u> κακῶσαί τινας τῶν ἀπὸ τῆς ἐκκλησίας.

---

41. NRSVue, "arrested."
42. NRSVue, "[And they] arrested."

CHAPTER 3

About that time <u>King Herod laid violent hands upon</u> some who belonged to the church.

Acts 21:27: οἱ ἀπὸ τῆς Ἀσίας Ἰουδαῖοι θεασάμενοι αὐτὸν ἐν τῷ ἱερῷ συνέχεον πάντα τὸν ὄχλον καὶ <u>ἐπέβαλον ἐπ' αὐτὸν τὰς χεῖρας</u>.

The Judeans from Asia, who had seen him in the temple, stirred up the whole crowd and <u>they laid hands on him</u>.[43]

In other words, the locution is one that seems to come naturally to the author of Luke's Gospel and Acts, while it occurs only twice in John (7:30, 44), in a context where Luke's parallel is in view. To summarize, Luke has language of laying violent hands on Jesus and his followers on three occasions in the gospel, all three of them additions to Mark. He uses the same language four times in Acts. On two of the occasions where Luke adds the language to Mark (Luke 20:19 and 22:53), the language occurs in connection with "hour" terminology, and this very combination is found here in John 7:30.

Barabbas (Mark 15:6–9 // Luke 23:18–19 // John 18:39–40)

MARK 15:6–9	LUKE 23:18–19	JOHN 18:39–40
Κατὰ δὲ ἑορτὴν ἀπέλυεν αὐτοῖς ἕνα δέσμιον ὃν παρῃτοῦντο. ἦν δὲ ὁ λεγόμενος Βαραββᾶς μετὰ τῶν στασιαστῶν δεδεμένος οἵτινες ἐν τῇ στάσει φόνον πεποιήκεισαν. καὶ ἀναβὰς ὁ ὄχλος ἤρξατο αἰτεῖσθαι καθὼς ἐποίει αὐτοῖς. ὁ δὲ Πιλᾶτος ἀπεκρίθη αὐτοῖς λέγων· Θέλετε ἀπολύσω ὑμῖν τὸν βασιλέα τῶν Ἰουδαίων;		ἔστιν δὲ συνήθεια ὑμῖν ἵνα ἕνα ἀπολύσω ὑμῖν ἐν τῷ πάσχα· βούλεσθε οὖν ἀπολύσω ὑμῖν τὸν βασιλέα τῶν Ἰουδαίων;

---

43. NRSVue, "The Jews from Asia, who had seen him in the temple, stirred up the whole crowd. They seized him."

John, from Mark, via Matthew and Luke

MARK 15:6–9	LUKE 23:18–19	JOHN 18:39–40
	Ἀνέκραγον δὲ παμπληθεὶ λέγοντες· Αἶρε <u>τοῦτον</u>, ἀπόλυσον δὲ ἡμῖν <u>τὸν Βαραββᾶν</u>· ὅστις ἦν διὰ στάσιν τινὰ γενομένην ἐν τῇ πόλει καὶ φόνον βληθεὶς ἐν τῇ φυλακῇ.	ἐκραύγασαν οὖν πάλιν λέγοντες· Μὴ <u>τοῦτον</u> ἀλλὰ <u>τὸν Βαραββᾶν</u>. ἦν δὲ ὁ Βαραββᾶς λῃστής.
Now at the festival he used to release a prisoner for them, anyone for whom they asked. Now a man called Barabbas was in prison with the rebels who had committed murder during the insurrection. So the crowd came and began to ask Pilate to do for them according to his custom. Then he answered them, "Do you want me to release for you the King of the Jews?"		"But you have a custom that I release someone for you at the Passover.
	Then <u>they</u> all <u>shouted</u> out together, "Away with <u>this man</u>![44] Release <u>Barabbas</u> for us!" (This was a man who had been put in prison for an insurrection that had taken place in the city and for murder.)	Do you want me to release for you the King of the Jews?" <u>They</u> <u>shouted</u> in reply, "Not <u>this man</u> but <u>Barabbas</u>!" Now Barabbas was a rebel.

Although John's narration of the Barabbas incident is brief, it has parallels with both Mark and Luke. Like Mark, John begins with a description of the Passover (Mark, "festival") custom, to release a prisoner of the crowd's choice

---

44. NRSVue, "this fellow," here adjusted to show the parallel with John.

(Mark 15:6 // Matt 27:15), though it is moved from the narrator's voice in Mark to Pilate's in John (18:39; see further on this below, p. 97). John then shares a six-word verbatim agreement with Mark, Θέλετε (Mark)/βούλεσθε οὖν (John) ἀπολύσω ὑμῖν τὸν βασιλέα τῶν Ἰουδαίων; ("Do you want me to release for you the King of the Jews?"). Yet John also appears to be influenced by Luke. Luke drops Mark's idea of the festival custom and restructures the material about Barabbas so that his criminal identity is explained only after he is introduced as a character in the drama. John shows knowledge of Luke's reworking of Mark, with the crowd shouting (Ἀνέκραγον/ἐκραύγασαν), saying (λέγοντες), "Not this one [τοῦτον] but Barabbas [τὸν Βαραββᾶν]," followed by an explanation of who Barabbas was. There is nothing in Luke to suggest that he has access to source material other than Mark here. There is no fresh content. It is purely literary reworking. John's parallels to the Lukan literary restructuring make best sense if the Fourth Gospel knows not only Mark but also Luke's redaction of Mark.

Doubled "Crucify!" and Threefold Declaration of Innocence (Luke 23:4, 14, 22 // John 18:38b; 19:4, 6)

MARK 15:12–14	LUKE 23:20–22	JOHN 19:6
ὁ δὲ Πιλᾶτος πάλιν ἀποκριθεὶς ἔλεγεν αὐτοῖς· Τί οὖν θέλετε ποιήσω ὃν λέγετε τὸν βασιλέα τῶν Ἰουδαίων; οἱ δὲ πάλιν ἔκραξαν· Σταύρωσον αὐτόν. ὁ δὲ Πιλᾶτος ἔλεγεν αὐτοῖς· Τί γὰρ ἐποίησεν κακόν; οἱ δὲ περισσῶς ἔκραξαν· Σταύρωσον αὐτόν.	πάλιν δὲ ὁ Πιλᾶτος προσεφώνησεν, θέλων ἀπολῦσαι τὸν Ἰησοῦν. οἱ δὲ ἐπεφώνουν λέγοντες· Σταύρου <u>σταύρου</u> αὐτόν. ὁ δὲ τρίτον εἶπεν πρὸς αὐτούς· Τί γὰρ κακὸν ἐποίησεν οὗτος; οὐδὲν <u>αἴτιον</u> θανάτου <u>εὗρον ἐν αὐτῷ</u>· παιδεύσας οὖν αὐτὸν ἀπολύσω.	ὅτε οὖν εἶδον αὐτὸν οἱ ἀρχιερεῖς καὶ οἱ ὑπηρέται ἐκραύγασαν λέγοντες· Σταύρωσον <u>σταύρωσον</u>. λέγει αὐτοῖς ὁ Πιλᾶτος· Λάβετε αὐτὸν ὑμεῖς καὶ σταυρώσατε, ἐγὼ γὰρ οὐχ <u>εὑρίσκω ἐν αὐτῷ αἰτίαν</u>.
Pilate spoke to them again, "Then what do you wish me to do with the man you call the King of the Jews?"	Pilate, wanting to release Jesus, addressed them again,	When the chief priests and the police saw him,

John, from Mark, via Matthew and Luke

MARK 15:12–14	LUKE 23:20–22	JOHN 19:6
They shouted back, "Crucify him!" Pilate asked them,	but they kept shouting, "Crucify, <u>crucify</u> him!" A third time he said to them,	they shouted, "Crucify! <u>Crucify</u>!"[46] Pilate said to them, "Take him yourselves and crucify him;
"Why, what evil has he done?"	"Why, what evil has he done? <u>I have found</u> in <u>him</u> <u>no case</u>[45] for the sentence of death; I will therefore have him flogged and then release him."	<u>I find</u> <u>no case</u> against <u>him</u>."
But they shouted all the more, "Crucify him!"		

Most commentators on Luke have no difficulty in assigning what the evangelist has written here to his own rewording of Mark. There is not the kind of additional content here that might lead to theories of additional sources—Mark is enough. And John appears to echo that reworded Lukan content, with the doubled imperative, "Crucify! Crucify (him)!" (Luke, Σταύρου σταύρου αὐτόν; John, σταύρωσον σταύρωσον), as well as the statement from Pilate that he cannot find (εὗρον/εὑρίσκω) any case (αἴτιον/αἰτίαν) for death in him (ἐν αὐτῷ). Moreover, the cluster of agreements makes coincidence highly unlikely, especially when it is noticed that this is now the third time that Pilate has proclaimed Jesus's innocence:

(1) Luke 23:4
ὁ δὲ Πιλᾶτος εἶπεν πρὸς τοὺς ἀρχιερεῖς καὶ τοὺς ὄχλους· Οὐδὲν <u>εὑρίσκω</u> <u>αἴτιον</u> <u>ἐν</u> τῷ ἀνθρώπῳ τούτῳ.

(1) John 18:38b
Καὶ τοῦτο εἰπὼν πάλιν ἐξῆλθεν πρὸς τοὺς Ἰουδαίους, καὶ λέγει αὐτοῖς· Ἐγὼ οὐδεμίαν <u>εὑρίσκω</u> <u>ἐν</u> αὐτῷ <u>αἰτίαν</u>·

(2) Luke 23:14
εἶπεν πρὸς αὐτούς· Προσηνέγκατέ μοι τὸν ἄνθρωπον τοῦτον ὡς ἀποστρέφοντα τὸν λαόν, καὶ ἰδοὺ ἐγὼ ἐνώπιον ὑμῶν ἀνακρίνας οὐθὲν <u>εὗρον</u> <u>ἐν</u> τῷ ἀνθρώπῳ τούτῳ <u>αἴτιον</u> ὧν κατηγορεῖτε κατ' αὐτοῦ.

(2) John 19:4
καὶ ἐξῆλθεν πάλιν ἔξω ὁ Πιλᾶτος καὶ λέγει αὐτοῖς· Ἴδε ἄγω ὑμῖν αὐτὸν ἔξω, ἵνα γνῶτε ὅτι οὐδεμίαν <u>αἰτίαν</u> <u>εὑρίσκω</u> <u>ἐν</u> <u>αὐτῷ</u>.

45. See note 47 below.
46. NRSVue, "Crucify him! Crucify him!" Adjusted also in the synopsis below.

CHAPTER 3

(3) Luke 23:20–22	(3) John 19:6
πάλιν δὲ ὁ Πιλᾶτος προσεφώνησεν, θέλων ἀπολῦσαι τὸν Ἰησοῦν. οἱ δὲ ἐπεφώνουν λέγοντες· <u>Σταύρου σταύρου</u> αὐτόν. ὁ δὲ τρίτον εἶπεν πρὸς αὐτούς· Τί γὰρ κακὸν ἐποίησεν οὗτος; οὐδὲν <u>αἴτιον</u> θανάτου <u>εὗρον</u> <u>ἐν αὐτῷ</u>· παιδεύσας οὖν αὐτὸν ἀπολύσω.	ὅτε οὖν εἶδον αὐτὸν οἱ ἀρχιερεῖς καὶ οἱ ὑπηρέται ἐκραύγασαν λέγοντες· <u>Σταύρωσον σταύρωσον</u>. λέγει αὐτοῖς ὁ Πιλᾶτος· Λάβετε αὐτὸν ὑμεῖς καὶ σταυρώσατε, ἐγὼ γὰρ οὐχ <u>εὑρίσκω</u> <u>ἐν αὐτῷ</u> <u>αἰτίαν</u>.
(1) Luke 23:4	(1) John 18:38b
Then Pilate said to the chief priests and the crowds, "I <u>find</u> <u>no</u> <u>case</u>[47] for an accusation <u>against</u> this man."	After he had said this, he went out to the Judeans again and told them, "I <u>find</u> <u>no</u> <u>case</u> <u>against</u> him.
(2) Luke 23:14	(2) John 19:4
and said to them, "You brought me this man as one who was inciting the people, and here I have examined him in your presence and have <u>not</u> <u>found</u> in this man a <u>case</u> for any of your charges <u>against him</u>.	Pilate went out again and said to them, "Look, I am bringing him out to you to let you know that I <u>find</u> no <u>case</u> <u>against him</u>."
(3) Luke 23:20–22	(3) John 19:6
Pilate, wanting to release Jesus, addressed them again, but they kept shouting, "<u>Crucify, crucify</u> him!" A third time he said to them, "Why, what evil has he done? I have <u>found</u> in him <u>no case</u> for the sentence of death; I will therefore have him flogged and then release him."	When the chief priests and the police saw him, they shouted, "<u>Crucify! Crucify!</u>" Pilate said to them, "Take him yourselves and crucify him; I <u>find</u> <u>no case</u> against him."

The parallels are clear and striking. But are there any indications that the language is characteristic of Luke? Is this the kind of thing that we might expect the evangelist to add on his own? The double imperative "Crucify! Crucify!" might

---

47. NRSVue, "basis," is adjusted to show the parallel with John. I have made a similar adjustment in 23:14 (NRSVue "and have not found this man guilty of any of your charges against him") and 23:22, "I have found in him no ground for the sentence of death." On all three occasions, Luke has the neuter αἴτιον, and John the feminine αἰτία in parallel.

be compared with Luke's tendency to double vocatives, as in "Master, Master" (Luke 8:24 R), "Martha, Martha" (Luke 10:41), "Simon, Simon" (Luke 22:31 R), and "Saul, Saul" (Acts 9:4; 22:7; 26:14), but the analogy is only partial, and John effects something similar on his own with his characteristically doubled, "Amen, amen," twenty-five times in the gospel.[48]

More telling is the language Luke uses for expressing Jesus's innocence. Although the Synoptics and John all find ways of underlining Jesus's innocence, it is only Luke and John who have this similar threefold declaration from Pilate, in which Pilate "finds" no case against Jesus. Luke frames Jesus's innocence similarly in Paul's speech in Antioch in Pisidia:

> Acts 13:28: Even though they found [εὑρόντες] no cause [αἰτίαν] for a sentence of death, they asked Pilate to have him killed.

Luke uses εὑρίσκω in much the same way in several other forensic contexts, where characters in the drama are looking but failing to "find" causes for arrest or grounds for condemnation:

> Luke 6:7: The scribes and the Pharisees were watching him to see whether he would cure on the Sabbath, so that they might <u>find</u> grounds to bring an accusation [ἵνα εὕρωσιν κατηγορεῖν αὐτοῦ] against him (contrast Matt 12:9 // Mark 3:2).

> Luke 19:47–48: Every day he was teaching in the temple. The chief priests, the scribes, and the leaders of the people kept looking for a way to kill him, but they did not <u>find</u> what they might do[49] [καὶ οὐχ εὕρισκον τὸ τί ποιήσωσιν], for all the people were spellbound by what they heard (contrast Mark 11:18).

> Luke 23:2: They began to accuse him, saying, "We <u>found</u> this man [Τοῦτον εὕραμεν] inciting our nation, forbidding us to pay taxes to Caesar and saying that he himself is the Messiah, a king" (contrast Matt 27:11 // Mark 15:2).

In each of these cases, leaders are attempting to find, claiming to find, or failing to find cause to arrest, kill, or condemn Jesus. And in each of these cases, the finding language is absent in the Synoptic parallels.[50] The last example is partic-

---

48. See John 1:51; 3:3, 5, 11; 5:19, 24, 25; 6:26, 32, 47, 53; 8:34, 51, 58; 10:1, 7; 12:24; 13:16, 20, 21, 38; 14:12; 16:20, 23; 21:18. There is one example of doubling in Mark, at 14:45, "Rabbi, Rabbi," and a handful in Matthew, "Lord, Lord" (Matt 7:21 // Luke 6:46; Matt 7:22; 25:11), and "Jerusalem, Jerusalem" (Matt 23:37 // Luke 13:34); cf. ναὶ ναί, οὒ οὔ ("Yes yes, no no," Matt 5:37).

49. NRSVue, "anything they could do."

50. The only possible example of the feature in Mark and Matthew is Mark 14:55, "Now

CHAPTER 3

ularly noteworthy because it provides the prelude, in Luke, to Pilate's threefold failure to find in Jesus what his accusers claim to have found, the threefold failure that is paralleled so strikingly in John. In other words, this appears to be a characteristic Lukan way of configuring forensic scenes, and in case we are in any doubt, the same feature also occurs five more times in Acts (in addition to Acts 13:28, quoted above):

> Acts 4:21 (Peter and John before the council in Jerusalem): After threatening them again, they let them go, <u>finding</u> [εὑρίσκοντες] no way to punish them because of the people.

> Acts 23:9 (Paul before the council in Jerusalem): Then a great clamor arose, and certain scribes of the Pharisees' group stood up and contended, "We <u>find</u> [εὑρίσκομεν] nothing wrong with this man. What if a spirit or an angel has spoken to him?"

> Acts 23:28–29 (Claudius Lysias to Felix about Paul): Since I wanted to know the charge [τὴν αἰτίαν] for which they accused him, I had him brought to their council. <u>I found</u> [εὗρον] that he was accused concerning questions of their law but was charged with nothing deserving death or imprisonment.

> Acts 24:5 (Tertullus to Felix about Paul): We have, in fact, <u>found</u> [εὑρόντες] this man a pestilent fellow, an agitator among all the Judeans throughout the world, and a ringleader of the sect of the Nazarenes.

> Acts 24:20 (Paul to Felix): Or let these men here tell what crime they had <u>found</u> [εὗρον] when I stood before the council.

There is, of course, no second volume of John's Gospel with which to compare these cases from Acts, but John is not short of its own forensic vocabulary, to the extent that the whole gospel is driven through with law-court imagery, and it is telling that the "finding" language occurs only here, in parallel with Luke. In other words, it is striking that a characteristic Lukan way of narrating stories like this, found six times in the gospel, and six times in Acts, including in contexts where the evangelist is rewording Mark, is shared here with John.

---

the chief priests and the whole council were looking for testimony against Jesus to put him to death, but they found none [οὐχ ηὕρισκον]." Overall figures for εὑρίσκω in forensic contexts are therefore 0/1/6/3+6.

John, from Mark, via Matthew and Luke

ORAL TRADITION OR LITERARY LINKS?

We have looked at five examples of Matthew's redaction of Mark that show up in John, and five examples of Luke's redaction of Mark that also show up in John. In these ten examples, there appears to be a good case that John knew the ways in which Matthew and Luke rewrote Mark. In each case, the Matthean and Lukan changes are easy to explain on the literary level, where the evangelists have made minor adjustments to their Markan source of the kind that we see throughout the triple tradition, adjustments that are straightforwardly explicable in the light of the way that they write elsewhere. Most commentaries on Matthew and Luke explain these as minor, literary, redactional adjustments to their Markan source. They do not need to appeal to different written sources or oral tradition. These are relatively minor, literary reworkings, and the fact that they appear in John is worthy of notice.

The key question here is whether there are other explanations. Is John's knowledge of Matthean and Lukan redaction the only option here? There are always other potential explanations for the data, the most prominent of which is usually the appeal to oral tradition. Surely, some will say, these agreements could be explained by John's familiarity with oral traditions shared by Matthew and Luke. We know that there were many oral traditions swirling around in the earliest years of the Jesus movement, and perhaps John, like Matthew and Luke, was in each of these cases dipping into the great reservoir. In fact, to judge from the watery metaphors preferred by New Testament scholars (see above, chapter 1), the supply of oral tradition was practically unlimited, and little literary parallels like the ones here are mere droplets in so huge a lake. But even if we grant the notion of the copious rivers of tradition, it does not address the issue at hand. In the cases discussed in this chapter, John appears to be paralleling Matthew's and Luke's literary reworking of Mark and not witnessing to some kind of alternative tradition. Each of these cases is in the nature of an enhancement of Mark, a literary alteration, a clarificatory detail.

Furthermore, most of them are in the narrators' voices. In the first example, the crown of thorns, Matthew appears to be dependent on his primary literary source, Mark, merely rewording in minor ways, in ways that commentators on Matthew have no difficulty in explaining as literary reworkings of Mark. And it is minor literary parallels like this that reappear in John. Moreover, this example, like the second (Joseph of Arimathea as a disciple) and third (Joseph's "new" tomb) examples, is found in the narrator's voice, and while the amorphous oral traditions may, of course, have featured small narrative embellishments like this, the Synoptic Gospels are generally much more varied in the narrators' voices than they are in speech material, and the appeal to oral tradition to explain them is unnecessary.

The examples from Luke are similar. In three of the five cases, these are minor comments in the narrator's voice, comments that are easy to understand as simple literary embellishments by Luke to his primary source Mark. Thus when Luke specifies that it was the "right" ear that was severed, it is the kind of minor enhancement that we see Luke making elsewhere, as when it emerges that it was the "right" hand of the man with a withered arm that Jesus healed. And when Luke is talking about Barabbas, he is simply restructuring the Markan account, and it is this literary restructuring that John parallels. In the case of Satan entering Judas, we have not a case of an independently observed or remembered tradition but a fresh cosmological narrative explanation of an action narrated similarly in Mark, as when the author of the Nature of the Rulers narrates a similar story to the one he finds in Gen 2–4 but adds a different cosmological narrative explanation of why the characters are behaving in this peculiar way.

There appear to be grounds, then, for drawing attention to these minor literary parallels. There is, of course, a rhetorical difficulty with appeals to minutiae. Minutiae are easy to ignore or dismiss, and those who draw attention to them can seem like the geeks of the guild, focusing on the detail at the expense of the bigger picture. It has to be said, though, that looking at these minutiae is not an alternative to looking at the bigger picture but is in addition to it. We saw in the previous chapter that there are striking resemblances between the literary structuring as well as the fundamental literary conceits of the Synoptics and John, and we will go on to look at key topics like the identities of the Beloved Disciple and Jesus later in this book (chapters 6 and 7). But it is also a question of the nature of the evidence. These small parallels between John and the Synoptics are diagnostic shards. The archaeologist who finds a small piece of Roman pottery in a Jerusalem tomb is interested in that tiny piece because of what it tells us about dating the entire tomb. We should be interested in the shards because of what they can reveal about the bigger picture. Sometimes, the devil is in the detail.

Chapter 4

John's Presupposition of Synoptic Narratives

The Fourth Gospel concludes twice with statements about the work's selectivity. The author knows of "many other signs" that Jesus performed before his disciples (John 20:30), so many, it turns out, that the world could not contain all of the books that could be written (21:25), yet he has chosen specific signs that he deems important in demonstrating that Jesus is the Messiah, the Son of God, "and that through believing, you might have life in his name" (20:31). This self-conscious selectivity is a feature found throughout the gospel. It is why there are seven signs, and only seven signs. It is why some of the most prominent features in the Synoptics, like the parables and the exorcisms, are absent. It is not accidental. Selectivity is sown into the literary fabric of the gospel. In this chapter, I would like to explore the extent to which the Fourth Gospel selects certain stories to tell, while presupposing certain Synoptic materials that are not themselves narrated. We will begin by noticing that selectivity is already a feature in the Synoptic Gospels. We will then explore the ways in which the Fourth Gospel underlines its selectivity, drawing attention to moments where the narrative makes full sense only when read alongside the Synoptics. We will conclude by asking why John's presupposition of the Synoptics is preferable to his presupposition of hypothetical, lost texts and traditions, and we will ask why any of this matters.

SELECTIVITY IN THE SYNOPTICS

Although selectivity is a particular emphasis in John's Gospel, it is something that is already present in the earliest Christian tradition.[1] Mark's Gospel often

---

1. The same selectivity about drawing on Jesus tradition is apparent as early as Paul. When he is giving advice to the Corinthians, he quotes a saying of Jesus about divorce and

CHAPTER 4

draws attention to material that it does not narrate. "Day after day I was with you in the temple, teaching," Jesus says at his arrest (Mark 14:49), but only a selection of that teaching is provided (Mark 11:27–12:44). The gospel gives the impression that its sayings have been drawn from a much larger body of material:

> Mark 4:2: He began to teach them many things in parables, and in his teaching he said to them. . . .
>
> Mark 4:33: With many such parables he spoke the word to them as they were able to hear it.

All three Synoptics often mention multiple healings,[2] giving the impression that they are selecting particular, noteworthy stories out of a far larger set of potential narratives. Moreover, Luke is adept at suggesting that he is selecting representative stories rather than threading together a tight chronological narrative, as Bultmann observed: "Luke knows that the few stories that have been passed on do not completely fit the course of events, but are only examples and illustrations; and so he frequently draws attention in some introductory phrase to the fact that the following section is really within a larger context. For this purpose he chooses a familiar formula from the LXX, *kai egeneto*, which is particularly used in Luke for introducing many stories from Mark."[3]

SELECTIVITY IN JOHN

There is a similar feature in John, but now it is much more prominent. The Fourth Gospel consistently draws attention to extended phases of time where no specific action is narrated,[4] which serves not only to increase the biographical

---

remarriage (1 Cor 7:10–11), but when he comes next to the question of unbelieving spouses, he instead offers his own advice (1 Cor 7:12–16).

2. Mark 1:32–34; 3:10; 6:13, 53–56; Matt 4:23–25; 8:16–17; 11:4–6; 12:15; 14:14, 34–36; 15:29–31; 21:14; Luke 4:40–41; 5:15; 6:17–19; 7:21–23; 8:2; 9:6; 10:17; 19:37.

3. Rudolf Bultmann, *History of the Synoptic Tradition*, trans. John Marsh (Oxford: Blackwell, 1963), 360. His examples are Luke 1:5, 8; 3:21; 5:1, 12, 17; 8:22; 9:18, 51; 11:1; 14:1; 17:11; 18:35; 20:1.

4. Brooke Foss Westcott, *The Gospel According to John: The Authorised Version with Introduction and Notes* (London: Murray, 1894), lxxviii, writes "The fragmentariness of St. John's record is shown conclusively by his notice of periods of teaching of undefined length of which he relates no more than their occurrence."

John's Presupposition of Synoptic Narratives

plausibility of the narrative but also to draw attention to the specific events that are narrated. One method used by the evangelist to achieve this is the phrase μετὰ ταῦτα, "after these things," a transitional piece of narration that works like "Some time later" or "On another day." There is a studied vagueness and generality about it that is similar to Luke's use of "And it came to pass." There are six examples of this in the narrator's voice:

> John 3:22: After these things [μετὰ ταῦτα], Jesus and his disciples went into the region of Judea, and he spent some time [διέτριβεν] there with them and baptized.
>
> John 5:1: After these things [μετὰ ταῦτα], there was a festival of the Judeans, and Jesus went up to Jerusalem.
>
> John 5:14: After these things [μετὰ ταῦτα], Jesus found him in the temple and said to him. . . .
>
> John 6:1: After these things [μετὰ ταῦτα], Jesus went to the other side of the Sea of Galilee (of Tiberias).
>
> John 7:1: And after these things [καὶ μετὰ ταῦτα], Jesus walked in Galilee. He did not want to walk in Judea because the Judeans were looking for an opportunity to kill him.
>
> John 21:1: After these things [μετὰ ταῦτα], Jesus showed himself again to the disciples by the Sea of Tiberias.[5]

Most of these examples are found in the selective first two years of Jesus's ministry (John 3–10), after the consecutive day-by-day narrative in John 1–2, and before the extended passion narrative of the second half of the gospel in John 11–21. The sense is given that Jesus frequently pauses to walk around, or to stay in a certain place, for extended periods. In the first example above, John 3:22, Jesus "spent some time" with the disciples in Judea, and the same word (διατρίβω) is often found in Acts where it is used to give a sense that Paul and others are staying, "tarrying" in the Authorized Version, for a prolonged period in a particular place (Acts 12:19; 14:3, 28; 15:35; 16:12; 20:6; 25:6, 14).

---

5. The phrase also occurs in a different usage in John 13:7, in Jesus's speech, "You do not know now what I am doing, but after these things [μετὰ ταῦτα], you will understand."

CHAPTER 4

Presupposing Synoptic Narratives

This selectivity, and the sense that the gospel is very deliberate about which stories it narrates, has a fascinating corollary. Not only does the evangelist underline that there are many events that the gospel does not narrate, but he also appears to presuppose several nonnarrated events, and in each case, the events concerned are found in one or more of the Synoptic Gospels. Although this feature in John has occasionally been noticed,[6] especially in relation to Johannine parallels with Mark and Luke, its potential to shed light on the relationship between John and the Synoptics has been underestimated. Let us look at each example in turn.

"John Had Not Yet Been Thrown into Prison" (John 3:24)

John 3:22–24: Μετὰ ταῦτα ἦλθεν ὁ Ἰησοῦς καὶ οἱ μαθηταὶ αὐτοῦ εἰς τὴν Ἰουδαίαν γῆν, καὶ ἐκεῖ διέτριβεν μετ' αὐτῶν καὶ ἐβάπτιζεν. ἦν δὲ καὶ ὁ Ἰωάννης βαπτίζων ἐν Αἰνὼν ἐγγὺς τοῦ Σαλείμ, ὅτι ὕδατα πολλὰ ἦν ἐκεῖ, καὶ παρεγίνοντο καὶ ἐβαπτίζοντο· οὔπω γὰρ ἦν βεβλημένος εἰς τὴν φυλακὴν ὁ Ἰωάννης.

After these things, Jesus and his disciples went into the region of Judea, and he spent some time there with them and baptized. John also was baptizing at Aenon near Salim because water was abundant there, and people kept coming and were being baptized. For John had not yet been thrown into prison.

The aside in John 3:24 is telling. It makes sense only if the reader is expected to know narratives like Matthew, Mark, and Luke, where John's arrest is narrated early in the story.[7] All three Synoptics narrate John's arrest before Jesus's ministry begins. Mark and Matthew both sequence the events directly:

Mark 1:14: Καὶ μετὰ τὸ παραδοθῆναι τὸν Ἰωάννην ἦλθεν ὁ Ἰησοῦς εἰς τὴν Γαλιλαίαν.

And after John was arrested, Jesus went to Galilee.

---

6. For partially overlapping examples of the phenomenon, see Westcott, *Gospel*, lxxxii, and J. Blinzler, *Johannes und die Synoptiker: Ein Forschungsbericht*, SBS 5 (Stuttgart: Katholisches Bibelwerk, 1965), 52–53.

7. See Margaret Davies, *Rhetoric and Reference in the Fourth Gospel*, JSNTSup 69 (Sheffield: Sheffield Academic, 1992), "We have to infer that readers and listeners were aware of his imprisonment and must have wondered how he could still be active. The Gospel, however, does not describe his subsequent imprisonment and execution" (357). Cf. Richard Bauckham, "John for Readers of Mark," in *The Gospels for All Christians: Rethinking the Gospel Audiences*, ed. Richard Bauckham (Grand Rapids: Eerdmans, 1998), 147–71, at 152–53, though Bauckham has John presupposing only Mark, and not Matthew and Luke.

Matt 4:12: Ἀκούσας δὲ ὅτι Ἰωάννης παρεδόθη ἀνεχώρησεν εἰς τὴν Γαλιλαίαν.

And when he heard that John had been arrested, he withdrew to Galilee.

In Matthew, the link between the two events, John's arrest and Jesus's move to Galilee, is particularly close—Jesus withdraws when he hears that John has been arrested. Luke also narrates the arrest here, although he waits to narrate the baptism of Jesus until afterward, and he adds some political detail, as well as the note that he was put in prison, which Matthew and Mark save for the story of his death later on (Matt 14:1–12 // Mark 6:14–29):

Luke 3:19–20: ὁ δὲ Ἡρῴδης ὁ τετραάρχης, ἐλεγχόμενος ὑπ᾽ αὐτοῦ περὶ Ἡρῳδιάδος τῆς γυναικὸς τοῦ ἀδελφοῦ αὐτοῦ καὶ περὶ πάντων ὧν ἐποίησεν πονηρῶν ὁ Ἡρῴδης, προσέθηκεν καὶ τοῦτο ἐπὶ πᾶσιν, καὶ κατέκλεισεν τὸν Ἰωάννην ἐν φυλακῇ.

But Herod the tetrarch, who had been rebuked by him concerning Herodias, the wife of his brother, and concerning all the evil things that Herod had done, added this to them all, and he locked up John in prison.

The Synoptic sequencing is clear: John had a ministry of baptism, then Jesus was baptized, and then John was arrested and locked up in prison, after which Jesus withdrew to Galilee where he began his public ministry. But in the Fourth Gospel, John the Baptist is still active later on, after Jesus has called the first disciples (John 1:35–51), performed his first sign, in Cana of Galilee (John 2:1–11), moved to Capernaum (2:12), and then visited Jerusalem (2:13–3:21). Any reader of John could easily be confused, and the evangelist thus adds the note that John had not yet been thrown into prison. We have not yet reached that point in the Synoptic narrative. In other words, this looks like an explanatory note for readers of the Synoptics to make clear where the new narrative fits in. Unlike the Synoptics, the Fourth Gospel never does go on to narrate John's arrest or death. It is simply taken for granted. The note in John 3:24 appears to have a clarificatory, explanatory function, and one that makes best sense on the thesis that John and his readers know the Synoptics.

"You Were Willing to Rejoice for a While in His Light" (John 5:35)

John 5:33: ὑμεῖς ἀπεστάλκατε πρὸς Ἰωάννην, καὶ μεμαρτύρηκεν τῇ ἀληθείᾳ· ἐγὼ δὲ οὐ παρὰ ἀνθρώπου τὴν μαρτυρίαν λαμβάνω, ἀλλὰ ταῦτα λέγω ἵνα ὑμεῖς σωθῆτε. ἐκεῖνος ἦν ὁ λύχνος ὁ καιόμενος καὶ φαίνων, <u>ὑμεῖς δὲ ἠθελήσατε ἀγαλλιαθῆναι πρὸς ὥραν ἐν τῷ φωτὶ αὐτοῦ</u>·

CHAPTER 4

You sent messengers to John, and he testified to the truth. Not that I accept such human testimony, but I say these things so that you may be saved. He was a burning and shining lamp, <u>and you were willing to rejoice for a while in his light</u>.

John the Baptist's arrest and death are not the only elements of John's biography that the Fourth Gospel fails to narrate. Other things are also taken for granted. The gospel famously does not narrate Jesus's baptism (Matt 3:13–17 // Mark 1:9–11 // Luke 3:21–22), but the author appears to know about it because he narrates its aftermath, when the dove descends on Jesus (Matt 3:16 // Mark 1:10 // Luke 3:22 // John 1:32), though now these words are transferred from the narrator to John's voice (see below, pp. 96–97). And now, in the discourse of which John 5:35 is a part, Jesus takes for granted a detail that has not been narrated in the Fourth Gospel but is narrated in the Synoptics, where Jesus's audience is said to have rejoiced for a while in John's light.

Jesus is here speaking to "the Judeans" (οἱ Ἰουδαῖοι, 5:15–18),[8] but there is no sign of the Judeans "rejoicing" in his light in John, not even "for a while." There is, however, an initially enthusiastic response to John's baptism in the Synoptics, of the kind that the Fourth Gospel appears to presuppose:

> Mark 1:5: And the whole of the region of Judea [πᾶσα ἡ Ἰουδαία χώρα], and all the people of Jerusalem [οἱ Ἱεροσολυμῖται πάντες] were going out to him and were baptized by him in the River Jordan, confessing their sins.

The same note appears in Matt 3:5–6, where it is "Jerusalem and all of Judea and the whole region of the Jordan" (Ἱεροσόλυμα καὶ πᾶσα ἡ Ἰουδαία καὶ πᾶσα ἡ περίχωρος τοῦ Ἰορδάνου) who are baptized by John.[9] The notion that Judean leaders are included in this group is explicit in Matt 3:7, where John directly

---

8. There is another possible case of John presupposing Synoptic narration in the same context. In John 5:18, "For this reason, the Judeans were seeking all the more to kill him" (διὰ τοῦτο οὖν μᾶλλον ἐζήτουν αὐτὸν οἱ Ἰουδαῖοι ἀποκτεῖναι), but this is the first mention of anyone trying to kill Jesus in John, so "all the more" is striking, and the reference could be to Mark 3:6, which comes in a similar Sabbath healing story, when Pharisees begin to plot with Herodians about "how they might kill Jesus" (ὅπως αὐτὸν ἀπολέσωσιν). This example is less certain, however, because the reference may simply be to John 5:16, "And therefore the Judeans were persecuting Jesus" (καὶ διὰ τοῦτο ἐδίωκον οἱ Ἰουδαῖοι τὸν Ἰησοῦν).

9. Luke, by contrast, does not place any stress on "Judea" and "Jerusalem" coming to be baptized by John but speaks only, in agreement with Matthew, about "the whole region of the Jordan" (Luke 3:3).

addresses "Pharisees and Sadducees" who are coming to be baptized (contrast Luke 3:7, "the crowds").

It does not appear to be the case that the Fourth Gospel is being vague or forgetful about Jesus's audience. When Jesus addresses the Judeans, he says "you sent messengers" (5:33), which is exactly what had happened in John. The Judeans sent "priests and Levites from Jerusalem" (1:19), and the narrator further clarifies that "they had been sent by the Pharisees" (1:24). This is the audience that is being addressed now in John 5, and it is striking that the reader now finds out more about their backstory, a backstory that coheres closely with the Synoptic narrative. There is nothing corresponding to the Judeans' enthusiasm for John's baptism in the Fourth Gospel. The best explanation for this is that it presupposes the narration in Matthew and Mark.

"The Other Side of the Sea of Galilee" (John 6:1)

John 6:1: Μετὰ ταῦτα ἀπῆλθεν ὁ Ἰησοῦς πέραν τῆς θαλάσσης τῆς Γαλιλαίας τῆς Τιβεριάδος.

After these things, Jesus went to the other side of the Sea of Galilee (of Tiberias).[10]

If John's Gospel had been the only early gospel to have survived, this statement would seem extraordinary, and we would have to speculate about prior narratives that might have provided more context. Jesus travels to "the other side" of the Sea of Galilee, as if this side of the lake has already been mentioned. But in fact, this is the first time that the "Sea of Galilee" has been mentioned at all. It makes sense to talk about "the other side of the Sea of Galilee" only if this side of the Sea of Galilee is somehow familiar.

Readers of Mark and Matthew know the Sea of Galilee as a major location for Jesus's early ministry. It is where Jesus calls Peter, Andrew, James, and John (Matt 4:18–22 // Mark 1:16–20), and activity tends to take place around the hub of Capernaum (Mark 1:21; 2:1; 9:33; Matt 8:5; 11:23; 17:24) and "the sea" (Mark 2:13; 3:7; 4:1). On one occasion, Jesus teaches the crowd, which is standing on the shore, from a boat in the sea (Mark 4:1), and Matthew's Gospel underlines the location of Jesus's home in Capernaum, by the sea:

---

10. My translation.

CHAPTER 4

Matt 4:13: καὶ καταλιπὼν τὴν Ναζαρὰ ἐλθὼν κατῴκησεν εἰς Καφαρναοὺμ τὴν παραθαλασσίαν ἐν ὁρίοις Ζαβουλὼν καὶ Νεφθαλίμ.

He left Nazara[11] and made his home in Capernaum by the sea, in the territory of Zebulun and Naphtali.

It is possible that the author of Mark's Gospel was the one to coin the term "Sea of Galilee." The Gospel of Mark is the first work in which the expression occurs, and John seems almost reluctant to use the term, qualifying it immediately with "of Tiberias" (John 6:1), the term he prefers on its only other mention in his gospel, in John 21:1.[12] But even if this is not the case, readers of Mark and Matthew are thoroughly familiar with life on this side of the Sea of Galilee, and when Jesus and the disciples eventually leave this area in a boat, they depart to "the other side" of the sea (4:35, εἰς τὸ πέραν). Mark and Matthew are both explicit about the different sides of the sea and use the same word that John uses in 6:1:

Mark 4:35: Καὶ λέγει αὐτοῖς ἐν ἐκείνῃ τῇ ἡμέρᾳ ὀψίας γενομένης· Διέλθωμεν εἰς τὸ <u>πέραν</u>.

And he says to them, on that day, when evening had come, "Let us cross over to the <u>other side</u>."

Mark 5:1: Καὶ ἦλθον εἰς τὸ <u>πέραν</u> τῆς θαλάσσης εἰς τὴν χώραν τῶν Γερασηνῶν.

And they came to the <u>other side</u> of the sea, into the region of the Gerasenes.

Mark 5:21: Καὶ διαπεράσαντος τοῦ Ἰησοῦ ἐν τῷ πλοίῳ πάλιν εἰς τὸ <u>πέραν</u> συνήχθη ὄχλος πολὺς ἐπ' αὐτόν, καὶ ἦν παρὰ τὴν θάλασσαν.

And when Jesus had crossed again in the boat to the <u>other side</u>, a great crowd gathered around him, and he was by the sea.

Mark 6:45: Καὶ εὐθὺς ἠνάγκασεν τοὺς μαθητὰς αὐτοῦ ἐμβῆναι εἰς τὸ πλοῖον καὶ προάγειν εἰς τὸ <u>πέραν</u> πρὸς Βηθσαϊδάν.

And immediately he compelled his disciples to get into the boat and to go on ahead to the <u>other side</u>, to Bethsaida.

---

11. NRSVue: "Nazareth."
12. See Eugene Boring, *An Introduction to the New Testament: History, Literature, Theology* (Louisville: Westminster John Knox, 2012), 674.

John's Presupposition of Synoptic Narratives

Mark 8:13: καὶ ἀφεὶς αὐτοὺς πάλιν ἐμβὰς ἀπῆλθεν εἰς τὸ <u>πέραν</u>.

And having left them, and having got into the boat again he went across to the <u>other side</u>.

Jesus's journeys from one side of the sea to the other are a major feature of these chapters of Mark's Gospel, including in the same context as the one in John 6, the feeding of the five thousand and the walking on the sea. To some extent, the same journeys are highlighted also in Matthew and Luke, though in Matthew, they are spread across a broader span of his gospel because of the disruption that his big discourses provide, and in Luke, it is a "lake" (λίμνη, Luke 5:1, 2; 8:22, 23, 33) rather than a "sea." Yet even in Matthew and Luke, details about Jesus's journeys on the lake are a major feature of the narrative, and it is never a surprise when travel across the water takes place. Not so John. The Fourth Gospel appears to be presupposing a narrative of exactly the kind that we find in the Synoptics.

The note in John 6:1 is so jarring that it has given birth to many theories about interpolations, drafts, layers, sources, and jumbled sheets. Perhaps John 6 originally came before John 5, in which case Jesus can be assumed to have traveled from Galilee (John 4:43–54), and specifically Cana (John 4:46), to "the other side of the Sea of Galilee" (John 6:1), before returning to Jerusalem (John 5). Perhaps John 6 was a special Galilean chapter inserted into an earlier edition of John. Or perhaps John is here copying from a hypothetical source like the signs gospel, in which the geography was clearer. The strength of these theories, none of which have any textual or manuscript evidence, is that they have noticed something genuinely striking about the sequencing of the Fourth Gospel. Their weakness, however, is that they miss the most straightforward explanation, that when John is read with knowledge of the Synoptics, its narrative can be seen to presuppose elements that are narrated there, especially items like this that are so markedly Markan.

"Did I Not Choose You, the Twelve?" (John 6:70)

John 6:66–71: Ἐκ τούτου πολλοὶ ἐκ τῶν μαθητῶν αὐτοῦ ἀπῆλθον εἰς τὰ ὀπίσω καὶ οὐκέτι μετ' αὐτοῦ περιεπάτουν. εἶπεν οὖν ὁ Ἰησοῦς τοῖς δώδεκα· Μὴ καὶ ὑμεῖς θέλετε ὑπάγειν; ἀπεκρίθη αὐτῷ Σίμων Πέτρος· Κύριε, πρὸς τίνα ἀπελευσόμεθα; ῥήματα ζωῆς αἰωνίου ἔχεις, καὶ ἡμεῖς πεπιστεύκαμεν καὶ ἐγνώκαμεν ὅτι σὺ εἶ ὁ ἅγιος τοῦ θεοῦ. ἀπεκρίθη αὐτοῖς ὁ Ἰησοῦς· <u>Οὐκ ἐγὼ ὑμᾶς τοὺς δώδεκα ἐξελεξάμην</u>; καὶ ἐξ ὑμῶν εἷς διάβολός ἐστιν. ἔλεγεν δὲ τὸν Ἰούδαν Σίμωνος Ἰσκαριώτου· οὗτος γὰρ ἔμελλεν παραδιδόναι αὐτόν, εἷς ἐκ τῶν δώδεκα.

CHAPTER 4

Because of this many of his disciples turned back and no longer went about with him. So Jesus asked the twelve, "Do you also wish to go away?" Simon Peter answered him, "Lord, to whom can we go? You have the words of eternal life. We have come to believe and know that you are the Holy One of God." Jesus answered them, "<u>Did I not choose you, the twelve</u>? Yet one of you is a devil." He was speaking of Judas son of Simon Iscariot, for he, though one of the twelve, was going to betray him.

The Fourth Gospel narrates the call of five disciples. The first three are Andrew, Simon Peter, and an anonymous character (John 1:35–42), then Philip and Nathanael (John 1:43–51). After this, there are no further calls in John. In this respect, John is like the Synoptics, which have calls only for the initial four or five disciples—Simon Peter, Andrew, James, and John (Matt 4:18–22 // Mark 1:16–20 // Luke 5:1–11, minus Andrew in Luke), and then Levi (Mark 2:13–14 // Luke 5:27–28) or Matthew (Matt 9:9–10). Unlike the Synoptics, however, there is no story or statement in John about an appointment of twelve disciples (Matt 10:1–4 // Mark 3:13–19 // Luke 6:12–16), let alone a commission for the twelve to go out on mission (Matt 10:5–15 // Mark 6:7–13 // Luke 9:1–6). So when, at the end of John 6, it appears that there is, after all, a group of twelve specially chosen disciples, it is really striking. The narrator mentions "the twelve" twice, as if they are a well-known entity, and Jesus uses the term, too, underlining his appointment with the rhetorical question, "Did I not choose you, the twelve?"

The example is an interesting one because "the twelve" terminology does not seem to be incidental. It is essential both to the story that is told in John 6 as well as to the way that the narrative unfolds in the rest of the gospel. This group, "the twelve," is a smaller, specially chosen group from among the larger set of "disciples." "The disciples" appear frequently from John 2 onward. They travel with Jesus, and they are his companions everywhere, showing up in Cana (John 2:2, 11), Capernaum (John 2:12), Jerusalem (2:17, 22), "the Judean region" (3:22), Samaria (4:8, 27, 31, 33), on a mountain on the other side of the Sea of Galilee (6:3, 8), on the sea (6:19), and now at the synagogue in Capernaum (6:24, 59). Unlike "the twelve," though, it seems that "many" in this larger group have no staying power. They find Jesus's teaching hard and cannot accept it (6:60), grumbling about it (6:61), and now turning their backs (6:66).

With their departure, the focus moves to "the twelve," and Jesus will go on, in the Farewell Discourses, to underline the importance of these specially "chosen" disciples (John 13:18; 15:16, 19).[13] Moreover, as in the Synoptics, the fact that Ju-

---

13. See further below, pp. 109–10, for the importance of this language about "choosing."

das is "one of the twelve" is a key element in the tragedy. He was one chosen by Jesus, yet he betrayed him. He is similarly labeled "one of the twelve" six times in the Synoptics (Matt 26:14 // Mark 14:10 // Luke 22:3; Matt 26:47 // Mark 14:43 // Luke 22:47).

There is a value in reading John here in light of the Synoptics. Rather than "the twelve" appearing suddenly and unexpectedly in a fragmentary narrative that has previously had no place for them, they appear at a key moment in a story that has presupposed their existence all along and that will continue to develop their story. As so often, reading John in the light of the Synoptics enhances narrative connections and tells a more compelling story.

"The Village of Mary and Her Sister Martha" (John 11:1)

John 11:1: Ἦν δέ τις ἀσθενῶν, Λάζαρος ἀπὸ Βηθανίας ἐκ <u>τῆς κώμης Μαρίας καὶ Μάρθας τῆς ἀδελφῆς αὐτῆς</u>.

Now a certain man was ill, Lazarus of Bethany, <u>the village of Mary and her sister Martha</u>.

The four examples discussed so far all involve Mark, with some parallel material in Matthew and Luke, but one of the most striking examples of this kind of narration occurs in a Johannine parallel with Luke's Gospel. John introduces his readers to a new character, previously not known, "a certain man" (τις) called Lazarus. He is then identified by means of two characters who apparently are familiar to the readers, Mary and Martha. Lazarus lives in Bethany, which is said to be "the village of Mary and her sister Martha." B. H. Streeter saw this as a clear sign that John was presupposing the already-known account of Luke, in which the sisters Mary and Martha appear as characters (Luke 10:38–42). It looks like the reader is expected to have some knowledge of Mary and Martha, who, unlike their brother, are not introduced as "certain women."[14] Once the reader is

---

In the Farewell Discourses, though, the inner group is not called "the twelve," because Judas makes his exit at John 13:30.

14. B. H. Streeter, *The Four Gospels: A Study of Origins* (London: Macmillan, 1924), 402. See also Davies, *Rhetoric and Reference*, 357. This example is not reversible. In Luke 10:38–39, Mary and Martha are not known characters—Luke introduces two unnamed characters, "a certain woman named Martha . . . and her sister named Mary" (γυνὴ δέ τις ὀνόματι Μάρθα . . . καὶ τῇδε ἦν ἀδελφὴ καλουμένη Μαριάμ). This is a further indication that John is familiar with Luke, and not Luke with John.

familiar with Lazarus, the way of alluding to Bethany changes, and in 12:1, after the raising story, Bethany becomes "the home of Lazarus" (ὅπου ἦν Λάζαρος).

Luke does not name the "village" (κώμη) in which Mary and Martha lived. It is just "a certain village" that Jesus enters (αὐτὸς εἰσῆλθεν εἰς κώμην τινά, Luke 10:38). At this point in Luke, the travel narrative has only just begun (9:51). But Bethany as the location of Mary and Martha's home does have a simple Synoptic explanation. John identifies this Mary as the woman who anoints Jesus (John 11:2; 12:1–8) in the passage that has the closest Synoptic parallel in the gospel (Matt 26:6–13 // Mark 14:3–9; cf. Luke 7:36–50; see pp. 23–31, above), and there, in Matthew and Mark, the anointing takes place in Bethany.

The same kind of phrasing around characters and their homes happens earlier in John, when Bethsaida is described as the "city of Andrew and Peter" (John 1:44). In this case, the two characters have just been introduced in John (1:35–42), and now the city is explained by means of them, like Bethany in John 11:1. The only difference is that John 1:44 presupposes the previous passage in John while John 11:1 presupposes a passage in Luke.

"You Will Be Scattered" (John 16:32)

John 16:32: ἰδοὺ ἔρχεται ὥρα καὶ ἐλήλυθεν ἵνα <u>σκορπισθῆτε</u> ἕκαστος εἰς τὰ ἴδια κἀμὲ μόνον ἀφῆτε·

Behold, an hour is coming, indeed it has come, when <u>you will be scattered</u>, each one to his home, and you will leave me alone.

Here John appears to presuppose an element in the Synoptic story that has not yet been narrated. The scattering of the disciples is prophesied in Mark and Matthew (Matt 26:31 // Mark 14:27), and at a similar point in the narrative, and using a related verb (σκορπίζω in John and διασκορπίζω in Mark and Matthew), but while Matthew and Mark go on to narrate the disciples fleeing (Matt 26:56 // Mark 14:50), John does not.[15] In other words, John here presupposes an element mentioned in the Synoptics that he will not go on to narrate. In fact, even though the Fourth Gospel's narrative presupposes the scattering of the disciples, it goes on to tell a story that one of them remained faithful, the Beloved Disciple at the cross (John 19:25–27, 35).

---

15. There is a partial parallel in John 18:8b–9, "'So if you are looking for me, let these people go.' This was to fulfill the word that he had spoken, 'I did not lose a single one of those whom you gave me.'" This appears, however, to be a reference back to Jesus's prayer in John 17:12, and the point stands that there is no narrative in John of the disciples actually fleeing.

"Am I Not to Drink the Cup That the Father Has Given to Me?" (John 18:11)

John 18:11: εἶπεν οὖν ὁ Ἰησοῦς τῷ Πέτρῳ· Βάλε τὴν μάχαιραν εἰς τὴν θήκην· <u>τὸ ποτήριον ὃ δέδωκέν μοι ὁ πατὴρ οὐ μὴ πίω αὐτό</u>;

Therefore Jesus said to Peter, "Put your sword back into its sheath. <u>Am I not to drink the cup that the Father has given to me</u>?

"The cup" as an image for the violent martyr's death is common in the Synoptics, and it is found there on several occasions, most notably when James and John are asked whether they can "drink the cup" that Jesus is about to drink (Matt 20:22–23; Mark 10:38–39), and when Jesus begs God to take this cup away (Matt 26:39; Mark 14:36; Luke 22:42). That incident, Jesus's prayer in Gethsemane (Matt 26:36–46 // Mark 14:32–42 // Luke 22:39–46), occurs immediately before the scene that is paralleled here in John, Jesus's arrest. The Gethsemane scene is famously omitted in John, to the surprise of some scholars, yet it looks like the Fourth Gospel actually knows and presupposes the narrative. This is the only reference to any kind of "cup" in John's Gospel,[16] and it is in large part because of our own familiarity with the Synoptics that we do not notice how anomalous it would be in John if we did not know the Synoptic story.

There is, of course, an earlier scene in John that evokes Jesus's Gethsemane prayer to the Father (John 12:27–33), when instead of silence, there is an answer so loud that the crowd thinks it is thunder, and we will address this fascinating moment in chapter 5 (pp. 104–5, below). Since that scene is in several senses a dramatic revision of the Synoptic Gethsemane story, it is striking that here, at Jesus's arrest, something more like the Synoptic Gethsemane story is presupposed. In other words, while the Fourth Evangelist chooses not to narrate Gethsemane, he nevertheless presupposes its outcome—that Jesus will indeed drink the cup that "the Father" has given him to drink, as when Jesus prays to "(Abba) Father" in the Synoptics.

Moreover, whereas in the Synoptics, the person who cuts off the high priest's slave's ear is anonymous, in John it is Simon Peter, one of the three disciples who should have been witnessing Jesus's agonized prayer in Gethsemane but who slept. For those who read John alongside the Synoptics, the poignant moment here is literally and metaphorically striking. Peter should have heard Jesus's prayer in Gethsemane and should have known that he has to drink the cup that his Father has given to him, yet far from realizing this, he shows the kind

---

16. Ποτήριον has figures of 7/7/5/1+0. As a metaphor for suffering and death, it has figures of 3/4/1/1+0.

CHAPTER 4

of violence that means he has not grasped anything. This kind of intertextual dramatic irony occurs on other occasions in John, too, and we will take a closer look at two further examples of this phenomenon below (pp. 102–3).

Teaching in the Synagogues and Temple (John 18:20)

John 18:20: ἀπεκρίθη αὐτῷ Ἰησοῦς· Ἐγὼ παρρησίᾳ λελάληκα τῷ κόσμῳ· <u>ἐγὼ πάντοτε ἐδίδαξα ἐν συναγωγῇ</u> καὶ ἐν τῷ ἱερῷ, ὅπου πάντες οἱ Ἰουδαῖοι συνέρχονται, καὶ ἐν κρυπτῷ ἐλάλησα οὐδέν·

Jesus answered, "I have spoken openly to the world; <u>I have always taught in synagogues</u> and in the temple, where all the Judeans come together. I have said nothing in secret."

Although John provides some teaching in the temple (John 7:14, 28; 8:20; 10:23), there is only one reference to teaching in the synagogue in the whole of the gospel, when, in 6:59, "He said these things while he was teaching in a synagogue at Capernaum." It would come as a surprise, therefore, when Jesus tells the high priest that he has "always" (πάντοτε) taught in the synagogues as well as the temple. But it is an idea that makes sense against the background of the Synoptics, which frequently depict Jesus teaching there (Matt 4:23; 9:35; 13:54; Mark 1:21, 39; 6:2; Luke 4:15, 16, 31–33, 44; 6:6; 13:10).[17] John seems to be presupposing a major feature of the Synoptic narratives, that Jesus regularly taught in synagogues.

"Then Annas Sent Him Bound to Caiaphas the High Priest" (John 18:24)

John 18:24: ἀπέστειλεν οὖν αὐτὸν ὁ Ἅννας δεδεμένον πρὸς Καϊάφαν τὸν ἀρχιερέα.

Then Annas sent him bound to Caiaphas the high priest.

This comes from the same passage as the previous example, and there are several strange features, all of which make sense if John is presupposing the Synoptic trial narratives. The major curiosity is that John does not actually narrate a trial before Caiaphas. In the place where we expect it, after Jesus is sent

---

17. Luke 4:44 is particularly noteworthy here in that it depicts Jesus preaching in the "synagogues of Judea" (καὶ ἦν κηρύσσων εἰς τὰς συναγωγὰς τῆς Ἰουδαίας). This verse may have been one of the inspirations for the Johannine idea that Jesus had an extended ministry in Judea.

bound to Caiaphas, there is only the last of Peter's denials (18:25–27), and then Jesus is sent to Pilate (18:28). To compound the curiosity, John appears to narrate a trial before Annas, who as well as being called Caiaphas's father-in-law (18:13) is apparently also called "the high priest" (18:19, 22). In order to see the issues here clearly, this is what the sequence in John looks like:

(a) John 18:12–14   Jesus is taken to Annas, the father-in-law of Caiaphas, "the high priest that year."
(b) John 18:15–18   Peter's first denial
(c) John 18:19–23   "The high priest" questions Jesus
(d) John 18:24   Annas sends Jesus bound to "Caiaphas the high priest"
(e) John 18:25–27   Peter's second and third denials
(f) John 18:28   Jesus is taken to Pilate

The "high priest," (c) in this sequence (John 18:19–23), has to be Annas, or the narrative makes no sense at all. Yet this raises several questions. Why does Annas play the key role here? Why is he called the high priest? And why is there no trial before Caiaphas, in spite of his being singled out as a key figure? Although this is one of the most exasperating pieces of narrative in the Fourth Gospel, these questions are straightforwardly answered if John is presupposing the Synoptics and supplementing their accounts with an overlapping narrative of his own.

If John is presupposing that a trial took place before Caiaphas, that trial is provided by Mark, Matthew, and to some extent Luke. In Mark's Gospel, there is a trial before the high priest and the council, but "the high priest" is unnamed (Mark 14:53–65). Matthew identifies him as Caiaphas (Matt 26:3, 57), which coheres with our knowledge from Josephus (*Ant.* 18.33–35). This would make sense of the odd and abrupt line that alludes to Jesus's encounter with Caiaphas but that does not narrate it. There is still, though, the curiosity of the role played by Annas. The detail that Annas was Caiaphas's father-in-law is unique to John, though it is plausible given that Annas seems to have had something of a high priestly dynasty.[18] But the notion that Annas and Caiaphas could both be called "high priest" at this point, around the late 20s or early 30s CE, takes its authority from Luke, who is unique in speaking of "the high priesthood of Annas and Caiaphas" (ἐπὶ ἀρχιερέως Ἄννα καὶ Καϊάφα, Luke 3:2). Luke does not further identify the "high priest" or the "high priests" in his trial narrative (Luke 22:66–71),[19]

---

18. Helen Bond, *Caiaphas: Friend of Rome and Judge of Jesus?* (Louisville: Westminster John Knox, 2004), 37, sees the detail in John as historically plausible.

19. The word is usually translated "chief priests" when it is plural (ἀρχιερεῖς), and "high

CHAPTER 4

and John's naming of both Caiaphas and Annas as "high priest" makes sense if his narrative is presupposing Luke as well as Mark and Matthew.

The isolation of a special trial before Annas appears to be a uniquely Johannine addition to the story, yet the narrative appears to acknowledge that Caiaphas was nevertheless the key figure. It is he who was "high priest that year,"[20] whom the reader has already met in 11:46–53, when he makes his prophecy about one man dying for the people, and it is he to whom Jesus is sent before the fatal referral to Pilate. Although not the most elegant piece of narrative, everything makes sense if John is presupposing the Synoptics, the joint high priesthood of Annas and Caiaphas from Luke, and the presupposition of Mark and Matthew's trial before the high priest, identified as Caiaphas by Matthew.

"We Do Not Know Where They Have Laid Him" (John 20:2)

John 20:1–2: Τῇ δὲ μιᾷ τῶν σαββάτων Μαρία ἡ Μαγδαληνὴ ἔρχεται πρωῒ σκοτίας ἔτι οὔσης εἰς τὸ μνημεῖον, <u>καὶ βλέπει τὸν λίθον ἠρμένον ἐκ τοῦ μνημείου</u>. τρέχει οὖν καὶ ἔρχεται πρὸς Σίμωνα Πέτρον καὶ πρὸς τὸν ἄλλον μαθητὴν ὃν ἐφίλει ὁ Ἰησοῦς, καὶ λέγει αὐτοῖς· Ἦραν τὸν κύριον ἐκ τοῦ μνημείου, καὶ <u>οὐκ οἴδαμεν ποῦ ἔθηκαν αὐτόν</u>.

Early on the first day of the week, while it was still dark, Mary Magdalene came to the tomb <u>and saw that the stone had been removed from the tomb</u>. So she ran and went to Simon Peter and the other disciple, the one whom Jesus loved, and said to them, "They have taken the Lord out of the tomb, and <u>we do not know where they have laid him</u>."

A reader who did not know the Synoptics would find two unusual features here. First, the story presupposes that a stone had been put in front of the tomb (20:1). It is an important element of this story that the stone has been removed. The stone does not feature in John's burial account (John 19:38–42) but appears to be presupposed from Mark's and Matthew's accounts, both of which emphasize that a stone was rolled at the entrance of the tomb (Matt 27:60 // Mark 15:46), and in Matthew it was sealed shut (Matt 27:65–66). This is not a question of redundancy. Not only do Matthew and Mark draw attention to the presence

---

priest" when it is singular (ἀρχιερεύς). But it is the same word in Greek, and it is much more common in the plural in the Synoptic Gospels.

20. This note is sometimes pressed to make the case that John was ignorant about Judean history in this period and supposed that the high priest changed each year. It is more likely that the phrase implies something like "that fateful year" (Bond, *Caiaphas*, 132).

of the stone in front of the tomb, but they make clear that Mary Magdalene and the other Mary witness this (Matt 27:61 // Mark 15:47), which provides the crucial link with the resurrection story, where the same women see the same tomb and the same stone (Mark 16:1–4; Matt 28:1–2). In John, it is not clear how Mary Magdalene even knows where the tomb is, let alone that a stone had been rolled against it, and the narrative makes best sense if the evangelist is presupposing these elements from the Synoptics.[21]

There is a related feature in the same story. John's reframing of the account focuses on just one of the women mentioned in the Synoptics, Mary Magdalene (John 20:1–18). The other women, variously "Mary of James, and Salome" (Mark 16:1), "the other Mary" (Matt 28:1), "Joanna, Mary of James, and the others" (Luke 24:10), are not mentioned here at all. Yet the Fourth Gospel presupposes that Mary is not alone. "We do not know where they have laid him," she says (John 20:2). As so often, the gospel chooses to focus on a particular character (see further below) and their engagements with Jesus, but the gospel narrative appears to presuppose that others are present, as in the Synoptic Gospels.

How Do We Know John Is Presupposing the Synoptic Gospels?

In a surprising number of cases, John appears to presuppose incidents that he does not narrate, and in each case, these incidents are narrated in the Synoptics. This looks like a sign that John knows the Synoptics. How certain can we be, though, that John is presupposing the Synoptics and not unknown sources that tell the same stories? Someone defending John's independence might object that the author has lost sources and traditions, something written like the signs gospel or something oral like the much-loved Synoptic-like traditions.

It is, of course, always possible to substitute hypothetical texts and traditions for known entities like Matthew, Mark, and Luke, and the appeal to the unknown will always have a certain attraction. There is a thrill when the ancient historian makes some kind of contact with what is no longer extant, and the temptation to search for what has been lost is ever present. Nevertheless, it is a temptation that should in this case be resisted. Oral tradition theories offer no help with explaining literary issues like these. John 3:24, the aside about the

---

21. Luke also omits to mention the stone in the burial story (Luke 23:50–56), and like John he does mention it in the resurrection story (Luke 24:2). Unlike John, though, Luke does connect the burial and resurrection stories with the presence of "the women who had come with Jesus from Galilee" (Luke 23:55; cf. 24:1, 10).

timing of John's arrest, makes sense only as an attempt to locate the action being narrated in a known narrative context, a context that we have at hand in the Synoptic Gospels. It is true that someone who knew Josephus might know about John's arrest, imprisonment, and death (*Ant.* 18.109–119), but there is no hint of how far John's and Jesus's public activities overlapped, or even that the two men even knew one another. The only reason for anxiety about how John's and Jesus's public activities intersected is something felt by readers of the Synoptic Gospels, for whom John's arrest appears to have preceded Jesus's public ministry.

Other features noted here are similar. To specify a location on "the other side of the Sea of Galilee" (John 6:1) presupposes a narrative in which this side of the Sea of Galilee provides the gravitational force, a narrative like the Gospel of Mark (and its parallels in Matthew and Luke). Oral traditions may, of course, have told stories like those found in Mark and parallels, located on either side of the Sea of Galilee, but that is the key point. Those traditions will, by definition, have featured stories about both sides of the Sea of Galilee. The note about "the other side" suggests knowledge of a narrative like Mark's where "this side" is the default, and where "the other side" requires a special note.

It is worth reflecting also on how oral traditions about Mary, Martha, and Lazarus could have led to the narration found in John 11:1–2, where Mary and Martha are known characters, and where Lazarus is a new character ("a certain man"). How likely is it that there was an oral tradition context in which Mary and Martha were well-known characters, while their brother Lazarus, raised from the dead after four days in the tomb, was completely unknown? This is, of course, possible, but it seems unlikely. The way that John sets up the story makes better sense if the well-known characters, Martha and Mary, are known because of their appearance in the Gospel of Luke (Luke 10:38–42), while the new character, Lazarus, "a certain man," is completely unknown.

In other words, several of these narrative notices make the best sense on a literary explanation, where the author of John is presupposing and pointing to material already narrated in the Synoptic Gospels. If a literary explanation makes the best sense, though, it raises the possibility that John is working not with the Synoptics but with a hypothetical written source that has parallels to the Synoptics, like the signs gospel. Could the signs gospel help us here? The difficulty with the signs gospel is that the source is already selective. As it is usually articulated, the signs gospel narrates only seven signs, seven signs that are then taken over by the author of the Fourth Gospel. But what is so striking about the examples discussed in this chapter is that they make good sense against the background of narratives like the Synoptics, with their broader narratives about the relation between John the Baptist and Jesus, about miracles that take

John's Presupposition of Synoptic Narratives

place on this side of the Sea of Galilee, about the choosing of the twelve, and about several details in the passion narratives. Attempts to reconstruct the signs gospel frequently leave the things presupposed in John to one side, and so have limited explanatory potential. In other words, is it worth prioritizing a weaker hypothetical source like the signs gospel when stronger known sources like the Synoptics are at hand?

Why Does It Matter?

If it is true that the author of John presupposes the Synoptic narratives, why does it matter? What does it add to our understanding of the Fourth Gospel? In a book arguing that John knows the Synoptics, the answer is in some ways obvious because this feature provides further evidence for that case. But there is more than that. If John is routinely leaving key materials unnarrated and expecting his readers to know those materials, it helps to answer one of the age-old questions about the gospel, and one we love to underline in our introductory lectures: why does John omit so much? Why is there no baptism, transfiguration, or Gethsemane? If John is presupposing the Synoptic narratives, he does not need to narrate every passage that readers might think essential. He knows these stories, but he chooses to emphasize other stories, and to add new material of his own, something we might in any case have guessed from the self-conscious selectivity with which we began the chapter.

Moreover, readers of the Synoptics have always been in the position of finding added value in John's narratives, of discovering some kind of hermeneutical key, and it turns out that this could be an element in the Fourth Gospel's design. In many of the cases cited in this chapter, reading John alongside the Synoptics actually improves the tale that is being told. If John expects his readers to know the Synoptics, it is not surprising that he mentions "the other side of the Sea of Galilee" in 6:1 because the story is already familiar, and John is building on it. There is something much more satisfying about this than the theories of dislocated passages, hypothetical earlier layers, interpolations, and other kinds of lost traditions. Or when Jesus underlines that he had chosen the twelve (6:70), this is not a foreign intrusion into a gospel that otherwise does not mention it but rather a key moment that caps a narrative that focuses on unfaithful disciples who are now contrasted with the inner circle. Or when Jesus tells Simon Peter to put away his sword because he must drink the cup that the Father has given him (18:11), this is poignant because the reader of the Synoptics knows that Peter, if he had not been asleep, would have known that Jesus was praying to his Father

CHAPTER 4

to take away the cup. At each point, where John is read as presupposing Synoptic narratives, it improves the narrative flow of the Fourth Gospel and invites the reader to see nuances in the gospel that are otherwise missed.

Further, if John expects his readers to know the Synoptics, and if he crafts his gospel around that expectation, it helps us to answer another age-old question: was John aiming to replace earlier gospels or to stand alongside them? Since John's narratives work so much better when they are read in conversation with the Synoptic narratives, it seems unlikely that the author had any hope of replacing the works that he takes for granted. He wanted to add, to enhance, to correct, and to change, but he could not hope to replace.

And finally, if John expected his readers to know the Synoptics, this sheds light on other important issues in the gospel's composition, two of which I would like to address next. In chapter 6 ("The Beloved Disciple for Readers of the Synoptics"), I would like to explore an old question under this fresh heading. If John was a reader of the Synoptics, and if his readers were readers of the Synoptics, too, how does that affect our reflections on the identity of the Beloved Disciple? But first, in chapter 5 ("John's Dramatic Transformation of the Synoptics"), I would like to ask a question about how John takes Synoptic narration and places it into the mouths of his characters, something that adds a whole layer of intertextual dramatic irony to the Fourth Gospel's narratives. This is territory that raises the fascinating possibility that the Synoptics are not simply John's source material, but they are also his intertexts.

Chapter 5

John's Dramatic Transformation of the Synoptics

When the gifted English novelist and dramatist Dorothy L. Sayers was writing *The Man Born to Be King*, a series of radio plays first broadcast on the BBC during the Second World War,[1] she wanted to avoid the excessive use of a narrator.[2] Like every good dramatist, she knew that the key to a compelling presentation was to place as much dialogue as possible in the mouths of the key players. And in supplying dialogue, she frequently found John's Gospel particularly helpful: "Indeed, when John is the authority for any scene, or when John's account is at hand to supplement those of the Synoptists, the playwright's task is easy. Either the dialogue is all there—vivid and personal on both sides—or the part of the interlocutor can be readily reconstructed from the replies given. And it is frequently John who supplies the reason and meaning of actions and speeches that in the Synoptists appear unexplained and disconnected."[3]

That sense of John as great drama is difficult to miss. The compelling interactions between Martha, Mary, and Jesus are what makes the story of the raising of Lazarus so vivid. The exchanges between Pilate and Jesus, and the carefully stage-managed action, are what makes John's passion narrative so memorable. It is not surprising that film directors like Franco Zeffirelli (*Jesus of Nazareth*, 1977) are irresistibly drawn to John. Where the Synoptics are terse and the exchanges brief, John takes time to develop lively stories in the dramatic mode.

---

1. *The Man Born to Be King* was broadcast as twelve plays on BBC Home Service beginning on 21 December 1941 and concluding on 18 October 1942. No official versions of the original broadcasts exist, but subsequent versions are available. The plays were published as Dorothy L. Sayers, *The Man Born to Be King: A Play-Cycle on the Life of Our Lord and Saviour Jesus Christ* (London: Gollancz, 1943).

2. See Barbara Reynolds, ed., *1937–1943: From Novelist to Playwright*, vol. 2 of *The Letters of Dorothy L. Sayers* (New York: St. Martin's, 1998), 302.

3. Sayers, *Man Born to Be King*, 51–52.

CHAPTER 5

The dramatic nature of John's narrative also attracts attention in the scholarly literature. It is disappointing, though, that reaction to Louis Martyn's emphasis on John as a "drama on two levels" frequently centers on the speculative second-level drama of the "Johannine community" rather than the far more compelling primary drama that plays out in the text itself.[4] After all, Martyn crafts his thesis around the dramatic narrative of the man born blind (John 9:1–41). Whatever one makes of Martyn's influential thesis, his astute depiction of John's Gospel as "drama" deserves more audience reflection than it has received.[5]

From Synoptic Narration to Johannine Direct Speech

Yet although the dramatic nature of the Fourth Gospel is now increasingly acknowledged,[6] there is an aspect of this phenomenon that is seldom noticed. Its author frequently engages in a dramatic transformation of the Synoptics, taking Synoptic narration and placing it on the characters' lips. This is the mark of a good dramatist, to multiply speaking roles when adapting a narrative source, especially a narrative source that places undue reliance on a narrator. The point is nicely illustrated by Dorothy L. Sayers in *Man Born to Be King*, here adapting the Markan narrator's comments about John appearing in the wilderness (Mark 1:2–4), proclaiming a baptism of repentance for the forgiveness of sins (Mark 1:4–5), wearing camel hair and a leather belt, and eating locusts and wild honey (Mark 1:6). All of this narrator's information she casts in the form of a family conversation:

> ISAAC (in a rapturous sing-song): "We're goin' to see the Prophet! We're goin' to see the Prophet! We're goin'—
> MOTHER: Sit still, Isaac darling.

---

4. J. Louis Martyn, *History and Theology in the Fourth Gospel*, 3rd ed. (Louisville: Westminster John Knox, 2003).
5. For Martyn, "the skilled dramatist is the evangelist himself" (*History and Theology*, 38).
6. See especially Jo-Ann Brant, *Dialogue and Drama: Elements of Greek Tragedy in the Fourth Gospel* (Peabody, MA: Hendrickson, 2004), George L. Parsenios, *Rhetoric and Drama in the Johannine Lawsuit Motif*, WUNT 258 (Tübingen: Mohr Siebeck, 2010), and literature cited in both places. Academic interest in John as drama goes back at least as far as F. R. M. Hitchcock, "Is the Fourth Gospel a Drama?," *Theology* 7 (1923): 307–17, and also from 1923, Hans Windisch, "John's Narrative Style," trans. David Orton, in *The Gospel of John as Literature: An Anthology of Twentieth-Century Perspectives*, ed. Mark Stibbe, NTTS 17 (Leiden: Brill, 1993), 29–32; see also C. R. Bowen, "The Fourth Gospel as Dramatic Material," *JBL* 49 (1930): 292–305, and C. M. Connick, "The Dramatic Character of the Fourth Gospel," *JBL* 67 (1948): 159–69.

DRIVER: What Prophet, sonny?
FATHER: This man John there's all the fuss about. He's been preaching in the desert yon side the river.
DRIVER: Oh, him! (with meaning) Ah!
FATHER: What d'you mean, "Oh, him!" [*sic*]
MIRIAM (rapidly): He goes about in a camel-hair shirt and a leather belt an' doesn't have nothing to eat only locusts and wild honey, doesn't he, mummy?
DRIVER: There's worse things than locusts, well fried.
MIRIAM: He's going to baptise a lot of people in the river. He dips them under the water and washes their sins away.
DRIVER: Huh!
ISAAC: An' the sins go swimming' away down the river—like—like—like little black wriggly-wiggly tadpoles.[7]

A similar phenomenon, minus the wriggly-wiggly tadpoles, is found at the beginning of John's Gospel, and it includes the same iconic piece of Markan narration, now reproduced as part of John the Baptist's speech:

MARK 1:2–3	JOHN 1:22–23
Καθὼς γέγραπται ἐν τῷ Ἠσαΐᾳ τῷ προφήτῃ· Ἰδοὺ ἀποστέλλω τὸν ἄγγελόν μου πρὸ προσώπου σου, ὃς κατασκευάσει τὴν ὁδόν σου· φωνὴ βοῶντος ἐν τῇ ἐρήμῳ· Ἑτοιμάσατε τὴν ὁδὸν κυρίου, εὐθείας ποιεῖτε τὰς τρίβους αὐτοῦ.	τί λέγεις περὶ σεαυτοῦ; ἔφη· Ἐγὼ φωνὴ βοῶντος ἐν τῇ ἐρήμῳ· Εὐθύνατε τὴν ὁδὸν κυρίου, καθὼς εἶπεν Ἠσαΐας ὁ προφήτης.
As it is written in Isaiah the prophet, "Behold I send my angel before your face, who will prepare your way. A voice crying in the wilderness, 'Prepare the way of the Lord; make straight his paths.'"	"What do you say about yourself?" He replied, "I am a voice crying in the wilderness: 'Make straight the way of the Lord,' as Isaiah the prophet said."

Now it is the Baptist himself who makes the self-identification as the "voice crying in the wilderness" prophesied by Isaiah. The secondary nature of John's

7. Sayers, *Man Born to Be King*, 63–64.

CHAPTER 5

formulation is clear not only from the way that his narrative presupposes the Synoptic "wilderness" location (Mark 1:4 and parr.), which John does not narrate,[8] but also from his condensing of the two clauses of the quotation from Isa 40. "Prepare the way of the Lord; make straight his paths" becomes "Make straight the way of the Lord" in a piece of typical Johannine paraphrase.[9]

The aftermath of Jesus's baptism in John provides a similar example:

MARK 1:10	JOHN 1:32
καὶ εὐθὺς ἀναβαίνων ἐκ τοῦ ὕδατος εἶδεν σχιζομένους τοὺς οὐρανοὺς καὶ τὸ πνεῦμα ὡς περιστερὰν καταβαῖνον εἰς αὐτόν·	καὶ ἐμαρτύρησεν Ἰωάννης λέγων ὅτι Τεθέαμαι τὸ πνεῦμα καταβαῖνον ὡς περιστερὰν ἐξ οὐρανοῦ, καὶ ἔμεινεν ἐπ' αὐτόν·
And immediately, coming out of the water, he saw the heavens torn open and the spirit as a dove descending into him.	And John witnessed, saying, "I saw the spirit descending as a dove from heaven, and it remained upon him."

Jesus's baptism is a famous apparent omission from John, but like several of the Synoptic features absent from John, this one is presupposed (see chapter 4, above), and its aftermath here depicted, not in the voice of the narrator, but in the voice of the Baptist, who has "witnessed" the spirit as a dove descending on Jesus, in language that is strikingly similar to that of the Synoptics.[10]

---

8. John is closer to Mark in his use of καθώς, but he is closer to Matthew and Luke in concentrating on Isa 40:1 and avoiding the quotation from Exod 23:20/Mal 3:1 found in Mark 1:2 but saved for later by both Matthew (11:10) and Luke (7:27); Matt 3:3: οὗτος γάρ ἐστιν ὁ ῥηθεὶς διὰ Ἠσαΐου τοῦ προφήτου λέγοντος· Φωνὴ βοῶντος ἐν τῇ ἐρήμῳ· Ἑτοιμάσατε τὴν ὁδὸν κυρίου, εὐθείας ποιεῖτε τὰς τρίβους αὐτοῦ. Luke 3:4: ὡς γέγραπται ἐν βίβλῳ λόγων Ἠσαΐου τοῦ προφήτου· Φωνὴ βοῶντος ἐν τῇ ἐρήμῳ· Ἑτοιμάσατε τὴν ὁδὸν κυρίου, εὐθείας ποιεῖτε τὰς τρίβους αὐτοῦ. On Matthew's and Luke's adaptation of Mark here, and the problems it poses for the two-source theory, see Mark Goodacre, "The Evangelists' Use of the Old Testament and the Synoptic Problem," in *New Studies in the Synoptic Problem: Oxford Conference, April 2008; Essays in Honour of Christopher M. Tuckett*, ed. Paul Foster et al., BETL 239 (Leuven: Peeters, 2011), 281–98, at 284–88.

9. On John's paraphrasing of Old Testament material, see above, p. 12.

10. As in the previous example, and often elsewhere, John shows knowledge of the minor agreements between Matthew and Luke against Mark. Here he shares their modification of Mark's εἰς αὐτόν ("into him") to ἐπ' αὐτόν ("upon him," Matt 3:16 // Luke 3:22).

Similarly, Synoptic narration becomes Jesus's direct speech in the feeding of the five thousand (Matt 14:13–21 // Mark 6:30–44 // Luke 9:10–17 // John 6:1–15):

MARK 6:42	JOHN 6:26
καὶ ἔφαγον πάντες καὶ ἐχορτάσθησαν·	Ἀμὴν ἀμὴν λέγω ὑμῖν, ζητεῖτέ με οὐχ ὅτι εἴδετε σημεῖα ἀλλ' ὅτι ἐφάγετε ἐκ τῶν ἄρτων καὶ ἐχορτάσθητε
And they all <u>ate</u> <u>and were satisfied</u>.	"Amen, amen I say to you, you are seeking me not because you see signs but because you <u>ate</u> from the bread <u>and were satisfied</u>."

John's familiarity with the Synoptics here is all the more likely given the rarity of the word χορτάζω ("to satisfy") in John. It has figures of 4/4/4/1. Each time it is used in Mark, it is with respect to being satisfied with bread, and on three occasions it is specifically used of the feeding narratives (here, Mark 8:4 and 8:8; the other time it is used in 7:27, the story of the Syro-Phoenician woman). Moreover, the word John uses earlier in the narrative is ἐμπίπλημι (John 6:12), so it seems likely that here the evangelist has cast the characteristic Markan narration into Jesus's direct speech.[11]

Several other examples could be cited. While in Mark the narrator explains the curious affair of the Passover amnesty (Mark 15:6–8), in John Pilate directly addresses the people and tells them what they already know: "But you have a custom that I release someone for you at the Passover. Do you want me to release for you the King of the Jews?" (John 18:39). This example is actually quite close to the kind of exposition that is one of the more clunky and unrealistic elements in certain dramas that attempt to avoid the use of a narrator. So too the division of Jesus's clothes, which is simply narrated in Mark 15:24, "[They] divided his clothes among them, casting lots to decide what each should take," is expanded (John 19:23) and partially moved to direct discourse in John 19:24: "So they said to one another, 'Let us not tear it, but cast lots for it to see who will get it.'"

---

11. C. K. Barrett, *The Gospel According to St. John: An Introduction with Commentary and Notes on the Greek Text*, 2nd ed. (Philadelphia: Westminster, 1978), 286, "The parallelism is close and supports the view that John knew Mark." Note also that the terminology is found here in triple tradition, Matt 14:20, καὶ ἔφαγον πάντες καὶ ἐχορτάσθησαν; Luke 9:17, καὶ ἔφαγον καὶ ἐχορτάσθησαν πάντες.

CHAPTER 5

ANALOGIES FROM MATTHEW

In cases like these, a good case can be made for John's dramatic transformation of elements in Synoptic narration. But while it is easy to see an analogy in contemporary dramatists' adaptation of narrative source material, it is important to ask whether there is anything that might illustrate the phenomenon at work in antiquity. Are there places where we can see authors moving source narrative into character speech? There are in fact several places where the same principle appears to be at work, one of them close to home, the Gospel of Matthew, and the other, not so far away, the Protevangelium of James.

While Mark frequently uses indirect discourse, Matthew often moves this into direct speech:

Mark 4:10: the twelve asked him about the parables.

Matt 13:10: the disciples came and asked him, "Why do you speak to them in parables?"

Mark 7:17: his disciples asked him about the parable.

Matt 15:15: But Peter said to him, "Explain this parable to us."[12]

Mark 7:26: She begged him to cast the demon out of her daughter.

Matt 15:22: "Have mercy on me, Lord, Son of David; my daughter is tormented by a demon."

Mark 9:9: As they were coming down the mountain, he ordered them to tell no one about what they had seen, until after the Son of Man had risen from the dead.

Matt 17:9: As they were coming down the mountain, Jesus ordered them, "Tell no one about the vision until after the Son of Man has been raised from the dead."

Examples like these could be multiplied,[13] but the opening of Matthew's passion narrative provides a particularly striking example of the phenomenon:

---

12. Note how in this example, we see the similar dramatic feature of turning the collective group into the named speaker, Peter, as often in John; see further below.

13. See also Mark 1:4 // Matt 3:2; Mark 5:13 // Matt 8:32; Mark 6:8–9 // Matt 10:9–10; Mark 3:2 // Matt 12:10; Mark 9:34 // Matt 18:1; Mark 14:10 // Matt 26:14–15; Mark 14:64 // Matt 26:65–66. E. P. Sanders, *The Tendencies of the Synoptic Tradition*, SNTSMS 9 (Cambridge: Cambridge

MATT 26:1–2	MARK 14:1
Καὶ ἐγένετο ὅτε ἐτέλεσεν ὁ Ἰησοῦς πάντας τοὺς λόγους τούτους, εἶπεν τοῖς μαθηταῖς αὐτοῦ· Οἴδατε ὅτι <u>μετὰ δύο ἡμέρας</u> <u>τὸ πάσχα</u> γίνεται, καὶ ὁ υἱὸς τοῦ ἀνθρώπου παραδίδοται εἰς τὸ σταυρωθῆναι.	Ἦν δὲ <u>τὸ πάσχα</u> καὶ τὰ ἄζυμα <u>μετὰ δύο ἡμέρας</u>.
When Jesus had finished saying all these things, he said to his disciples, "You know that <u>after two days</u> <u>the Passover</u> is coming, and the Son of Man will be handed over to be crucified."	It was <u>two days before</u> <u>the Passover</u> and the Festival of Unleavened Bread.

In Mark, it is the narrator who provides the relatively bland chronological note, whereas in Matthew, it is Jesus who gives the time note, now in direct speech that is expanded to incorporate a much richer theological statement about the destiny of the Son of Man. The prospect for the dramatizing principle to influence developing Christian thought and practice is further illustrated in another of Matthew's transformations:

MATT 26:27	MARK 14:23
<u>καὶ λαβὼν ποτήριον</u> καὶ <u>εὐχαριστήσας</u> <u>ἔδωκεν αὐτοῖς λέγων</u>· Πίετε <u>ἐξ αὐτοῦ</u> <u>πάντες</u>.	<u>καὶ λαβὼν ποτήριον</u> <u>εὐχαριστήσας</u> <u>ἔδωκεν αὐτοῖς</u>, καὶ ἔπιον <u>ἐξ αὐτοῦ</u> <u>πάντες</u>.
Then he took a cup, and <u>after giving thanks he gave it to them</u>, saying, "Drink <u>from it</u>, <u>all of you</u>."	Then he took a cup, and <u>after giving thanks he gave it to them</u>, and <u>all of them</u> drank <u>from it</u>.

With typical Matthean dexterity, the alteration of just one word in the clause (from ἔπιον ἐξ αὐτοῦ πάντες to πίετε ἐξ αὐτοῦ πάντες ἐξ αὐτοῦ πάντες) enables the evangelist to move Mark's narrative description to Jesus's direct

---

University Press, 1969), 256–62, has a still more expansive list. But Sanders sees it as a sign of the imitation of popular speech rather than of writing in the dramatic mode: "In this instance the First Gospel is closer to popular speech than the Second.... Whatever one may conclude about the relation of Matthew and Luke to Mark, it is clear that in at least one respect Matthew's Gospel stood nearer to popular speech than Luke's, whose literary abilities here come to light" (262). Cf. Rudolf Bultmann, *History of the Synoptic Tradition*, trans. John Marsh (Oxford: Blackwell, 1963), 258–59.

CHAPTER 5

speech, an imperative that has forever found its way into many versions of the eucharistic prayer. A quirk of Matthean redaction has become a mainstay of liturgical tradition.

Analogies from the Protevangelium

The theory that Matthew redacted Mark is uncontroversial, and it is straightforward to see the evangelist dramatically transforming his source, in a way analogous to what I am proposing for John. But if further illustration is needed, the Protevangelium of James likewise frequently transforms its source material in the same way.[14]

MATT 1:19	PROT. JAS. 14.4
Ἰωσὴφ δὲ ὁ ἀνὴρ αὐτῆς, δίκαιος ὢν καὶ μὴ θέλων αὐτὴν δειγματίσαι, ἐβουλήθη <u>λάθρᾳ ἀπολῦσαι αὐτήν</u>.	τί οὖν αὐτὴν ποιήσω; <u>λάθρᾳ αὐτὴν ἀπολύσω</u> ἀπ' ἐμοῦ.
Her husband Joseph, being a righteous man and unwilling to expose her to public disgrace, planned to <u>dismiss her quietly</u>.	"What therefore shall I do with her? I will <u>dismiss her</u> from me <u>quietly</u>."

MATT 2:4	PROT. JAS. 21.4
καὶ συναγαγὼν πάντας τοὺς ἀρχιερεῖς καὶ γραμματεῖς τοῦ λαοῦ ἐπυνθάνετο παρ' αὐτῶν <u>ποῦ ὁ Χριστὸς</u> γεννᾶται.	καὶ μετεπέμψατο καὶ τοὺς ἀρχιερεῖς καὶ ἀνέκρινεν αὐτοὺς ἐν τῷ πραιτωρίῳ λέγων αὐτοῖς· Πῶς γέγραπται περὶ <u>τοῦ Χριστοῦ</u>· <u>ποῦ γεννᾶται</u>;

---

14. See Mark Goodacre, "The Protevangelium of James and the Creative Rewriting of Matthew and Luke," in *Connecting Gospels: Beyond the Canonical/Non-canonical Divide*, ed. Francis Watson and Sarah Parkhouse (Oxford: Oxford University Press, 2018), 57–76. Other examples from second-century works could be provided. Compare, e.g., Gos. Pet. 16, "And someone of them said: 'Give him to drink gall with vinegary wine.' And having made a mixture, they gave it to him to drink," with Mark 15:36, "And someone ran, filled a sponge with sour wine, put it on a stick, and gave it to him to drink" (parr. Matt 27:48 // Luke 23:36 // John 19:28, none of which have the direct speech).

MATT 2:4	PROT. JAS. 21.4
And assembling all the high priests and scribes of the people, he inquired of them <u>where</u> the Christ was <u>to be born</u>.	He also sent for the high priests and questioned them in his palace: "What has been written about the Christ? Where is he supposed <u>to be born</u>?"

ALTERING DRAMATIS PERSONAE

Like Matthew and like the Protevangelium, then, John sometimes rewrites his source narration by moving it into his characters' voices. But this is not, of course, the only way to add drama to a story. In one of the examples above, where Matthew recasts Markan narration, Peter is named as the disciple who asked Jesus to "explain this parable to us" (Mark 7:17 // Matt 15:15). This naming of anonymous characters, alongside a tendency to create more intimate, one-to-one encounters, is an even more elaborate feature of John. The anointing pericope (Matt 26:6–13 // Mark 14:3–9 // John 12:1–8), for example (see pp. 25–30, above), adds compelling dramatic details by naming the anonymous protagonist as Mary, so extending the story begun in John 11 and reducing the anonymous complainants to one antagonist, Judas, whose motivations in the betrayal, already hinted at in the Synoptics (love of money), become explicit.[15]

Something similar happens in the story of Jesus's arrest (Mark 14:47 // John 18:10–11). Where in the Synoptics the assailant and the victim whose ear is cut off are unnamed (Matt 26:51 // Mark 14:47 // Luke 22:50), in John they become Peter and Malchus (John 18:10–11). Or at the tomb, the two or three women (Matt 28:1: Mary Magdalene and the other Mary; Mark 16:1: Mary Magdalene, Mary the mother of James, and Salome; Luke 24:10: Mary Magdalene, Joanna, and Mary mother of James) become one, Mary Magdalene, now the sole spokesperson for a group that is still presupposed in John's first person plural in 20:2, "We do not know where they have laid him."[16]

---

15. Note, however, that John, too, can introduce anonymous characters to add dramatic color to his narrative—e.g., the boy unique to John's feeding of the five thousand (John 6:9) and the anonymous disciple known to the high priest (John 18:15–16), as well as retaining anonymous characters from the Synoptics, like the παιδίσκη at Peter's denial (Matt 26:69; Mark 14:66, 69; Luke 22:56; John 18:17).

16. Cf. F. Neirynck, "John and the Synoptics: The Empty Tomb Stories," in *Evangelica II: 1982–1991; Collected Essays by Frans Neirynck*, ed. F. Van Segbroeck (Leuven: Leuven University Press, 1991), 571–99, at 579: "Mary Magdalene in 20,1 is an example of Johannine dramatization."

CHAPTER 5

Another one of John's iconic incidents, the story of doubting Thomas (John 20:24–29), may itself be a dramatic development of Matthew's and Luke's motif of doubting disciples at Jesus's resurrection. In Matthew, "they doubted" (οἱ δὲ ἐδίστασαν, Matt 28:17), and in Luke, Jesus asks, "Why are you frightened, and why do doubts arise in your hearts?" (Luke 24:38, Τί τεταραγμένοι ἐστέ, καὶ διὰ τί διαλογισμοὶ ἀναβαίνουσιν ἐν τῇ καρδίᾳ ὑμῶν). Similarly, the narrator in Luke adds, "While in their joy they were disbelieving and still wondering" (ἔτι δὲ ἀπιστούντων αὐτῶν ἀπὸ τῆς χαρᾶς καὶ θαυμαζόντων, Luke 24:41). The first of these is another example, if Luke knows Matthew, of recasting narration into character speech.[17]

This issue may also explain why it is John among the evangelists who has by far the richest tapestry of character disciples. There are new speaking roles for Philip (John 1:43–51; 6:5, 7; 12:21–22; 14:8–9), Nathanael (1:43–51), Andrew (1:40–42; 6:8; 12:22), Thomas (11:16; 14:5; 20:24–29), and Judas not Iscariot (14:22), as well as Mary and Martha (11:1–12:8) and Mary Magdalene (20:1–18).

Intertextual Dramatic Irony

If this kind of dramatic adaptation of the Synoptics is straightforward to see in the evangelist's character changes and additions of discourse, it is worth asking whether there are other ways in which John makes sense as a dramatic adaptation of the Synoptics. I would like to suggest that one such issue is the use of intertextual dramatic irony. We saw in the previous chapter several examples of occasions where John makes much better sense if his gospel is presupposing elements that are narrated in the Synoptics. On occasions, John's presupposition of elements in the Synoptic narrative greatly enrich the sense of dramatic irony in his own narrative. We should, of course, use the term "intertextual" with caution, but these are occasions where the Synoptic Gospels are more like John's intertexts than his sources, places where knowing what they say adds something special to John.

If John is expecting his readers to know elements in the Synoptics, this adds to the dramatic irony involved in certain Johannine passages.[18] One of the classic pieces of Johannine irony occurs in the crowd's exchange in John 7:41–42:

---

17. Cf. Jeffrey Peterson, "Matthew's Ending and the Genesis of Luke-Acts: The Farrer Hypothesis and the Birth of Christian History," in *Marcan Priority Without Q: Explorations in the Farrer Hypothesis*, ed. John C. Poirier and Jeffrey Peterson, LNTS 455 (London: T&T Clark, 2015), 140–59, at 153.

18. On the well-trodden paths of studies on Johannine irony, see especially Paul D. Duke, *Irony in the Fourth Gospel* (Atlanta: John Knox, 1985). These studies tend to focus solely on

John 7:41–42: ἄλλοι ἔλεγον· Οὗτός ἐστιν ὁ χριστός· οἱ δὲ ἔλεγον· Μὴ γὰρ ἐκ τῆς Γαλιλαίας ὁ χριστὸς ἔρχεται; οὐχ ἡ γραφὴ εἶπεν ὅτι ἐκ τοῦ σπέρματος Δαυὶδ, καὶ ἀπὸ Βηθλέεμ τῆς κώμης ὅπου ἦν Δαυὶδ, ἔρχεται ὁ χριστός;

Others said, "This is the Messiah." But some asked, "Surely the Messiah does not come from Galilee, does he? Has not the scripture said that the Messiah is descended from David and comes from Bethlehem, the village where David lived?"

The point of the dramatic irony is that Jesus's ultimate origin is from above, from the Father, a key element in John's Christology and the point of much of John 7 (especially John 7:25–29). Attentive readers know this, but the crowd in this scene does not. But the irony is all the more marked if the readers also know the Synoptic narratives. Thus the readers know that in spite of the appearance of Jesus coming from Galilee, he was actually born in Bethlehem, David's city. John never in his gospel connects Jesus with Bethlehem, unlike Matthew and Luke (Matt 2:1–12; Luke 2:1–20), nor does he ever call Jesus "Son of David," also unlike Matthew and Luke, for both of whom this is key, and a particular point of emphasis in the birth narratives (Matt 1:1–17; 2:20; Luke 1:27, 32; 2:4, 11). The theory of John's independence from the Synoptics casts its first readers in the same position as the puzzled crowd. They are left scratching their heads about whether Jesus was born in Bethlehem and whether he is descended from David. If John is presupposing these Synoptic elements, the reader is not puzzled but rewarded for the insider knowledge.

A similar case of intertextual dramatic irony occurs in John 8:41, where Jesus is once again in dispute with the Judeans, here about fatherhood—the fatherhood of God, of Abraham, of the devil. In the midst of this argument, they say, Ἡμεῖς ἐκ πορνείας οὐ γεγεννήμεθα· ἕνα πατέρα ἔχομεν τὸν θεόν, "We are not born from fornication. We have one Father, God." The line about fornication is a curious one if John's first readers were ignorant of the Synoptic narratives, but it works well as a piece of dramatic irony if the readers knew the Matthean and Lukan story that Jesus was conceived out of wedlock (Matt 1:18–25; Luke 1:26–38). It is a slur against Jesus but a slur that readers of Matthew and Luke know to be unjustified.

---

the intra-Johannine irony without exploring the possibilities of understanding the gospel's intertextual dramatic irony.

CHAPTER 5

Dramatic Revision

There are several ways, then, in which John makes good sense as a dramatic reworking of the Synoptics, and this is an approach that coheres with other recent studies that draw attention to drama and lawsuit motifs in John as well as the importance of testimony and witness. Nevertheless, some difficulties remain. First, given that John's theology is often so different from the Synoptics' theology, what are we to make of the places where John does more than dramatically appropriate Synoptic material? Second, it might be said that for all this talk about drama, John in fact has the most vocal narrator in the gospel tradition, a narrator who often makes his presence felt.

To begin with the first of these issues, I have spoken above of "dramatic appropriation," but it would be a mistake to see John's recasting of the Synoptics solely in terms of this kind of dramatic adaptation. The value of the examples discussed above is that they are easier to spot because of the contextual and verbal agreements between the gospels, but there are many other cases where John's dramatic transformation is a matter of correcting as well as recasting Synoptic narration. The narrator in Mark, for example, claims that John's baptism is a "baptism of repentance for the forgiveness of sins" (Mark 1:4 // Luke 3:3; cf. Matt 3:1), and the people come from far and wide, "confessing their sins" (Mark 1:5 // Matt 3:6).[19] But this differs from John's portrait of the Baptist. For the Fourth Evangelist, only Jesus removes sin, and he announces not a call to a baptism of repentance, or of confession of sin, but instead a call to focus on the one who deals with sin. So John the Baptist still talks about the removal of sin, but he talks about it in the context of the one who removes sin: "Behold the lamb of God, who takes away the sin of the world" (John 1:29; cf. 1:36). And unlike John, who in the Synoptics baptizes Judeans for the forgiveness of sin, Jesus here takes away the sin "of the world." This is an important dramatic revision of the Synoptics, with Synoptic narration dramatized at the same time as its theology is corrected.

John's version of Jesus's prayer of agony provides a similar example of a corrective, dramatic recasting of some Synoptic narrative:

John 12:27–30: Νῦν ἡ ψυχή μου τετάρακται, καὶ τί εἴπω; πάτερ, σῶσόν με ἐκ τῆς ὥρας ταύτης. ἀλλὰ διὰ τοῦτο ἦλθον εἰς τὴν ὥραν ταύτην. πάτερ, δόξασόν σου τὸ

---

19. Mark's John's baptism of repentance has important points of contact with Josephus's John's baptism of purification and virtue (*Ant.* 18.5.2). It is therefore likely to have closer contact with the historical John the Baptist than has the Fourth Gospel. See Joel Marcus, *John the Baptist in History and Theology*, SPNT (Columbia: University of South Carolina Press, 2018).

John's Dramatic Transformation of the Synoptics

ὄνομα. ἦλθεν οὖν φωνὴ ἐκ τοῦ οὐρανοῦ· Καὶ ἐδόξασα καὶ πάλιν δοξάσω. ὁ οὖν ὄχλος ὁ ἑστὼς καὶ ἀκούσας ἔλεγεν βροντὴν γεγονέναι· ἄλλοι ἔλεγον· Ἄγγελος αὐτῷ λελάληκεν. ἀπεκρίθη Ἰησοῦς καὶ εἶπεν· Οὐ δι' ἐμὲ ἡ φωνὴ αὕτη γέγονεν ἀλλὰ δι' ὑμᾶς.

"Now my soul is troubled. And what should I say—'Father, save me from this hour'? No, it is for this reason that I have come to this hour. Father, glorify your name." Then a voice came from heaven, "I have glorified it, and I will glorify it again." The crowd standing there heard it and said that it was thunder. Others said, "An angel has spoken to him." Jesus answered, "This voice has come for your sake, not for mine."

The occasion is, of course, different. The location is not Gethsemane, and the timing is earlier. But the echoes of Mark 14:32–42 (and parallels) are clear. While Mark's narrative consists partly of Jesus's speech, there are elements in indirect speech that move into direct speech in John. The "hour" is only in the narrator's voice in Mark, "he prayed that, if it were possible, the hour might pass from him" (Mark 14:35), but on Jesus's lips in John, "And what should I say? 'Father, save me from this hour'?" (John 12:27).

What is happening here is a "dramatic" transformation in both senses of the word—John dramatizes the Markan scene but also radically changes its vision of Jesus's suffering. The momentary torment in John replaces the hours of agony in Mark; the serenity of embracing God's will is practically immediate. Moreover, Jesus's prayer is a solitary affair in Mark—he has taken only Peter, James, and John with him, and they all slept and missed everything. But Jesus's prayer is fully public in John, with a voice from heaven witnessed by the entire crowd—a voice so loud that it was like thunder. No one missed it! This is radical transformation, dramatic reworking, public witness.

The Narrator's Presence in John

Nevertheless, for all of these cases of the dramatic transformation of the Synoptics, one important caveat has to be made. In spite of the fact that John apparently loves recasting and revising in the dramatic mode, he still has perhaps the most prominent narrator in the gospel tradition, a narrator so obtrusive that he sometimes speaks for extended passages. In the second half of John 3, for example, Jesus's discussion with Nicodemus apparently morphs into the narrator's reflections on and developments of the conversation, appearing in such a way that it is difficult to be sure when Jesus stops speaking and the narrator starts, providing nightmares for editors of red-letter Bibles.

CHAPTER 5

Yet the forceful presence of the narrator in John itself participates in the drama. He is not like the narrator of Thackeray's *Vanity Fair* who only pretends to having overheard the story he is narrating while at a dinner party one night. He performs a role akin to the speaker of the prologue, as well as the chorus in classical drama. Indeed, his role is even more important than that. He is, in fact, one of the characters in the drama. Although not immediately obvious since John is not actually written as a play or designed to be performed by multiple characters,[20] the obtrusive narrator gradually emerges as the key witness in the narrative. He is laying on Jesus's bosom at the Last Supper; he witnesses Jesus's death with the three Marys (Magdalene, mother, and wife of Clopas); and he witnesses both the vacated tomb and the resurrected Jesus.

The narrator of John's Gospel is actually one of its major characters, the disciple whom Jesus loved. And this phenomenon may explain one piece of first-person narration in the prologue:

> John 1:14: And the Word became flesh and tabernacled among us, and <u>we have seen his glory</u>, the glory as of a father's only son, full of grace and truth.[21]

It is a passage that may provide one further example of John's dramatic transformation of the Synoptics. The line has a noticeable parallel with Luke 9:32, when at the transfiguration, they talk about building tabernacles and "they <u>saw his glory</u>."[22] An iconic Synoptic moment has been transformed into a Johannine perspective on the whole ministry of Jesus.

"We beheld his glory." One of the characters present in the Synoptic narrative is now apparently the one telling the story. Could it be that this will help shed light on one of the greatest mysteries in the study of John, the identity of the Beloved Disciple? This will be the subject of the next chapter.

---

20. But see Thomas E. Boomershine, "The Medium and Message of John: Audience Address and Audience Identity in the Fourth Gospel," in *The Fourth Gospel in First-Century Media Culture*, ed. Anthony Le Donne and Tom Thatcher (New York: T&T Clark, 2011), 92–120.

21. Jo-Ann Brant, *John*, PCNT (Grand Rapids: Baker, 2011), 34, sees this verse as evoking Greek drama, "The Greek word *skēnē* is the term adopted in Greek theater for the background building and platform upon which plays were enacted and from which we derive the English word 'scene.' The verb that John uses to describe how humans witness to the incarnation, *theaomai*, is semantically related to our word for theater: and we were spectators to [*etheasametha*] his glory."

22. The note is a redactional addition by Luke to Mark (and Matthew).

Chapter 6

The Beloved Disciple for Readers of the Synoptics

Talking about John's Gospel without mentioning the Beloved Disciple would be like talking about *E. T.* without mentioning Elliott. Any attempt to understand the gospel that does not engage seriously with its most enigmatic and inviting literary trait is bound to disappoint. Yet the proliferation of literature makes this topic unlikely to yield anything new. It would surely be a fool's errand to attempt fresh insight.[1] Every potential candidate for the "the disciple whom Jesus loved" has its passionate advocates, and every case has been scrutinized in detail. Is it John the Elder, Lazarus, Thomas, Mary Magdalene, Nathanael, or Paul? Is it an ideal figure not connected with any known character? Is it a paradigm of the perfect disciple or the perfect witness? Is the anonymity relevant, and does it preclude the reader from making an identification with a historical or a fictional character?

There is, surprisingly, one issue that has not been addressed in any detail, and it involves looking at John's Gospel alongside the Synoptics. For most of Christian history, John has been read in light of the Synoptic Gospels. Although scholarly discussions of the Beloved Disciple frequently treat John in isolation, this is quite the opposite of the way that John has been viewed for most of its history. Readers of John have always been readers of the Synoptics. Readers of the Beloved Disciple have always read the character in the light of Synoptic characters. The point is surely significant.

In this chapter, I would like to ask what a reading of John's Beloved Disciple looks like for readers who are already familiar with the Synoptics. For those who read John as the Fourth Gospel, who could the Beloved Disciple be? And if, as I

---

1. Brad Blaine, *Peter in the Gospel of John: The Making of an Authentic Disciple* (Atlanta: Society of Biblical Literature, 2007), 26, says, "Speculating on the identity of BD is something of a rite of passage in Johannine scholarship."

CHAPTER 6

have argued in this book, the author knew and used the Synoptic Gospels, could it be that he invites his readers to make an identification with a known Synoptic character? The discussion can proceed in several steps. First, I will attempt to show that for readers of the Synoptics, the Beloved Disciple has to be one of the twelve. I will then attempt to illustrate that the obvious candidate is the traditional one, John son of Zebedee. I will then address the obstacles that this identification usually faces, and I will conclude by suggesting that the author of the gospel himself invites the audience to read this character as John.

One of the Twelve

In spite of the appeal of candidates like Mary Magdalene, Lazarus, and John the Elder,[2] readers of the Synoptics will view the Beloved Disciple as one of the twelve. The first explicit appearance of the character is in the famous note at the Last Supper:

> John 13:23: ἦν ἀνακείμενος εἷς ἐκ τῶν μαθητῶν αὐτοῦ ἐν τῷ κόλπῳ τοῦ Ἰησοῦ, ὃν ἠγάπα ὁ Ἰησοῦς.
>
> One of his disciples—the one whom Jesus loved—was reclining close to Jesus's heart.[3]

The gospel itself flags this as a key moment (21:20), and we would be wise to take it seriously. The reader of the Synoptics knows that those reclining with Jesus at the Last Supper were the twelve, his inner circle. This is evident in all three Synoptics (Matt 26:20 // Mark 14:17 // Luke 22:14),[4] but it is particularly clear in Matthew:

---

2. The most comprehensive treatment of the identity of the Beloved Disciple is James H. Charlesworth, *The Beloved Disciple: Whose Witness Validates the Gospel of John?* (Valley Forge, PA: Trinity International, 1995). Charlesworth is right to identify the Beloved Disciple as one of the twelve, but the identification with Thomas is weak.

3. The benefit of this NRSVue translation is that it aligns the Beloved Disciple, reclining "close to Jesus's heart," with John 1:18, "the only Son, himself God, who is close to the Father's heart." Both are translating εἰς τὸν κόλπον (John 1:18) or ἐν τῷ κόλπῳ (John 13:23).

4. Luke uses his characteristic ἀπόστολος, which applies only to the twelve in his gospel (Luke 6:13; 9:10; 17:5; 22:14; 24:10). Overall the word has figures of 1/1/6/1+28. John's one use of the word is here, in 13:16, οὐδὲ ἀπόστολος μείζων τοῦ πέμψαντος αὐτόν ("nor is an apostle greater than the one who sent him"), and may be influenced by Luke 22:14.

Matt 26:20: Ὀψίας δὲ γενομένης ἀνέκειτο μετὰ τῶν δώδεκα μαθητῶν.

When it was evening, he reclined[5] with the twelve disciples.

The cast of characters is set, and when the Fourth Gospel is read with knowledge of the Synoptics, it is the twelve who immediately come to mind. As in the Synoptics, one of them will betray him, and one of them will deny him, but now there is a third key character, the one who will love him to the end.

The whole drama of John's Farewell Discourses takes place as a conversation between Jesus and his inner circle. There are several named characters in John 13–14, and for readers of the Synoptics, each of them is a known member of the twelve. Peter is the most prominent (13:6–9), alongside Judas Iscariot and the Beloved Disciple (13:21–30), but after Judas leaves, there are roles for Thomas who wants to know where Jesus is going (14:5–7), Philip who wants Jesus to show him the Father (14:8–14), and "Judas not Iscariot" who asks about revelation (14:22–23). Each piece of dialogue locates a one-to-one encounter in the context of teaching the broader group, with singular addresses morphing into the plural appeals to the disciples as a whole, before the discourse overall moves to addressing "the disciples" repeatedly as a group (15:8; 16:17, 29; 18:1).

As in the Synoptics, Judas's betrayal is regarded as all the more tragic because he is a member of this inner circle. Already in John 6:71, Judas is going to betray Jesus "though one of the twelve" (εἷς ἐκ τῶν δώδεκα). In Matthew, Mark, and John, Jesus says, "Amen (Amen), I say to you: one of you will betray me" (Matt 26:21 // Mark 14:18 // John 13:21), and the betrayal is poignant because Judas dips his bread into the same bowl as Jesus and the other disciples (Matt 26:23 // Mark 14:20 // John 13:26–30, cf. Luke 22:21).

The term "the twelve" is not used here in the Farewell Discourse, presumably because of Judas's early exit (John 13:30), but the identity of the group is repeatedly underlined. They are the ones Jesus has "chosen," and they have been with Jesus from the beginning. The idea that the Beloved Disciple could be some Johnny come lately, whether the Elder or otherwise, makes no sense of the rhetoric here. The twelve are those who were "chosen" by Jesus, and now their chosen status is reaffirmed:[6]

---

5. NRSVue, "took his place with."

6. On John here presupposing the Synoptic narratives about the appointment of the twelve, see above, pp. 81–83. The "choosing" language may derive from Luke 6:13, which uses it in a similar context: καὶ ἐκλεξάμενος ἀπ' αὐτῶν δώδεκα, οὓς καὶ ἀποστόλους ὠνόμασεν.

CHAPTER 6

John 6:70: Οὐκ ἐγὼ ὑμᾶς τοὺς δώδεκα ἐξελεξάμην;

"Did I not choose you, the twelve?"

John 13:18: οὐ περὶ πάντων ὑμῶν λέγω· ἐγὼ οἶδα τίνας ἐξελεξάμην·

"I am not speaking of all of you. I know whom I have chosen."

John 15:16: οὐχ ὑμεῖς με ἐξελέξασθε, ἀλλ' ἐγὼ ἐξελεξάμην ὑμᾶς.

"You did not choose me, but I chose you."

John 15:19: ὅτι δὲ ἐκ τοῦ κόσμου οὐκ ἐστέ, ἀλλ' ἐγὼ ἐξελεξάμην ὑμᾶς ἐκ τοῦ κόσμου, διὰ τοῦτο μισεῖ ὑμᾶς ὁ κόσμος.

"Because you do not belong to the world, but I have chosen you out of the world, therefore the world hates you."

Moreover, these "chosen" addressees have been with Jesus from the beginning. Not only does Jesus specifically draw attention to the time Philip has spent with him, but he presupposes that all those present for these discourses have been there from the first:

John 14:9: Τοσούτῳ χρόνῳ μεθ' ὑμῶν εἰμι καὶ οὐκ ἔγνωκάς με, Φίλιππε;

"Have I been with you all this time, Philip, and you still do not know me?"

John 15:27: καὶ ὑμεῖς δὲ μαρτυρεῖτε, ὅτι ἀπ' ἀρχῆς μετ' ἐμοῦ ἐστε.

"You [plural] also are to testify, because you have been with me from the beginning."[7]

Philip has been with Jesus since the first week (John 1:43–45), when Jesus first appeared in Galilee (John 1:43). It looks like the Beloved Disciple might have a similar pedigree.

---

7. Martin Hengel, *The Johannine Question* (London: SCM, 1989), 127, asserts without argument that "this does not mean 'since the baptism of John', as it does in Acts 1:21, but as in 1 John 1:1ff. refers to the origin of their testimony in the person and word of the Son of God." The latter in fact aligns itself closely with the Fourth Gospel's theme of witness from the beginning of Jesus's ministry. John's "from the beginning" is also reminiscent of Luke 1:2: καθὼς παρέδοσαν ἡμῖν οἱ ἀπ' ἀρχῆς αὐτόπται καὶ ὑπηρέται γενόμενοι τοῦ λόγου. Similar language also features in John 6:64, in a discipleship context: ᾔδει γὰρ ἐξ ἀρχῆς ὁ Ἰησοῦς τίνες εἰσὶν οἱ μὴ πιστεύοντες καὶ τίς ἐστιν ὁ παραδώσων αὐτόν.

JOHN SON OF ZEBEDEE

Any reader of the Synoptics would assume that the "disciple whom Jesus loved" was one of the twelve reclining with Jesus at his Last Supper, and John 13–17 provides repeated indications that this is the group from which the Beloved Disciple is drawn. But is it possible to be more precise than this? Are there any pointers to a specific disciple? It is, of course, not Peter, who appears alongside the Beloved Disciple in 20:2–12, 21:7, and 21:20–23, and the steady refusal to name the disciple in the body of the gospel makes it highly unlikely that he could be Philip, Nathanael, Andrew, Thomas, or Judas not Iscariot, all of whom play important roles in a way that would undermine the author's decision to keep the character anonymous. The same issue also renders the candidacy of Lazarus and Mary Magdalene problematic, though there are further issues with these identifications, like gender in Mary's case (19:26–27),[8] and the lack of "disciple" terminology in both cases.[9]

For readers of the Synoptics, there are two disciples who, with Peter, are constantly in Jesus's inner circle—James and John, the sons of Zebedee, sometimes also with Andrew. They are the first called by Jesus (Matt 4:18–22 // Mark 1:16–20 // Luke 5:1–11; see also Mark 1:29), as well as the primary audience of Jesus's last discourse (Mark 13:3). They are always the first four disciples to be named (Matt 10:2 // Mark 3:16–18 // Luke 6:14), in the order Simon, James, John, Andrew (Mark's Gospel), and Simon, Andrew, James, John (Matthew and Luke). The inner three, Peter, James, and John, have three special appearances with Jesus, at Jairus's house (Mark 5:37 // Luke 8:51), at the transfiguration (Matt 17:1 // Mark 9:2 // Luke 9:28), and in Gethsemane (Matt 26:37 // Mark 14:33), all three of

---

8. The difficulty of the masculine grammar, alongside the fact that the Beloved Disciple is addressed by Mary Magdalene in John 20:2, effectively rules out any strong version of this identification, but see Sandra Schneiders, "'Because of the Woman's Testimony . . .': Reexamining the Issue of Authorship in the Fourth Gospel," *NTS* 44 (1998): 513–35, for a measured case for Mary Magdalene's identification with the Beloved Disciple in John 19:26 as part of a broader textual paradigm of ideal characters in the gospel. See also Esther de Boer, *The Gospel of Mary: Listening to the Beloved Disciple* (London: T&T Clark, 2005), especially 157–90. As de Boer and others note, the language of Jesus's loving the beloved disciple does percolate through from the Gospel of John into the Gospels of Philip and Mary.

9. Ben Witherington III, "What's in a Name? Rethinking the Historical Figure of the Beloved Disciple in the Fourth Gospel," in *Aspects of Historicity in the Fourth Gospel*, vol. 2 of *John, Jesus, and History*, ed. Paul N. Anderson, Felix Just, SJ, and Tom Thatcher, SymS (Atlanta: Society of Biblical Literature, 2009), 203–12, notes that Lazarus is depicted as "he whom you love" (John 11:3; cf. 11:36), but this is only one half of the requirement to be a "beloved disciple." Lazarus is never described as Jesus's "disciple."

which focus on themes of suffering, death, and resurrection. The two brothers, James and John, feature in two further stories, the request to sit at Jesus's right and left in Matthew and Mark (Matt 20:20–28 // Mark 10:35–45), and the fire from heaven in Luke (Luke 9:51–56). And although James never appears without John, John sometimes appears alone (Mark 9:38–41 // Luke 9:49–50, the strange exorcist), or paired with Peter (Luke 22:8).

After Peter (forty times), John is the most frequently named disciple in the Synoptic Gospels (twenty-one times), a fact that makes his almost complete absence from the Fourth Gospel all the more striking.[10] Readers of the Synoptic Gospels naturally imagine that he is a major candidate for Jesus's closest disciple. Indeed, readers of Acts would have still more reason to think of John as the major player alongside Peter, with whom he appears constantly (Acts 3:1–11; 4:1–31; 8:14–25), as James recedes completely into the background, appearing only in the disciple list (Acts 1:13) before his death in Acts 12:2. The picture in Acts is corroborated also in Paul's letters, in which James son of Zebedee never appears, while John appears alongside Peter in Gal 2:9 (along with James, presumably Jesus's brother, 1:19).

For readers of the Synoptics, then, John is the obvious contender to be the Beloved Disciple of the Fourth Gospel. He is one of the twelve, reclining with Jesus at the Last Supper, and he is one of the three disciples who are constantly given special treatment by Jesus. Moreover, he is the only disciple other than Peter and Judas to be explicitly mentioned in connection with the Last Supper, when in Luke 22:8, it is "Peter and John" who are sent by Jesus to prepare the meal (22:7–13; contrast Matt 26:17–19, "the disciples," and Mark 14:12–16, "two of his disciples").

---

10. Peter appears twelve times in Matthew, fourteen times in Mark, and fourteen times in Luke: Matt 4:18; 10:2; 14:28–33; 16:13–20, 21–23; 17:1–8, 24–27; 18:21–22; 19:27–30; 26:31–35, 36–46, 58, 69–75; Mark 1:16–20, 29–31, 36; 3:16; 5:37; 8:31–3; 9:2–8; 10:28–31; 11:20–24; 13:3; 14:26–31, 32–42; 14:54, 66–72; 16:7; Luke 4:38–39; 5:1–11; 6:14; 8:45 R, 51; 9:18–20, 28–36; 12:41; 18:28–30; 22:7–13, 31–34, 54–62; 24:12, 34. John appears eighteen times with James or Peter, or both: Matt 4:21; 10:2; 17:1–8; 20:20–28; 26:36–46 (cf. also 27:56, the mother of the sons of Zebedee); Mark 1:16–20, 29–31; 3:17; 5:37; 9:2–8; 10:35–45; 13:3; 14:32–42; Luke 5:10; 6:14; 8:51; 9:28–36, 51–56. He also appears alone twice (Mark 9:38–41 // Luke 9:49–50) and with Peter once (Luke 22:7–13). Judas Iscariot appears thirteen times, Andrew seven times, and Matthew four times. Everyone else appears only in the disciple lists (Philip, Bartholomew, Thomas, James son of Alphaeus, Thaddaeus/Lebbaeus/Judas son of James, Simon the Cananaean/Zealot, Matt 10:2–4 // Mark 3:13–19 // Luke 6:12–16).

The Beloved Disciple for Readers of the Synoptics

Difficulties

It is unsurprising that traditional readers of the New Testament have concluded that the Beloved Disciple's name was John. Unlike New Testament scholars, they are not trained to read the gospels in isolation from one another, and to be obsessed about what is distinctive in each. To most scholars, however, reading the Beloved Disciple as John is symptomatic of the worst kind of harmonizing approach, the same kind of approach that conflates characters like Mary Magdalene with "the sinner" of Luke 7:36–50, and the woman taken in adultery in John 8:1–10. Many of us have spent hours in the classroom and on the written page railing against popular harmonizing readings that we see as historically problematic and ethically troubling. Why, then, is it even worth discussing the potential for reading the Beloved Disciple as John son of Zebedee?

The question is focused by noticing apparent difficulties with the identification between the Beloved Disciple and John. The most striking of these is that the Beloved Disciple seems to be a "Jerusalem disciple," a point made with force by scholars like Martin Hengel and Richard Bauckham.[11] His first explicit appearance is in John 13, and he makes no appearances in the Galilean sections of the gospel, which would be strange for a clearly Galilean disciple like John son of Zebedee. Moreover, in 18:15–16, not only is he "known to the high priest" (ὁ δὲ μαθητὴς ἐκεῖνος ἦν γνωστὸς τῷ ἀρχιερεῖ), but he has the kind of access to the high priest's residence that enables him to bring Peter into the courtyard. This does not sound like the Galilean fisherman. It surely rules out John, the son of Zebedee.

As compelling as this sounds, the idea that the Beloved Disciple has a special profile as a Jerusalem disciple is illusory. It is true that most of the explicit references to the disciple occur while Jesus is in Jerusalem, in John 13–20, but these chapters cover only a few days. The action in John 13–17 (Last Supper and Farewell Discourses) all take place on (what we call) Thursday evening; John 18 (arrest and trials) takes the reader from Thursday evening into Friday; John 19 (sentence and crucifixion) is on Friday; and John 20 (resurrection) is mainly the following Sunday, with an appearance to Thomas a week later.

---

11. Hengel, *Johannine Question*, 124–26. Richard Bauckham, *The Testimony of the Beloved Disciple* (Grand Rapids: Baker, 2007), 36, "More recently, a number of scholars have recognized that the Gospel does not portray the disciple as one of the twelve, who accompanied Jesus throughout the ministry, but a Jerusalem disciple." Bauckham pays tribute to Hengel here but argues that he has unnecessarily complicated the picture (*Testimony*, 73–92, reproduced from Bauckham, "The Beloved Disciple as Ideal Author," *JSNT* 49 [1993]: 21–44). Even when reading John in isolation from the Synoptics, though, it is arguable that the Beloved Disciple appears as one of the twelve, "chosen" by Jesus, from the beginning (see pp. 108–10, above).

CHAPTER 6

In that extended weekend, everyone is a Jerusalem disciple. And John son of Zebedee is prominent in the same phase in the Synoptic Gospels. As well as being present in the disciple group, he appears repeatedly by name in this Jerusalem phase (Matt 26:36–46; Mark 13:3; 14:32–42; Luke 22:7–13). According to Matthew, even John's mother was a Jerusalem disciple that weekend (Matt 27:56).[12] Only Judas and Peter are more prominent.

Moreover, there are signs that the historical son of Zebedee was also a Jerusalem disciple. Not only is he prominent in the early chapters of Acts, as the key apostle in Jerusalem, alongside Peter (Acts 3:1–11; 4:1–31; 8:14–25), but also he is one of the pillar apostles on Paul's second visit to Jerusalem, in the late 40s or early 50s (Gal 2:9). Paul does not here have to explain to the Galatians who this pillar John might be. Like Cephas (Gal 1:18), but unlike James (qualified as "the Lord's brother," Gal 1:19),[13] Paul can expect his readers to know who John is, and it is taken for granted that he is a pillar apostle in Jerusalem. He is apparently one of the key characters that you would expect to meet in Jerusalem.

What, then, of John 18:15–16, which seems so clearly to ground the Beloved Disciple in Jerusalem, with access to the high priest's courtyard, in such a way as to contrast him with Peter, who has no such access? It is true that this does not look like the son of Zebedee who fished alongside Peter on Lake Gennesaret, and who lived in Capernaum. But the appeal to John 18:15–16 is a red herring. The idea that the character who appears here is the Beloved Disciple has no basis in the text:

> John 18:15–16: Simon Peter and <u>another disciple</u> [ἄλλος μαθητής] followed Jesus. Since <u>that disciple</u> [ὁ μαθητὴς ἐκεῖνος] was known to the high priest, he went with Jesus into the courtyard of the high priest, but Peter was standing outside at the gate. So <u>the other disciple, the one who was known to the high priest</u> [ὁ μαθητὴς ὁ ἄλλος ὁ γνωστὸς τοῦ ἀρχιερέως], went out, spoke to the woman who guarded the gate, and brought Peter in.

---

12. On the mother of the sons of Zebedee as a disciple in Matthew, see my "Mary, Mary and Another Mother: How Matthew Read Women in Mark's Gospel," forthcoming. It is possible that the presence of the mother of the sons of Zebedee in Matthew stimulated the evangelist's imagination to place the Beloved Disciple at the cross, all the more as both James and John had said that they were able to drink Jesus's cup (Matt 20:22). Now the Beloved Disciple is with his adopted mother at the cross (John 19:25–27).

13. It is curious that Paul needs to explain who this James is. Perhaps this is because of other Jameses who were well known as apostles at the time, like James son of Alphaeus (Matt 10:3 // Mark 3:18 // Luke 6:15) or even James, John's brother, who may still have been alive at the time of Paul's first visit to Jerusalem.

The Beloved Disciple for Readers of the Synoptics

This anonymous disciple is a new character who has not previously been introduced. When he is first mentioned, he is simply "another disciple" (ἄλλος μαθητής), and there is no indication that this is someone that the reader has met before. His identity is defined not in terms of prior narrative appearances but in terms of information relevant to the plot, and how Simon Peter was able to find his way into the high priest's courtyard, something that is left unexplained in the Synoptics where he simply walks in (Matt 26:58 // Mark 14:54 // Luke 22:54–55). This new disciple is eventually called "the other disciple" (John 18:16), but even here, the reference is to the previous verse that established his identity (John 18:15), and the narrator still clarifies which "other disciple" it is, "the one who was known to the high priest" (John 18:16). The narrator's concerns all focus on this scene, with no reference to previous action.

If this were a fresh appearance of an already established character, the reader might have expected to see a pointer of the kind that is common in John. When Nicodemus reappears in John 7:50, he is "the one who had come to him before" (ὁ ἐλθὼν πρὸς αὐτὸν πρότερον). In 19:39, he had "at first come to Jesus by night" (ὁ ἐλθὼν πρὸς αὐτὸν νυκτὸς τὸ πρῶτον). On Caiaphas's second appearance, the narrator underlines again the earlier appearance, "Caiaphas was the one who had advised the Jews that it was better to have one person die for the people" (John 18:14).

There are no grounds, then, for seeing the anonymous disciple who was known to the high priest as the Beloved Disciple, even if it is true that John son of Zebedee is indeed a Jerusalem disciple for much of his life. The key question, though, is whether the Fourth Gospel ever suggests that the Beloved Disciple was also from Galilee or associated with Galilee in some way. Is he exclusively a Jerusalem disciple, or does he have roots in Galilee? We have already seen the extent to which the evangelist underlines how those reclining with him at the Last Supper, in John 13–17, were "chosen" to be with him "from the beginning" (John 13:18; 14:9; 15:16, 19, 27), but there are further important pointers to the Beloved Disciple being depicted as a Galilean.

A Galilean Disciple

What, then, are the indicators that the Beloved Disciple is being depicted as anything other than a Jerusalem disciple? Where are his Galilean credentials? The answer to this question depends in part on a feature of John's Gospel that distinguishes it from the Synoptics: the surprisingly limited amount of Galilean material. We are talking about only a handful of passages, compared to multiple passages that take place in Jerusalem and Judea. As in the Synoptics, the passion narrative dominates the second half of the gospel (see above, pp. 36–37), but the first half of the gospel takes the reader to Galilee only as an occasional reminder of Jesus's original location:

STORY	SETTING
John 1:43–51: Philip and Nathanael	Galilee (1:43); Bethsaida (1:44); Nazareth (1:45–46)
John 2:1–11: Water into wine	Cana (2:1, 11); Capernaum (2:12)
John 4:43–54: Officer's son	Galilee (4:43, 45); Cana (4:46); Capernaum (4:46)
John 6:1–71: Five thousand; walking on the sea; bread of life	Sea of Galilee (6:1); Capernaum (6:17, 24, 59); Tiberias (6:23)
John 7:1–13: Jesus stays in Galilee and goes to Jerusalem in secret	Galilee (7:1, 3, 9)
John 21:1–24: Appearance by the Sea of Tiberias	Sea of Tiberias (21:1)

After Jesus departs for Jerusalem in John 7:9, he never returns to Galilee until after the resurrection (John 21:1–24). The entire gospel is primarily located in Jerusalem and Judea, with only a handful of Galilean encounters in the early chapters. That the Beloved Disciple appears primarily in Judean material is in large part a consequence of the gospel's focus on Judea.

Nevertheless, this still raises the question about whether the Beloved Disciple ever has a Galilean connection. Is there anything that links him positively with John son of Zebedee? For readers familiar with the Synoptics, there are three passages that point in this direction: (a) John 1:35–42, the "two disciples"; (b) John 21, fishing and following at the Sea of Tiberias; and (c) John 1:14, "We beheld his glory." Let us take each in turn.

The Two Disciples in John 1:35–42

For the reader familiar with the Synoptics, the stories found in John 1 provide multiple pointers to material the Synoptics narrate, presupposing but also changing and developing the action that takes place there. One of the most striking is the call of Andrew and Peter (John 1:35–42), which, in spite of major differences from the Synoptics (Matt 4:18–22 // Mark 1:16–20 // Luke 5:1–11), evokes elements from those call stories, like the importance of seeing (Matt 4:18, 21; Mark 1:16, 19; Luke 5:2, 8; John 1:36, 38, 39, 42), but especially the theme of following Jesus:

MATTHEW	MARK	LUKE	JOHN
4:20: οἱ δὲ εὐθέως ἀφέντες τὰ δίκτυα ἠκολούθησαν αὐτῷ. 4:21b–22: καὶ ἐκάλεσεν αὐτούς. οἱ δὲ εὐθέως ἀφέντες τὸ πλοῖον καὶ τὸν πατέρα αὐτῶν ἠκολούθησαν αὐτῷ.	1:18: καὶ εὐθὺς ἀφέντες τὰ δίκτυα ἠκολούθησαν αὐτῷ. 1:20: καὶ εὐθὺς ἐκάλεσεν αὐτούς. καὶ ἀφέντες τὸν πατέρα αὐτῶν Ζεβεδαῖον ἐν τῷ πλοίῳ μετὰ τῶν μισθωτῶν ἀπῆλθον ὀπίσω αὐτοῦ.	5:11: καὶ καταγαγόντες τὰ πλοῖα ἐπὶ τὴν γῆν ἀφέντες πάντα ἠκολούθησαν αὐτῷ.	1:37: καὶ ἤκουσαν οἱ δύο μαθηταὶ αὐτοῦ λαλοῦντος καὶ ἠκολούθησαν τῷ Ἰησοῦ. 1:40: ἦν Ἀνδρέας ὁ ἀδελφὸς Σίμωνος Πέτρου εἷς ἐκ τῶν δύο τῶν ἀκουσάντων παρὰ Ἰωάννου καὶ ἀκολουθησάντων αὐτῷ.
4:20: Immediately they left their nets and followed him. 4:22: Immediately they left the boat and their father and followed him.	1:18: And immediately they left their nets and followed him. 1:20: Immediately he called them, and they left their father Zebedee in the boat with the hired men and went after him.[14]	5:11: When they had brought their boats to shore, they left everything and followed him.	1:37: The two disciples heard him say this, and they followed Jesus. 1:40: One of the two who heard John speak and followed him was Andrew, Simon Peter's brother.

---

14. NRSVue, "followed him" (adjusted to show the difference in Greek).

CHAPTER 6

The "following" theme will return later (John 21, below) in a story explicitly focusing on Peter and the Beloved Disciple, but the current passage in John is a functional equivalent of the Synoptic call of the first disciples. The passage occurs in proximity to the material about John the Baptist (Matt 3:1–17 // Mark 1:2–11 // Luke 3:1–22), with only the temptation story (Mark 1:12–13) and the move to Galilee (Mark 1:14–15) intervening in Mark and Matthew:[15]

Matt 3:1–12	Mark 1:2–8	John 1:19–28	John the Baptist
Matt 3:13–17	Mark 1:9–11	John 1:29–34	Spirit descends
Matt 4:1–11	Mark 1:12–13		Temptation
Matt 4:12–17	Mark 1:14–15		Move to Galilee
Matt 4:18–22	Mark 1:16–20	John 1:35–42	Call of Simon and Andrew, and James and John, or anonymous disciple

Readers of the Synoptics find themselves in familiar territory when they turn to the Fourth Gospel. What is curious about the story in John, though, is that there is a certain coyness about the identity of one of these first disciples. There are three disciples in John's story, two of whom are named, and one of whom is anonymous. The reader of the Synoptics naturally reads the anonymous disciple as one of the sons of Zebedee:

MATTHEW	MARK	LUKE	JOHN
4:18: he saw **two brothers, Simon, who is called Peter, and Andrew his brother**.	1:16: he saw **Simon and his brother Andrew**.	5:2: he saw two boats there.... 5:3: He got into one of the boats, the one belonging to **Simon**. 5:8: But	1:35: The next day John again was standing with **two of his disciples**.... 1:37: The two

15. Luke has the same relative order here as Mark, Matthew, and John, but there is more intervening material. His genealogy (Luke 3:23–38) comes after the baptism of Jesus rather than at the beginning of the gospel (Matt 1:1–18); Luke 4:16–30 (rejection at Nazareth) is brought forward from Matt 13:54–58 // Mark 6:1–6, and Jesus's day in Capernaum (Luke 4:31–44) is brought forward from Mark 1:21–39. This is, in other words, one of those occasions where John aligns with Mark and Matthew more closely than Luke does.

The Beloved Disciple for Readers of the Synoptics

MATTHEW	MARK	LUKE	JOHN
4:21: he saw two other brothers, **James son of Zebedee and his brother John**.	1:19: he saw **James son of Zebedee and his brother John**.	when **Simon Peter** saw it. . . . 5:10: and so also were **James and John, sons of Zebedee**, who were partners with Simon.	disciples heard him. . . . 1:40: One of the two who heard John speak and followed him was **Andrew, Simon Peter's brother**. . . . 1:42: "You are **Simon son of John**. You are to be called Cephas" (which is translated **Peter**).

The first four of Jesus's disciples in Matthew and Mark are the two sets of brothers—Simon Peter and Andrew, alongside James and John. In Luke, Andrew drops out (but see 6:14), but Simon Peter, James, and John are all present. In the Johannine story, then, it would be fair for a reader of the Synoptics to imagine that the anonymous third disciple was one of the sons of Zebedee.

But is there anything more than this? There is a hint that may further tilt Synoptic readers toward identifying the anonymous disciple here as one of the sons of Zebedee. When Andrew goes to find Simon, the narrator leans heavily on the notion that they are brothers:

John 1:40–41: ἦν Ἀνδρέας ὁ ἀδελφὸς Σίμωνος Πέτρου εἷς ἐκ τῶν δύο τῶν ἀκουσάντων παρὰ Ἰωάννου καὶ ἀκολουθησάντων αὐτῷ· εὑρίσκει οὗτος πρῶτον <u>τὸν ἀδελφὸν τὸν ἴδιον Σίμωνα</u> καὶ λέγει αὐτῷ· Εὑρήκαμεν τὸν Μεσσίαν.

One of the two who heard John speak and followed him was Andrew, Simon Peter's brother. He first found <u>his own brother Simon</u> and says to him, "We have found the Messiah."

It is possible that τὸν ἴδιον ("his own") adds nothing more than a little emphasis to τὸν ἀδελφόν ("brother"), and several translations, including the NRSVue, translate the sentence this way ("his brother Simon"). Other translations, however, see τὸν ἴδιον as adding something of substance and translate it "his own brother" (KJV, NASB, NET), which invites the reader to think about other brothers. Is there another brother in the vicinity? A reader of the Synoptics who is familiar with the two pairs of brothers might well infer that at least one of the second pair of brothers, the sons of Zebedee, is here too.[16]

The difficulty with leaning too heavily on this passage is that it is not clear whether this anonymous disciple should be read as the Beloved Disciple. Many commentators have imagined that this is a subtle first appearance of the character, but others have argued against the identification. The major argument against the identification is that this disciple is not "loved" and he is not given the kind of prominence that the Beloved Disciple is given later in the narrative. Yet it would hardly be appropriate for the narrator to call the anonymous disciple "loved" before he has even met Jesus, and at this point in the narrative, his discipleship is still with John (John 1:35, 37) and not Jesus, so it would not make any sense for him to be "John's disciple whom Jesus loved." On balance, it is fair for readers of John to infer that this is a subtle, early appearance of the disciple Jesus loved, and it is fair for readers of the Synoptics to notice that the character aligns more closely with one of the sons of Zebedee than with any other known character.

John 21:1–25

The preeminent appearance of the Beloved Disciple is, of course, at the end of the gospel.[17] This final resurrection story has speaking roles for only three characters, Jesus, Peter, and the Beloved Disciple, and the gospel ends with a grand sign-off that attributes everything to that disciple's witness. Unlike many other gospels, however, the author does not unmask its authenticating figure, and the tantalizing enigma about his identity begins in earnest. Yet for the reader familiar with the Synoptics, it is actually not much of a mystery. The reader infers that the character is John, the son of Zebedee. There are three reasons for this.

---

16. The exhaustive discussion of this verse by Frans Neirynck, "The Anonymous Disciple in John 1," *ETL* 66 (1990): 5–37 (= Neirynck, *Evangelica II: 1982–1991; Collected Essays by Frans Neirynck*, ed. F. Van Segbroeck [Leuven: Leuven University Press, 1991], 617–50), is inconclusive, but my point here is to ask the question of how this passage reads for those familiar with the Synoptic Gospels, and what inferences such readers would make.

17. I am treating the gospel as a whole and do not share the common view that John 21 was a later addition. But even if it was, the chapter would illustrate that one of John's earliest readers, with a remarkable command of his style and storytelling, read the Beloved Disciple as a Galilean disciple, who fished and followed Jesus, just like the sons of Zebedee.

"Follow Me"

In the Synoptic Gospels, John son of Zebedee is one of the first four disciples who are called to "follow" Jesus (Matt 4:22 // Mark 1:20 // Luke 5:11), just like the anonymous disciple in John 1:35–42 (above). As in the Synoptics, true discipleship is characterized by following Jesus, and unlike Peter, the Beloved Disciple has exemplified this, following Jesus to the cross (19:25–27), witnessing his death (John 19:35), and seeing and believing at the vacated tomb (20:8). Unlike Peter, he does not need to be exhorted to "follow me" (John 21:19, 22), and his love, by contrast with Peter's, can be taken for granted (John 21:15–19). In the same setting, the Sea of Galilee, at which John son of Zebedee first followed Jesus (Matt 4:22 // Mark 1:20 // Luke 5:11), the Beloved Disciple is still seen to be following Jesus:

John 21:20: Ἐπιστραφεὶς ὁ Πέτρος βλέπει τὸν μαθητὴν ὃν ἠγάπα ὁ Ἰησοῦς ἀκολουθοῦντα.

When Peter turned, he sees the disciple whom Jesus loved following.[18]

Moreover, there is a clear echo here of the story of the anonymous disciple in John 1:35–42, the kind of echo that further suggests a link from the Beloved Disciple appearing explicitly in John 21, to his appearing implicitly in John 1, to the identification with one of the sons of Zebedee:

John 1:38: στραφεὶς δὲ ὁ Ἰησοῦς καὶ θεασάμενος αὐτοὺς ἀκολουθοῦντας	John 21:20–22: Ἐπιστραφεὶς ὁ Πέτρος βλέπει τὸν μαθητὴν ὃν ἠγάπα ὁ Ἰησοῦς ἀκολουθοῦντα.... τοῦτον οὖν ἰδὼν ὁ Πέτρος λέγει τῷ Ἰησοῦ· Κύριε, οὗτος δὲ τί;
λέγει αὐτοῖς, Τί ζητεῖτε;	λέγει αὐτῷ ὁ Ἰησοῦς....
When Jesus turned and saw them following,	When Peter turned, he sees the disciple whom Jesus loved following.... When Peter saw him,
he says to them, "What are you looking for?"	he says to Jesus, "Lord, what about him"? Jesus says to him....[19]

18. This is sometimes translated "following them" (e.g., NET, NRSVue), but the object of ἀκολουθοῦντα is not specified, and given the weight the work gives to "following" language, it is a better inference that the Beloved Disciple is following Jesus, as in 1:38.

19. My translation in both cases to reflect the similarities as clearly as possible.

CHAPTER 6

The Miraculous Haul of Fish (*Luke 5:1–11 // John 21:1–14*)

Although the postresurrection setting in John requires the telling of a slightly different story, the parallels between the miraculous haul of fish in both gospels are clear. The gospels share key details in common, including the location (Lake of Gennesaret/Sea of Tiberias), the nature of the miracle (a huge haul of fish), and some of the personnel.

LUKE 5:1–10	JOHN 21:3–11
Once while he was <u>standing</u> beside the Lake of Gennesaret and the crowd was pressing in on him to hear the word of God.... When he had finished speaking, <u>he said</u> to Simon, "Put out into the deep water and <u>let down your nets</u> for a catch."	Just after daybreak, Jesus <u>stood</u> on the shore,[20] but the disciples did not know that it was Jesus. <u>He said</u> to them, "<u>Cast the net</u> to the right side of the boat, and you will find some."
Simon answered, "Master, we have worked all <u>night</u> long but have <u>caught nothing</u>. Yet if you say so, I will let down the nets." When they had done this, they caught <u>so many fish</u> that their nets were beginning to burst.	Simon Peter said to them, "I am going fishing." They said to him, "We will go with you." They went out and got into the boat, but that <u>night</u> they <u>caught nothing</u>. So they cast it, and now they were not able to haul it in because there were <u>so many fish</u>.
So they signaled their partners in the other boat to come and help them. And they came and filled both boats, so that they began to sink. But when Simon Peter saw it, he fell down at Jesus's knees, saying, "Go away from me, Lord, for I am a sinful man!" For he and all who were with him were astounded at the catch of fish that they had taken, and so also were James and John, sons of Zebedee, who were partners with Simon.	That disciple whom Jesus loved said to Peter, "It is the Lord!" When Simon Peter heard that it was the Lord, he put on his outer garment, for he had taken it off, and jumped into the sea. But the other disciples came in the boat, dragging the net full of fish, for they were not far from the land, only about a hundred yards off. So Simon Peter went aboard and hauled the net ashore, full of large fish, a hundred fifty-three of them, and though there were <u>so many</u>, the net was not torn.

---

20. NRSVue, "beach."

The Beloved Disciple for Readers of the Synoptics

This is not the kind of verbatim agreement that would help us to diagnose direct literary borrowing, but the point in this context is not to argue for John's dependence on Luke,[21] but to see how readers of Luke and John might see the parallels as an invitation to read the passages side by side, and to read the Lukan personnel in the Johannine story. Peter is the key figure in each narrative, but just as the Beloved Disciple appears alongside him in John 21, so too do the sons of Zebedee appear alongside him in Luke 5. The Beloved Disciple does seem, after all, to be a Galilean disciple. It hardly gets any more Galilean than this in John. Apart from John 6, there is no other passage that has so lengthy a focus on Galilee in the Fourth Gospel.

Nevertheless, there is an oddity that needs addressing. Something is different here. After the sustained refusal to name the Beloved Disciple throughout the gospel, this narrative apparently begins with a list of candidates:

John 21:2: ἦσαν ὁμοῦ Σίμων Πέτρος, καὶ Θωμᾶς ὁ λεγόμενος Δίδυμος, καὶ Ναθαναὴλ ὁ ἀπὸ Κανᾶ τῆς Γαλιλαίας, καὶ οἱ τοῦ Ζεβεδαίου, καὶ ἄλλοι ἐκ τῶν μαθητῶν αὐτοῦ δύο.

Gathered there together were Simon Peter, Thomas called the Twin, Nathanael of Cana in Galilee, the sons of Zebedee, and two others of his disciples.

The mention of "two others of his disciples" frustrates any sense that the named disciples here provide a full candidate short list, so the Beloved Disciple could indeed be someone other than James, John, Thomas, or Nathanael. Nevertheless, even the "two others" are clearly part of the "disciple" group (cf. John 21:1), which is usually a tight-knit group in John, especially in the second half of the gospel, where they are taken to one side for special instruction. As we saw above, the fact that this group of "disciples" has been "chosen" to be with Jesus "from the beginning" excludes popular gospel candidates like Lazarus, and popular nongospel candidates like John the Elder.

The use of the term "sons of Zebedee" is interesting for several reasons. Not only does it explicitly place John son of Zebedee in the narrative in which the Beloved Disciple is most prominent, but also it reveals that the "sons of Zebedee" are indeed characters known to the audience. When John's Gospel introduces a fresh character, there is usually a note that explains his or her identity, as in 3:1, "Now there was a Pharisee named Nicodemus, a leader of the Judeans," and 11:1, "Now a certain man was ill, Lazarus of Bethany, the village of Mary and her sister

---

21. See Michael D. Goulder, *Luke: A New Paradigm*, JSNTSup 20 (Sheffield: Sheffield Academic, 1989), 323–26 for the case that John 21 is derived from Luke 5:1–11 (and other Synoptic passages). For the argument that John knew Luke, see chapter 3 above.

CHAPTER 6

Martha." But here, the implied reader apparently already knows who "the sons of Zebedee" are. The book is almost finished, and it turns out that all along, its readers knew about the sons of Zebedee. The terminology, moreover, provides another link to Luke 5. It is the only time that the phrase "sons of Zebedee" occurs in Luke, and the only time that it occurs in John.[22]

Some scholars have suggested that the naming of the sons of Zebedee here precludes either one from being the Beloved Disciple. The suggestion is groundless. The literary trope of waiting until the end of the work to reveal the key character, or the author, is common in antiquity. The Protevangelium of James, for example, reveals the name of its author only in its last paragraph:

> Now I, James, wrote this history in Jerusalem when tumult arose on the death of Herod, and withdrew into the desert until the tumult in Jerusalem ceased. And I praise the Lord God who gave me the wisdom to write this history. (Prot. Jas. 25.1)

Similarly, the Gospel of Peter appears to bring its author to the fore only at the end, and in an incident that clearly parallels John 21:

> But we, the twelve disciples of the Lord, wept and mourned and each one, grieving for what had happened, returned to his own home. But I, Simon Peter, and my brother Andrew took our nets and went to the sea. And there was with us Levi, the son of Alphaeus, whom the Lord. . . . (Gos. Pet. 59–60)

It is unfortunate that this is the point at which the Akhmim codex breaks off, but it seems likely that what we have here is the beginning of the end of the gospel, with the author revealing his identity by the sea, as he prepares to let down his nets.

Works like these are, of course, explicit about their authors' identities in a way that the Fourth Gospel is not, but the point is that it is common to withhold key information relevant to the author's identity until the very end of a work. Something similar could easily be imagined with respect to the Fourth Gospel, albeit that its author is much more coy. Other works parallel that pseudepigraphic hesitation. Both Qoheleth (Ecclesiastes) and Wisdom of Solomon imply that they are written by Solomon without naming him (Eccl 1:1; 12:9;

---

22. It is more common in Matthew and Mark. See Matt 4:21; 10:2; 20:20; 26:37; 27:56; Mark 1:9, 20; 3:17; 10:35.

The Beloved Disciple for Readers of the Synoptics

Wis 9:7–8).[23] It is worth remembering, too, that the surest way to tease the solution to a mystery is to place an idea subtly in the reader's mind. By explicitly mentioning the apparently well-known "sons of Zebedee," John 21 succeeds in evoking call stories at the Sea of Galilee, fishing, and following Jesus, subtly teasing the reader about the identity of the Beloved Disciple.

The Disciple Who Would Not Die

There is a third feature of the story that encourages readers of the Synoptics to identify the Beloved Disciple with John son of Zebedee. Before the author identifies himself as the Beloved Disciple (John 21:24), he deals with an apparent rumor:

> Peter turned and saw the disciple whom Jesus loved following; he was the one who had reclined next to Jesus at the supper and had said, "Lord, who is it that is going to betray you?" When Peter saw him, he said to Jesus, "Lord, what about him?" Jesus said to him, "If it is my will that he remain until I come, what is that to you? Follow me!" So the rumor spread among the brothers and sisters that this disciple would not die. Yet Jesus did not say to him that he would not die, but, "If it is my will that he remain until I come, what is that to you?" (John 21:20–23)

The idea that one of Jesus's disciples would not die before the parousia is an intriguing one. How could something like this have arisen, and how could it have been so influential that the evangelist feels the need to quell it, and right at the climax of the work? For readers of the Synoptics, there is no mystery. There is only one passage that explicitly brings up the question of the disciples' deaths alongside the promise of Jesus's return:

---

23. See Hugo Méndez, *The Gospel of John: A New History* (Oxford: Oxford University Press, 2025), 152. Méndez also draws attention to Clare Rothschild, *Hebrews as Pseudepigraphon: The History and Significance of the Pauline Attribution of Hebrews*, WUNT 235 (Tübingen: Mohr Siebeck, 2009), for the suggestion that the Epistle to the Hebrews gestures at Pauline authorship without naming him.

CHAPTER 6

MATT 16:28	MARK 9:1	LUKE 9:22
ἀμὴν λέγω ὑμῖν ὅτι εἰσίν τινες τῶν ὧδε ἑστώτων οἵτινες οὐ μὴ γεύσωνται θανάτου ἕως ἂν ἴδωσιν τὸν υἱὸν τοῦ ἀνθρώπου ἐρχόμενον ἐν τῇ βασιλείᾳ αὐτοῦ.	καὶ ἔλεγεν αὐτοῖς· Ἀμὴν λέγω ὑμῖν ὅτι εἰσίν τινες τῶν ὧδε ἑστηκότων οἵτινες οὐ μὴ γεύσωνται θανάτου ἕως ἂν ἴδωσιν τὴν βασιλείαν τοῦ θεοῦ ἐληλυθυῖαν ἐν δυνάμει.	λέγω δὲ ὑμῖν ἀληθῶς, εἰσίν τινες τῶν αὐτοῦ ἑστηκότων οἳ οὐ μὴ γεύσωνται θανάτου ἕως ἂν ἴδωσιν τὴν βασιλείαν τοῦ θεοῦ.
"Amen I say to you, there are some standing here who will not taste death before they see the Son of Man coming in his kingdom."	And he said to them, "Amen I say to you, there are some standing here who will not taste death before they see the kingdom of God coming with power."	"Truly I say to you, there are some standing here who will not taste death before they see the kingdom of God."[24]

The Synoptics are all close here. Mark and Matthew share a remarkable seventeen-word verbatim string, and Mark and Luke a ten-word verbatim string. In all three, the saying comes at a pivotal point in the narrative. Peter has just confessed that Jesus is Messiah, but crucially, he has failed to link his messianic identity to Jesus's suffering and death (Matt 16:13–27 // Mark 8:27–38 // Luke 9:18–26). And now, as the narrative turns toward Jerusalem, it is this verse that segues from teaching about Jesus's death to the transfiguration (Matt 17:1–13 // Mark 9:2–13 // Luke 9:28–36). "Some of those standing there" (Matt 16:28 // Mark 9:1 // Luke 9:27), of course, includes the presence of the key Synoptic disciples, Peter, James, and John, who then become the explicit audience in the following verse (Matt 17:1 // Mark 9:2 // Luke 9:28).[25]

The link between the Johannine rumor and the Synoptic verse is strengthened by the fact that elsewhere the Fourth Gospel has a very similar saying. For

---

24. My translations.
25. See Dale Allison, "'Jesus Did Not Say to Him That He Would Not Die': John 21:20–23 and Mark 9:1" (paper presented at the Annual Meeting of the Society of Biblical Literature, Baltimore, MD, 2013), 30n70, for a long list of those, from Cyril of Alexandria onward, who identified "some standing here" with Peter, James, and John. I am grateful to the author for sending me a copy of this paper, which is to appear in a future book on John.

ease of comparison, let us take just Mark this time (since Matthew and Luke are so similar) and put it alongside both John 8:51 and John 8:52:

MARK 9:1	JOHN 8:51	JOHN 8:52
Ἀμὴν λέγω ὑμῖν ὅτι εἰσίν τινες τῶν ὧδε ἑστηκότων οἵτινες <u>οὐ μὴ γεύσωνται θανάτου</u> ἕως ἂν ἴδωσιν τὴν βασιλείαν τοῦ θεοῦ ἐληλυθυῖαν ἐν δυνάμει.	ἀμὴν <u>ἀμὴν λέγω ὑμῖν</u>, ἐάν τις τὸν ἐμὸν λόγον τηρήσῃ, θάνατον οὐ μὴ θεωρήσῃ εἰς τὸν αἰῶνα.	Ἐάν τις τὸν λόγον μου τηρήσῃ, <u>οὐ μὴ γεύσηται θανάτου</u> εἰς τὸν αἰῶνα·
And he said to them, "<u>Amen I say to you</u>, there are some standing here <u>who will not taste death</u> before they see the kingdom of God coming with power."	"Amen, <u>amen I say to you</u>, if anyone keeps my word, they will not see death forever."	"If anyone keeps my word, <u>they will not taste death</u> forever."[26]

Dale Allison points out just how close John is here to the Synoptics.[27] All the Johannine variations are straightforwardly explicable in line with John's characteristic language, and the expression that they have in common, "will not taste death" (οὐ μὴ γεύσωνται/γεύσηται θανάτου) is striking. Although familiar to us because of its occurrences in the Synoptics, John, and Thomas, it is easy to miss that it is highly unusual, and there is only one known earlier example in Greek literature.[28]

For those reading John 21 in the light of the Synoptics, then, there are several pointers to the identity of the Beloved Disciple as John son of Zebedee. But the closely knit pivotal section in the Synoptics comprising Peter's confession, the prophecy about "some standing here," and the transfiguration draws the reader's attention to a striking parallel at the outset of the gospel that gives its author a voice that provides an even stronger clue.

---

26. My translations.
27. Allison, "Jesus Did Not Say," 7–8.
28. Theocritus, *Epigr.* 16 (third century BCE).

CHAPTER 6

"We Beheld His Glory" (John 1:14)

At the end of the previous chapter, we noted the apparent oddity that a gospel that is so rich in drama, moving Synoptic narration into the mouths of Johannine characters, still has so prominent a narrator, who will speak for whole paragraphs at a time. Yet the gospel's prominent narrator is himself a key character in the drama, and there are two occasions in the gospel when he speaks in the first person, once at the beginning, and once at the end:

John 1:14: Καὶ ὁ λόγος σὰρξ ἐγένετο καὶ ἐσκήνωσεν ἐν ἡμῖν, <u>καὶ ἐθεασάμεθα τὴν δόξαν αὐτοῦ</u>, δόξαν ὡς μονογενοῦς παρὰ πατρός, πλήρης χάριτος καὶ ἀληθείας.

And the Word became flesh and tabernacled among us, <u>and we have seen his glory</u>, the glory as of a father's only son, full of grace and truth.

John 21:24: Οὗτός ἐστιν ὁ μαθητὴς ὁ μαρτυρῶν περὶ τούτων καὶ ὁ γράψας ταῦτα, καὶ οἴδαμεν ὅτι ἀληθὴς αὐτοῦ ἡ μαρτυρία ἐστίν.

This is the disciple who is testifying to these things and has written these things down, <u>and we know that his testimony is true</u>.[29]

John 1:14 is, of course, one of the most famous verses in the gospel, but the christological meteor of "the Word became flesh" can blaze so brightly that it outshines the extraordinary switch to first-person narration in the next clause. Here, before the narrative proper has begun, the narrator reveals himself as a participant in the events.

A reader familiar with the Synoptics would have several reasons for aligning the first-person narration in John 1:14 with the Synoptic transfiguration story (Matt 17:1–8 // Mark 9:2–8 // Luke 9:28–36). One of the most memorable features in that story is the idea that Peter, James, and John could set up "tabernacles" (σκηναί) for Jesus, Moses, and Elijah (Matt 17:4 // Mark 9:5 // Luke 9:33), and now here, in the Fourth Gospel, the Word "tabernacled among us" (ἐσκήνωσεν ἐν ἡμῖν). The parallel would be just a curiosity if it were not for two other elements that make the link clearer. The statement "We have seen his glory" has a close parallel in the Lukan version of the transfiguration:

---

29. My translations in both verses.

The Beloved Disciple for Readers of the Synoptics

MATT 17:4	MARK 9:5-6	LUKE 9:32-33
		ὁ δὲ Πέτρος καὶ οἱ σὺν αὐτῷ ἦσαν βεβαρημένοι ὕπνῳ· διαγρηγορήσαντες <u>δὲ εἶδον τὴν δόξαν αὐτοῦ</u> καὶ τοὺς δύο ἄνδρας τοὺς συνεστῶτας αὐτῷ. καὶ ἐγένετο ἐν τῷ διαχωρίζεσθαι αὐτοὺς ἀπ' αὐτοῦ εἶπεν ὁ
ἀποκριθεὶς δὲ ὁ Πέτρος εἶπεν τῷ Ἰησοῦ· Κύριε, καλόν ἐστιν ἡμᾶς ὧδε εἶναι· εἰ θέλεις, ποιήσω ὧδε τρεῖς σκηνάς, σοὶ μίαν καὶ Μωϋσεῖ μίαν καὶ Ἠλίᾳ μίαν.	καὶ ἀποκριθεὶς ὁ Πέτρος λέγει τῷ Ἰησοῦ· Ῥαββί, καλόν ἐστιν ἡμᾶς ὧδε εἶναι, καὶ ποιήσωμεν τρεῖς σκηνάς, σοὶ μίαν καὶ Μωϋσεῖ μίαν καὶ Ἠλίᾳ μίαν. οὐ γὰρ ᾔδει τί ἀποκριθῇ, ἔκφοβοι γὰρ ἐγένοντο.	Πέτρος πρὸς τὸν Ἰησοῦν· Ἐπιστάτα, καλόν ἐστιν ἡμᾶς ὧδε εἶναι, καὶ ποιήσωμεν σκηνὰς τρεῖς, μίαν σοὶ καὶ μίαν Μωϋσεῖ καὶ μίαν Ἠλίᾳ μὴ εἰδὼς ὃ λέγει.
		Now Peter and his companions were weighed down with sleep, but as they awoke <u>they saw his glory</u> and the two men who stood with him. Just as they were leaving him, Peter
Then Peter said to Jesus, "Lord, it is good for us to be here; if you wish, I will set up three tents here, one for you, one for Moses, and one for Elijah."	Then Peter said to Jesus, "Rabbi, it is good for us to be here; let us set up three tents: one for you, one for Moses, and one for Elijah." He did not know what to say, for they were terrified.	said to Jesus, "Master, it is good for us to be here; let us set up three tents: one for you, one for Moses, and one for Elijah," not realizing what he was saying.

CHAPTER 6

This is the only time, anywhere in the Synoptics, that anyone is said to have seen Jesus's glory, and now, something very close to the Lukan narration appears in the first person in the Fourth Gospel,[30] where the glory is further defined in christological terms that provide a further parallel with all three Synoptics:

MATT 17:5	MARK 9:7	LUKE 9:32, 35	JOHN 1:14
			Καὶ ὁ λόγος σὰρξ ἐγένετο καὶ ἐσκήνωσεν ἐν ἡμῖν, καὶ
		διαγρηγορήσαντες δὲ <u>εἶδον τὴν δόξαν αὐτοῦ</u>. . . .	<u>ἐθεασάμεθα τὴν δόξαν αὐτοῦ</u>,
Οὗτός ἐστιν ὁ <u>υἱός μου ὁ ἀγαπητός</u>, ἐν ᾧ εὐδόκησα· ἀκούετε αὐτοῦ.	Οὗτός ἐστιν ὁ <u>υἱός μου ὁ ἀγαπητός</u>, ἀκούετε αὐτοῦ.	Οὗτός ἐστιν ὁ <u>υἱός μου ὁ ἐκλελεγμένος</u>, αὐτοῦ ἀκούετε.	δόξαν ὡς <u>μονογενοῦς παρὰ πατρός</u>,
			πλήρης χάριτος καὶ ἀληθείας.
		And when they had woken up, <u>they saw his glory</u>. . . .	And the Word became flesh and tabernacled among us, and <u>we saw his glory</u>, glory as of the
"This is <u>my beloved son</u>, in whom I am well pleased; listen to him."	"This is <u>my beloved son</u>; listen to him."	"This is <u>my chosen son</u>; listen to him."	<u>only begotten of the father</u>, full of grace and truth.

The "beloved," "only," or "chosen" son of the Synoptics is very similar to John's "only begotten of the father." To the reader of the Synoptics, the climax of the

---

30. For a similar move from the Synoptic narration to first-person testimony in the transfiguration story, see 2 Pet 1:16–18. See also Acts of John 90 where John recounts his experience on the mountain.

The Beloved Disciple for Readers of the Synoptics

Johannine prologue evokes the Christology, the tabernacles, and the glory of the transfiguration story. And one of the three who witnessed this was John, the son of Zebedee.[31]

FROM READERS OF THE SYNOPTICS TO THE AUTHORSHIP OF JOHN

In this chapter, we have explored the viewpoint of a hypothetical, imagined reader of the Synoptics, posing the question, What would someone with knowledge of the Synoptics make of John's Gospel? How would that person read the figure of the Beloved Disciple? The hypothetical, however, does not have to remain hypothetical, and what we imagine can in this case come to life. This is because reading John alongside the Synoptics is not just an idea. It is a practice with a long historical precedent. For as long as Christian history takes us, John's Gospel has been read by readers with knowledge of the Synoptics. That means that the Beloved Disciple has always been read in the light of the Synoptics. Is it any wonder, under these circumstances, that readers of the fourfold gospel have always concluded that the Beloved Disciple was John, from Clement to da Vinci to Zeffirelli?

The difficulty for scholars and students of the New Testament is that while we love reception history, we loathe harmonizing. We are happy to learn from the history of John's reception, but we become anxious if we appear to be harmonizing the Gospels ourselves. The kind of reading that I have been attempting here does not come naturally to academics. It goes against everything that we do in the classroom. In our New Testament introductions, it is a key learning objective to have students able to distinguish between the Synoptics, on the one hand, and John, on the other. We need them to see the differences. I do it myself. A whole class is given over to stressing just how different John is from the Synoptics. The difficulty, though, is that we are in danger of believing our own rhetoric, of carrying our important and necessary pedagogical stresses into our research to the extent that we forget the reception history of the works we are studying. The Fourth Gospel has always been read alongside the Synoptics, and the Beloved Disciple has been identified with John for a reason.

Nor can the discussion end here. I have been arguing in this book that the author of the Fourth Gospel was himself a reader of the Synoptics and that he expects his readers to be presupposing, building on, and engaging with their nar-

---

31. See again Allison, "Jesus Did Not Say," for the idea that John 1:14 evokes the Synoptic transfiguration story, and the consequence that the Beloved Disciple's identity is John son of Zebedee.

CHAPTER 6

ratives too. And if readers of the fourfold gospel have, across the centuries, concluded that the Beloved Disciple was John, could it be that they were right all along and that the author was effectively inviting them to make the identification?

So conservative a conclusion may at first appear startling. Several centuries of canonical readings of the Fourth Gospel have assumed that the Beloved Disciple is John son of Zebedee, and while it is an identification that works well enough for it to have become a part of the Christian imagination, it is quite different for it to be part of the scholar's thinking. What is the point of New Testament scholarship if it is not going to challenge accepted dogma? Where is the fun in thinking that what scholars love to call "the Fourth Gospel" is, after all, "the Gospel of John"?

Perhaps the most marked difficulty here has been the failure of most scholarship on John to distinguish between two different but related questions: (1) Is it plausible to read the Beloved Disciple as John son of Zebedee? And (2) was the historical John son of Zebedee the author of the Fourth Gospel? Arguments against John son of Zebedee's authorship have frequently been conflated with arguments against his identity as the Beloved Disciple,[32] but the two questions are different. Pierson Parker, for example, listed twenty-one reasons why John son of Zebedee could not have been the author of the Fourth Gospel and the Beloved Disciple, but most of these are subjective, quasi-fundamentalist arguments like, "It is difficult to imagine how the emotional and wrathful 'son of thunder' wrote such a tranquil Gospel," and "It is difficult to imagine a bold person of action like John the son of Zebedee writing a contemplative Gospel."[33] Martin Hengel's argument similarly focuses on the impossibility that the historical John son of Zebedee authored the gospel—"this Gospel cannot come from a Galilean fisherman."[34]

A moment's reflection will confirm that it is more than possible for a work to imply a claim to apostolic authority without actually being authored by that person.[35] In fact, examples of authentic authorial representation are the exception rather than the rule among Christian works from this era. The Gospel of

---

32. Pierson Parker, "John the Son of Zebedee and the Fourth Gospel," *JBL* 81 (1962): 35–43. The article is focused more precisely on the question of John son of Zebedee as author of the gospel. Most of his reasons focus on the implausibility of John son of Zebedee as the gospel's actual author, so they are largely irrelevant to the case being argued in this chapter. Nevertheless, his article has proved persuasive to many.

33. Parker, "John the Son of Zebedee," 37, 39.

34. Hengel, *Johannine Question*, 130. Nevertheless, Hengel retains a place for idealized elements of John son of Zebedee to be incorporated into the characterization of a Beloved Disciple who is historically John the Elder.

35. For John as a pseudepigraphal work, see especially Hugo Méndez, "Did the Johannine Community Exist?," *JSNT* 42 (2020): 350–74.

Thomas authenticates its "secret sayings of the living Jesus" by appealing to the authority of Didymus Judas Thomas (incipit; cf. 13), in language that is reminiscent of John. Few scholars take this authorial self-representation seriously as history, and the same is true with respect to other early Christian works like the Protevangelium of James, the Gospel of Peter, or another Johannine work, the Apocryphon of John.[36] In all these cases, the authorial self-representation is a literary fiction used to authenticate the new work.

One of the reasons that this conclusion can seem challenging is that the figure of the Beloved Disciple is so superbly crafted that we think we can see him, and we want to believe in him. Unlike the presentation of several of the other authenticating figures in early Christian gospels, there is a subtlety in the way that the Beloved Disciple appears in the narrative, at first only a hint in another character's story (1:35–42), leading to an absence that lasts for the first half of the gospel, and then a presence at the key moments in the Christian proclamation, on the night that Jesus was handed over (13:21–30), at the crucifixion (19:25–27), witnessing Jesus's death (19:35), seeing and believing at the vacated tomb (20:1–10), and following Jesus at his resurrection (21:1–25). The refusal to name him invites the reader to focus on his function in the narrative, as the key authenticating witness to the key moments in Jesus's story. As in the "we passages" of Acts (16:10–17; 20:5–15; 21:1–8; 27:1–28:16), the use of the first person plural at key points (John 1:14 and 21:24) locates the narrator in the action as a witness without making a fuss over their identity.

Rather than using the character's name, the author uses a term, "the disciple whom Jesus loved," that implies but does not narrate a fascinating backstory that can only be imagined. And since the move has engaged generations of readers' imaginations, the framing is clearly a successful one. The reader of the Synoptics has all the clues that point to John son of Zebedee, yet the invitation to read him in John's narrative is complemented by some character development that is not found there. The Beloved Disciple is, effectively, an idealized witness to the key events in the earliest Christian tradition, but the genius of the Fourth Gospel's narrative is that the reader of the Synoptics still has the sense that the character is a familiar one. We have seen his story.

---

36. For further reflections on the role played by authorial self-representation (more commonly called "authorial fiction") in early Christian literature, with specific reference to the Gospel of Thomas, see my *Thomas and the Gospels: The Case for Thomas's Familiarity with the Synoptics* (Grand Rapids: Eerdmans, 2012), 174–79.

Chapter 7

John's Christological Transformation of the Synoptics

If there is one area where the Gospel of John differentiates itself radically from the Synoptics, it is Christology. This is the key contrast between the Synoptics and John. The Synoptic Jesus announces the kingdom of God, but John's Jesus proclaims himself. The Synoptic Jesus speaks allusively in parables, but John's Jesus announces his true identity. One of the most striking features of John's Gospel is one of the most famous features of Christian theology, Jesus's proclamation, "I am the way, the truth, and the life. No one comes to the Father except through me" (John 14:6). There is nothing like this in the Synoptics, and surely here, at last, we will see some clear blue water between the Synoptics and John.

John's christological differences from the Synoptics are not illusory. They are real. There is nowhere in the Synoptics that Jesus says, "I am the light of the world," "I am the bread of life," "I am the good shepherd," "I am the resurrection and the life," or "I am the true vine." The reader only familiar with the Synoptics would be surprised to see these multiple "I am" sayings. This sounds like a different Jesus. He is less mysterious and far more direct. The old academic cliché is that "the proclaimer has become the proclaimed," but like many clichés, there is a lot of truth in it. Every one of the "I am" sayings begins with ἐγώ εἰμι. These sayings are not just about who Jesus is but about the emphasis that Jesus, and nobody else, is the one. It is not just "I am" but "*I* am."

What sense, then, does it make to see John using the Synoptics when his Christology is so different? How could John's depiction of Jesus be in any kind of continuity with the Synoptics' depiction of Jesus? In this final chapter, I would like to reflect on how John achieves a christological transformation of the Synoptics, in continuity with them, but attempting to surpass them in boldness, in clarity, and, most importantly, in Jesus centeredness. We will begin by looking

John's Christological Transformation of the Synoptics

at John's surprising similarities to the Synoptics in the terms it uses for Jesus, its repeating almost every Synoptic title for Jesus. We will then turn to the "I am" sayings and look at how they all utilize Synoptic imagery, and we will argue that even the most distinctive elements of John's Christology, including the relationship between "the Father" and "the Son," derive from the Synoptics.

"The Messiah, the Son of God"

Although many studies of John's Christology begin at the beginning, with the Word made flesh, one of the strongest statements about Jesus's identity comes at the end, in the first conclusion to the gospel:

> John 20:30-31: Now Jesus did many other signs in the presence of his disciples that are not written in this book. But these are written so that you may believe [πιστεύητε][1] that Jesus is the Messiah, the Son of God, and that through believing you may have life in his name.

In spite of this characteristically Johannine ending, it has to be said that a claim like this would not be out of place in the Synoptics, all three of which place Jesus's identity as "Messiah" and "Son of God" at the heart of their gospels. There are studies galore on these terms in both the Synoptics and John, and it is probably not worth laboring the point that these are key elements in a Christology that is shared by all four canonical Gospels, but there is a key piece of continuity between the Synoptics and John that repays a closer look. Mark famously has Peter's confession at Caesarea Philippi, "You are the Messiah," at around the midpoint of his gospel (Mark 8:29), and in Matthew this is expanded to "You are the Messiah, the Son of the living God" (Matt 17:16), and it is this Matthean expansion that is paralleled most closely in John. Peter's confession in John has Jesus as only "the Holy One of God" (John 6:69), echoing Mark's Capernaum demoniac (Mark 1:24), so that the fuller and more christologically precise confession can be saved for Martha's mouth in John 11:27:

---

1. NRSVue, "continue to believe." There is a long debate about how to translate πιστεύητε here, all the more given the significant variant πιστεύσητε. The NIV has "that you may believe."

CHAPTER 7

MATT 17:16	MARK 8:29	LUKE 9:20	JOHN 11:27
ἀποκριθεὶς δὲ Σίμων Πέτρος εἶπεν·	ἀποκριθεὶς ὁ Πέτρος λέγει αὐτῷ·	Πέτρος δὲ ἀποκριθεὶς εἶπεν·	λέγει αὐτῷ· Ναί, κύριε· ἐγὼ πεπίστευκα ὅτι
<u>Σὺ εἶ ὁ χριστὸς ὁ υἱὸς τοῦ θεοῦ</u> τοῦ ζῶντος.	<u>Σὺ εἶ ὁ χριστός.</u>	Τὸν χριστὸν τοῦ θεοῦ.	<u>σὺ εἶ ὁ χριστὸς ὁ υἱὸς τοῦ θεοῦ</u> ὁ εἰς τὸν κόσμον ἐρχόμενος.
Simon Peter answered,	Peter answered him,	Peter answered,	She said to him, "Yes, Lord, I believe that
<u>"You are the Messiah, the Son of</u> the living <u>God."</u>	<u>"You are the Messiah."</u>	"The Messiah of God."	<u>you are the Messiah, the Son of God</u>, the one coming into the world."

The agreement here between Matthew and John (σὺ εἶ ὁ χριστὸς ὁ υἱὸς τοῦ θεοῦ) is an eight-word verbatim string.[2] It is striking that John is so often at its closest to the Synoptics when it comes to questions of Jesus's identity, as if these are the elements in the Synoptics that the author most wants to underline.

For some readers, the fact that John and the Synoptics share the idea that Jesus is "the Messiah, the Son of God" will be unremarkable. Surely all early Christians believed this. Aren't "Messiah" and "Son of God" the basics, the 101 of who Jesus is? It is true that Paul repeatedly depicts Jesus as Messiah and Son of God, but Paul never conjoins the two, "the Messiah, the Son of God," in the way that we see here. John does it twice, here in Martha's confession (John 11:27) and at the first conclusion to the gospel (John 20:31). Matthew also does it twice, in Peter's confession (Matt 17:16) and in the questioning before Caiaphas (Matt 26:63, ἵνα ἡμῖν εἴπῃς εἰ σὺ εἶ ὁ χριστὸς ὁ υἱὸς τοῦ θεοῦ, "tell us if you are the Messiah, the Son of God"). And Mark comes close to the same formulation in

---

2. See further above, p. 28, for the eight-word verbatim string between Matthew and John in the anointing. The longest verbatim string (nine words) is shared between Matthew, Mark, and John (see above, pp. 8–9). This means that all three of the longest verbatim string agreements between John and the Synoptics include, or are exclusive to, Matthew.

his parallel, Σὺ εἶ ὁ χριστὸς ὁ υἱὸς τοῦ εὐλογητοῦ; ("Are you the Messiah, the Son of the Blessed?" Mark 14:61).

Even aside from the parallel conjoining of "the Messiah, the Son of God" in Matthew and John, it is worth noting that other early Christian works prefer different terminology for Jesus. The Gospel of Thomas, for example, never uses the terms "Messiah" or "Son of God" about Jesus, either separately or combined, nor do the Gospel of Mary, the Dialogue of the Savior, and many others. The difficulty is that our familiarity with the Synoptic Gospels and John gives us the sense that combined "Messiah" and "Son of God" language is normative, and everything different is an aberration. Further, it is easy to be so dazzled by the distinctiveness of the Johannine Christology, the Word made flesh, and the "I am" sayings, that we overlook John's striking agreement with the Synoptics on what John in fact centralizes, that Jesus is "the Messiah, the Son of God," and that salvation is about believing in him.

EVERY SHARED TITLE

It is not just a question of this central shared tenet, "the Messiah, the Son of God," important though that is. It is rarely pointed out that practically every other major christological term in the Synoptics is also found in John:

TITLE	MATTHEW	MARK	LUKE	JOHN
Messiah (Christ)[3]	1:1, 16, 17, 18; 2:4; 11:2; 16:16, 20; 23:10; 26:63, 68; 27:17, 22	1:1; 8:29; 9:41; 14:61; 15:32	2:11, 26; 4:41; 9:20; 22:67; 23:2, 35, 39; 24:26, 46	1:17, 41; 4:25, 29; 7:26, 27, 31, 41, 42; 9:22; 10:24; 11:27; 12:34; 17:3; 20:31
Son of God	4:3, 6; 8:29; 14:33; 16:16; 26:63; 27:40, 43, 54; cf. 3:17; 17:5	3:11; 5:7; 14:61;[4] 15:39; cf. 1:11; 9:7	1:32,[5] 35; 3:38; 4:3, 9, 41; 8:28;[6] 22:70; cf. 3:22; 9:35	1:14, 18, 49; 3:16, 17, 18; 5:25; 10:36; 11:4, 27; 19:7; 20:31; cf. 3:35; 5:19, 20, 21, 22, 23, 26; 6:40; 8:36; 13:32; 14:13; 17:1

3. This list includes only places where Jesus is called "Messiah" (Christ), and not places like Mark 13:21–22, Luke 3:15, and John 1:20 ("I am not the Messiah").
4. "Son of the Blessed."
5. "Son of the Most High."
6. "Son of the Most High God."

CHAPTER 7

TITLE	MATTHEW	MARK	LUKE	JOHN
Son of Man	8:20; 9:6; 10:23; 11:19; 12:8, 32, 40; 13:37, 41; 16:13, 27, 28; 17:9, 12, 22; 19:28; 20:18, 28; 24:27, 30, 37, 44; 25:31; 26:2, 24, 45, 64	2:10, 28; 8:31, 38; 9:9, 12, 31; 10:33, 45, 48; 13:26; 14:21, 41, 62	5:24; 6:5, 22; 7:34; 9:22, 26, 44, 58; 11:30; 12:8, 10, 40; 17:22, 24, 26, 30; 18:8, 31; 19:10; 21:27, 36; 22:22, 48, 69; 24:7	1:51; 3:13, 14; 5:27; 6:27, 53, 62; 8:28; 9:35; 12:23, 34 (twice); 13:31
Lord[7]	3:3; 7:21 (twice), 22 (twice); 8:2, 6, 8, 21, 25; 9:28, 38; 12:8; 14:28, 30; 15:22, 25, 27; 16:22; 17:4, 15; 18:21; 20:30, 31, 33; 21:3; 24:42; 25:11 (twice), 37, 44; 26:22	2:28; 5:19; 7:28; 11:3	1:43; 2:11; 5:8, 12; 6:5, 46 (twice); 7:6, 13, 19; 9:54, 59, 61; 10:1, 17, 39, 40, 41; 11:1, 39; 12:41, 42; 13:15, 23; 17:5, 37; 18:6, 41; 19:8 (twice), 31, 34; 22:33, 38, 49, 61; 24:3, 34	6:23, 68; 9:38; 11:2, 3, 12, 21, 27, 32, 34, 39; 13:6, 9, 13, 14, 25, 36, 37; 14:5, 8, 22; 20:2, 13, 18, 20, 25, 28; 21:7 (twice), 12, 15, 16, 17, 20, 21
Teacher[8]	8:19; 9:11; 12:38; 17:24; 19:16; 22:16, 24, 36; 23:8; 26:18	4:38; 5:35; 9:17, 38; 10:17, 20, 35; 12:14, 19, 32; 13:1; 14:14	7:40; 8:49; 9:38; 10:25; 11:45; 12:13; 18:18; 19:39; 20:21, 28, 39; 21:7; 22:11	1:38; 3:2; 11:28; 13:13, 14; 20:16

7. The examples listed are those that explicitly refer to Jesus; there are many other examples of "Lord" language for God. There are also occasions where others are addressed as "Sir," which are not included here.

8. These are examples of διδάσκαλος, which is usually translated "Teacher" but is sometimes translated "Master." I have excluded any examples that do not directly refer to Jesus.

John's Christological Transformation of the Synoptics

TITLE	MATTHEW	MARK	LUKE	JOHN
Rabbi	26:25, 49	9:5; 11:21; 14:45		1:38, 49; 3:2, 26; 4:31; 6:25; 9:2; 11:8
Rabbouni		10:51		20:16
Prophet[9]	13:57; 21:11, 46; cf. 16:14	6:4; cf. 6:15; 8:28	1:76; 4:24; 7:16, 39; 13:33; 24:19; cf. 9:8, 19	4:19, 44; 6:14; 7:40, 52; 9:17
Jesus of Nazareth	26:71; cf. 2:23; 21:11	1:24; 10:47; cf. 1:9; 14:67; 16:6	4:34; 18:37; 24:19	1:45; 18:5, 7; 19:19
King of the Jews	2:2; 27:11, 29, 37	15:2, 9, 12, 18, 26	23:3, 37, 38	18:33, 39; 19:3, 19, 21 (twice)
King of Israel	27:42	15:32		1:49; 12:13
Holy One of God		1:24	4:34	6:69
The coming one[10]	3:11; 11:3; 21:9; 23:39	11:9	7:19, 20; 13:35; 19:38[11]	1:15, 27;[12] 3:31 (twice);[13] 11:27;[14] 12:13; cf. 6:14
Savior			2:11	4:42

These fourteen different Synoptic titles for Jesus are all found in John. The only ones missing in John are "Master" (ἐπιστάτης), which is unique to Luke and used sometimes instead of "Rabbi" or "Teacher,"[15] "Emmanuel," which occurs

---

9. This list includes only places where Jesus is called a "prophet" or where people speculate that he may be one.
10. Or "the one who is coming," ἐρχόμενος.
11. "Blessed is the king who comes in the name of the Lord" (Εὐλογημένος ὁ ἐρχόμενος βασιλεὺς ἐν ὀνόματι κυρίου).
12. Both "the one who comes after me" (Ὁ ὀπίσω μου ἐρχόμενος).
13. "The one who comes from above" and "the one who comes from heaven."
14. "The one who is coming into the world" (ὁ εἰς τὸν κόσμον ἐρχόμενος).
15. This has figures of 0/0/7/0; two of Luke's seven are the doubled vocative in Luke 8:24. Luke uses it in parallel to Διδάσκαλε ("Teacher") in Mark 4:38 // Luke 8:24, as well as in Mark 9:38 // Luke 9:49, and in parallel to Ῥαββί ("Rabbi") in Mark 9:5 // Luke 9:33.

CHAPTER 7

only in Matt 1:23 in a quotation of Isa 7:14, and "Son of David," which is particularly common in Matthew.[16] Some might find it unremarkable that John features titles like "Messiah," "Son of God," "Son of Man," and "Lord," but what is so striking is that even some of the more unusual Synoptic titles turn up in John. Thus Matthew, Mark, and John all have "Rabbi," but Luke does not. Only Mark and John have the related "Rabbouni." Mark, Luke, and John have "Holy One of God," but Matthew does not. Matthew, Mark, and John have "King of Israel," but Luke does not. And only Luke and John have "Savior." It is almost as if John has been through the Synoptics, and made a list of every title that Jesus is given, and has determined to use as many of them as he can, though in reality, it is more likely that he was so immersed in the Synoptic Gospels and their overlapping Christologies that he found himself using, repeating, underlining, and developing their preferred terminology for Jesus.

The point here is that scholars frequently play down the extent of John's continuity with the Synoptic Christology and rarely pause to note the possibility that John's basic christological vocabulary is derived from the Synoptics. The reason, of course, is that it is always so much easier to see what is distinctive in John and to ignore what is similar. What, then, of the distinctive tenets of John's Christology, and especially the "I am" sayings? Let us take a closer look at them.

The "I Am" Sayings

There are seven "I am" sayings in John, or six if one sees "I am the door for the sheep" as the same as "I am the good shepherd," both of which occur in the same context:

> "I am the bread of life" (John 6:35, 48); "I am the bread that came down from heaven" (John 6:41); "I am the living bread that came down from heaven" (John 6:51).
>
> "I am the light of the world" (John 8:12; 9:5).
>
> "I am the door for the sheep" (John 10:7, 9); "I am the good shepherd" (John 10:11, 14).

---

16. "Son of David" as a title for Jesus has figures of 8/2/2/0. John does, however, appear to be aware of the "Son of David" Christology, and the story of Jesus's birth in Bethlehem, on which see above, pp. 102–3.

"I am the resurrection and the life" (John 11:25).

"I am the way, and the truth, and the life. No one comes to the Father except through me" (John 14:6).

"I am the true vine, and my Father is the vinegrower" (John 15:1); "I am the vine; you are the branches" (John 15:5).

All of these are unique to John. None of these have any direct parallels in the Synoptics. So perhaps here, at last, we have some strong evidence of John's distinctiveness from the Synoptics. The situation is not so clear. The imagery from all of the "I am" sayings is paralleled in the Synoptics. This table presents a summary of the relevant parallels:[17]

"I AM" SAYING IN JOHN	SYNOPTIC IMAGERY
6:35, 48: Ἐγώ εἰμι ὁ ἄρτος τῆς ζωῆς ("I am the bread of life") 6:41: Ἐγώ εἰμι ὁ ἄρτος ὁ καταβὰς ἐκ τοῦ οὐρανοῦ ("I am the bread that came down from heaven") 6:51: ἐγώ εἰμι ὁ ἄρτος ὁ ζῶν ὁ ἐκ τοῦ οὐρανοῦ καταβάς ("I am the living bread that came down from heaven")	Matt 14:13–21 // Mark 6:32–44 // Luke 9:10–17: Feeding of the five thousand Matt 15:32–39 // Mark 8:1–10: Feeding of the four thousand Matt 16:5–12 // Mark 8:14–21: Discussion about bread (ἄρτος) Matt 6:11 // Luke 11:3: "Give us this day our daily bread" (ὁ ἄρτος) Matt 26:26 // Mark 14:22 // Luke 22:19: Jesus takes bread (ἄρτος), "This is my body, which is given for you"
8:12, 9:5: Ἐγώ εἰμι τὸ φῶς τοῦ κόσμου ("I am the light of the world")	Matt 5:14: Ὑμεῖς ἐστε τὸ φῶς τοῦ κόσμου ("You are the light of the world")

---

17. Paul Anderson similarly draws attention to the parallels between the language and imagery of the "I am" sayings in John and related language in the Synoptics. See "The Origin and Development of the Johannine *Egō Eimi* Sayings in Cognitive-Critical Perspective," *JSHJ* 9 (2011): 139–206. While I am arguing that John adapts the Synoptic imagery, Anderson argues that "in bioptic perspective, these theologically rich metaphors can be clearly identified as central components of Jesus' teaching about his mission and the character of God's working in the world" (195–96).

CHAPTER 7

"I AM" SAYING IN JOHN	SYNOPTIC IMAGERY
10:7: ἐγώ εἰμι ἡ θύρα τῶν προβάτων ("I am the door for the sheep") 10:9: ἐγώ εἰμι ἡ θύρα ("I am the door") 10:11, 14: Ἐγώ εἰμι ὁ ποιμήν ὁ καλός ("I am the good shepherd")	Luke 13:24: "Strive to enter through the narrow door [θύρα]"; cf. Matt 7:13–14 Matt 18:10–14 // Luke 15:3–7: Parable of the lost sheep Matt 26:31 // Mark 14:27: "Strike the shepherd (ὁ ποιμήν) and the sheep will be scattered"
11:25: Ἐγώ εἰμι ἡ ἀνάστασις καὶ ἡ ζωή ("I am the resurrection and the life")	Matt 9:18–26 // Mark 5:21–43 // Luke 8:40–56: Jairus's daughter Luke 7:11–17: Widow of Nain's son Matt 11:5 // Luke 7:22: "The dead are raised" Mark 8:31–33; 9:30–32; 10:32–34 (and parallels): Prophecy of resurrection Luke 16:19–31: Rich man and Lazarus Matt 22:23–33 // Mark 12:18–27 // Luke 20:27–40: Question about resurrection (ἀνάστασις) Matt 25:31–46: Sheep and the goats Matt 28; Mark 16; Luke 24: Jesus's resurrection
14:6: Ἐγώ εἰμι ἡ ὁδός καὶ ἡ ἀλήθεια καὶ ἡ ζωή ("I am the way, and the truth, and the life")	Mark 1:3 (and parallels): "Prepare the way [ἡ ὁδός] of the Lord" Mark 8:27; 9:33–34; 10:17, 32, 46, 52: "the way" (ἡ ὁδός) = the way of the cross Matt 7:13–14: "Enter through the narrow gate; for the gate is wide and the way [ἡ ὁδός] is easy that leads to destruction, and there are many who take it. For the gate is narrow and the way [ὁδός] is hard that leads to life [ζωή], and there are few who find it" Luke 10:25–37; 24:13–35: Parable and story "on the way [ὁδός]" Luke 10:31; 12:58; 19:36; 24:32, 35: "on the way" (ἐν τῇ ὁδῷ)

John's Christological Transformation of the Synoptics

"I AM" SAYING IN JOHN	SYNOPTIC IMAGERY
15:1: Ἐγώ εἰμι ἡ ἄμπελος ἡ ἀληθινή, καὶ ὁ πατήρ μου ὁ γεωργός ἐστιν ("I am the true vine, and my Father is the vinegrower") 15:5: ἐγώ εἰμι ἡ ἄμπελος, ὑμεῖς τὰ κλήματα ("I am the vine; you are the branches")	Matt 26:29: "I will never again drink of this fruit of the vine [ἡ ἄμπελος] until that day when I drink it new with you in the kingdom of my Father [ὁ πατήρ μου]; cf. Mark 14:25 // Luke 22:18 Matt 21:33–46 // Mark 12:1–12 // Luke 20:9–19: Parable of the tenants in the vineyard Matt 20:1–16: Parable of the laborers in the vineyard Matt 21:28–32: Parable of the two sons Luke 13:6–9: Parable of the barren fig tree

"I Am the Bread of Life" (John 6:35, 41, 48, 51)

The first "I am" saying in John takes "bread" as its key image, and it is an image that reverberates throughout the Synoptic Gospels. The context in which it is found in John (John 6:25–60) is just after the feeding of the five thousand (John 6:1–15), which is the one miracle story that John shares with all three Synoptics (Matt 14:13–21 // Mark 6:32–44 // Luke 9:10–17), and bread plays the key part in the story. This is, of course, literal bread being eaten by the multitudes, as in the subsequent feeding of the four thousand (Matt 15:32–39 // Mark 8:1–10), but it soon develops into a symbol of something greater, the full meaning of which is hidden from the disciples (Matt 16:5–12 // Mark 8:14–21).

As well as in this context, there are several Synoptic references to bread that associate it with Jesus. "Give us today our daily bread" is a key petition in Matthew's and Luke's Lord's Prayer (Matt 6:11 // Luke 11:3),[18] and the image is developed in Luke's parable of the friend at midnight who comes asking for bread (Luke 11:5–8).

In the Last Supper, in all three Synoptics, Jesus makes it clear that he is the bread that future believers will eat in his memory. After taking the bread, blessing it, and breaking it, Jesus says, "Take, this is my body" (Matt 26:26 // Mark 14:22 // Luke 22:19). For all the debates across Christian history about how to interpret this, one point is certain, that the Synoptic Jesus is identifying himself with the

---

18. See also the "bread" and stone temptation in Matt 4:3–4 // Luke 4:3–4, and the child who asks for "bread" in Matt 7:9.

CHAPTER 7

bread in a context that is all about salvation. So when John's Jesus says, "I am the bread of life," in a context that goes on to reflect on salvation, this is not a long way from the Synoptic statements, all the more given the fact that John's discourse takes a decidedly eucharistic turn (John 6:50–58). Moreover, in Luke, it is the breaking of bread in the story of the road to Emmaus (Luke 24:13–35) that leads to the two disciples recognizing Jesus (Luke 24:30–31, 35).

"I Am the Light of the World" (John 8:12; 9:5)

MATT 5:14	JOHN 8:12; CF. 9:5
Ὑμεῖς ἐστε <u>τὸ φῶς τοῦ κόσμου</u>.	Ἐγώ εἰμι <u>τὸ φῶς τοῦ κόσμου</u>.
"You are <u>the light of the world</u>."	"I am <u>the light of the world</u>."

In Matthew's Sermon on the Mount, Jesus tells the disciples that they are "the salt of the earth" (Ὑμεῖς ἐστε τὸ ἅλας τῆς γῆς, Matt 5:13) and "the light of the world" (Ὑμεῖς ἐστε τὸ φῶς τοῦ κόσμου, Matt 5:14). Now, in John, Jesus characterizes himself in exactly the same way, as "the light of the world." It is a striking parallel. Could Matthew and John both have found their way to the same fascinating image? Perhaps. But this expression, "the light of the world," is found in only these two contexts in the New Testament. Moreover, according to TLG, these are the first two occurrences of this phrase in all extant Greek literature to this point.

"I Am the Door" (John 10:7, 9) and "I Am the Good Shepherd" (John 10:11, 14)

Although John 10:1–21 is usually characterized as the good shepherd discourse, the first "I am" saying in the passage makes Jesus "the door for the sheep" (ἐγώ εἰμι ἡ θύρα τῶν προβάτων, 10:7), and then, more tersely "the door" (ἐγώ εἰμι ἡ θύρα, 10:9). As Andrew Lincoln says, "The 'I Am' statement can be seen as a Johannine Christological application, in the context of pastoral imagery, of the Synoptic saying of Jesus about the narrow gate that leads to life (Matt 7:13–14) or salvation (Luke 13:23–25)."[19] What makes the link with the Synoptics particularly telling is the use of the word θύρα ("door"), four times in the passage (John 10:1, 2, 7, 9), echoing the use of the word in Luke 13:24 (contrast Matt 7:13–14, πύλης, "gate").

---

19. Andrew Lincoln, *The Gospel According to St. John*, BNTC (London: Continuum, 2005), 296.

The imagery is a little awkward, and this may come from adopting the word from Luke.

The discourse eventually morphs more happily into Jesus as the "good shepherd" (Ἐγώ εἰμι ὁ ποιμὴν ὁ καλός, John 10:11, 14), an image that evokes not only multiple Old Testament passages in which leaders, and especially David, are described as shepherds, but also the Synoptic Gospels. Shepherd and sheep imagery is found regularly in the Synoptics, and it is pretty obvious that the shepherd in these contexts evokes the divine, and especially Jesus. The parable of the lost sheep (Matt 18:10–14 // Luke 15:3–7) depicts the shepherd going in search for the one sheep that has departed in an allegory that aligns the shepherd with Jesus, but the image features in several other contexts and is a particular favorite of Matthew. Matthew 2:6 quotes Mic 5:4, which prophesies a ruler "who will shepherd [ποιμαίνω] my people Israel," and the parable of the sheep and the goats (Matt 25:31–46), which is unique to Matthew, has Jesus allegorized as "a shepherd" (ποιμήν) who "separates the sheep from the goats" (Matt 25:32). But Mark also uses the image twice. In Mark 6:34, just before the feeding of the five thousand, Jesus has compassion for the crowd because they are like "sheep without a shepherd" (ὡς πρόβατα μὴ ἔχοντα ποιμένα), paralleled in a different context in Matthew (Matt 9:36). And at the Last Supper, when predicting Peter's denial, Jesus quotes Zech 13:7, "Strike the shepherd [ποιμήν], and the sheep will be scattered" (Mark 14:27 // Matt 26:31).

"I Am the Resurrection and the Life" (John 11:25)

The fourth (or fifth) of the "I am" sayings, Ἐγώ εἰμι ἡ ἀνάστασις καὶ ἡ ζωή ("I am the resurrection and the life," John 11:25), is perhaps the least surprising. "Resurrection" and "life" are core vocabulary in John's Gospel, and the saying occurs just before the climactic moments in this story, Martha's confession (John 11:27), and Lazarus's resurrection (John 11:38–44). The terminology is also key in the Synoptics, which have resurrection stories, Jairus's daughter in all three (Matt 9:18–26 // Mark 5:21–43 // Luke 8:40–56), the widow of Nain's son in Luke (Luke 7:11–17), and further reports that "the dead are raised" (Matt 11:5 // Luke 7:22). All three have Jesus announcing that "he is not the God of the dead but of the living" (Matt 22:32 // Mark 12:27 // Luke 20:38), in a story all about the nature of the resurrection (Matt 22:23–33 // Mark 12:18–27 // Luke 20:27–40). And the resurrection of Jesus is, of course, the climactic event in the Synoptics, prophesied multiple times (Matt 16:21–23 // Mark 8:31–33 // Luke 9:22; Matt 17:22–23 // Mark 9:30–32 // Luke 9:43–45; Matt 20:17–19; Matt 10:32–34 // Luke 18:31–34), and narrated in varying degrees of detail (Matt 28; Mark 16; Luke 24).

CHAPTER 7

It might be said that these are mainly stories of actual, physical resurrection rather than resurrection and life imagery, so it is worth noting that resurrection also appears in parable material like Matthew's sheep and the goats (Matt 25:31–46), which ends with "the righteous" being welcomed "into eternal life" (εἰς ζωὴν αἰώνιον, Matt 25:46), and Luke's rich man and Lazarus (Luke 16:19–31), which ends with the line, "If they do not listen to Moses and the prophets, neither will they be convinced even if someone rises from the dead" (Luke 16:31), which some see as the inspiration for John's Lazarus story, in which this "I am" saying occurs.[20]

"I Am the Way, the Truth, and the Life" (John 14:6)

When Thomas says to Jesus, "Lord, we do not know where you are going. How can we know the way?" (John 14:5), Jesus replies with the fifth (or sixth) of the "I am" sayings, Ἐγώ εἰμι ἡ ὁδὸς καὶ ἡ ἀλήθεια καὶ ἡ ζωή· οὐδεὶς ἔρχεται πρὸς τὸν πατέρα εἰ μὴ δι' ἐμοῦ ("I am the way, and the truth, and the life; no one comes to the Father except through me," 14:6). As in every other case, the imagery is paralleled in the Synoptic Gospels. Although there are uniquely three words in this "I am" saying, "way," "truth," and "life," the key word is the first one, "the way," or "the road" (ὁδός), because the context is all about the road and the journey, and the word comes three times in the passage (14:4, 5, 6).[21] "Way, truth, and life" appears to mean something like "the true, living way." This image is striking because it is a major one in the Synoptic Gospels, so important that it has been seen as central to Mark's theology.[22] From the opening of Mark's Gospel (Mark 1:2–3), with its composite quotation of Exodus, Malachi, and Isaiah, there is an emphasis on Jesus's mission as progress on the way of the Lord, and this is progress toward the passion. The way in the wilderness is the way prophesied in Deutero-Isaiah, but the triumphal procession is paradoxically inverted as the way of the cross. As soon as Jesus turns toward Jerusalem, "the way" features repeatedly in Mark's narration and Jesus's speech, including at key structural moments in the

---

20. See especially Margaret Davies, *Rhetoric and Reference in the Fourth Gospel*, JSNTSup 69 (Sheffield: Sheffield Academic, 1992), 256.

21. On "life" (ζωή), note the usage in Matt 7:14, discussed below. The typically Johannine reference to "truth" comes also in the next "I am" saying, when Jesus says, "I am the true vine" (John 15:1, below).

22. See Joel Marcus, *The Way of the Lord: Christological Exegesis of the Old Testament in the Gospel of Mark* (Louisville: Westminster John Knox, 1992), and Rikki E. Watts, *Isaiah's New Exodus in Mark* (Grand Rapids: Baker, 2000).

narrative.[23] In Mark, the way of the Lord is the way of the passion. The way is prophesied by Isaiah, proclaimed by John, and walked by Jesus.

The feature is also found in Matthew, who uses the word ὁδός twenty times,[24] perhaps most notably in Matt 7:13–14, "Enter through the narrow gate," his version of the saying that in Luke 13:24 uses the "door" language that we saw above. In Matthew, it is a "gate" (πύλης) rather than a door, but the "way" or "road" language is striking: "for the gate is wide and the road [ὁδός] is easy that leads to destruction, and there are many who take it. For the gate is narrow and the road [ὁδός] is hard that leads to life [ζωή], and there are few who find it." As in John 14:6, "the way" (ὁδός) is connected with "life" (ζωή).

The way or road (ὁδός) motif is also huge in Luke's writing, though it is not often realized just how important it is.[25] The early Christian movement is characterized as "the Way" (ἡ ὁδός) on repeated occasions in Acts (Acts 9:2; 19:9, 23; 22:4; 24:14, 22), and he uses a variety of descriptors for the godly path, not only "the Way of the Lord" (Acts 18:25) but also "the Way of God" (Acts 18:26, cf. Matt 22:16 // Mark 12:14 // Luke 20:21) and "the Way of salvation" (Acts 16:17).

The symbolic use of "the way" provides the setting for several iconic Lukan passages, like the good Samaritan (Luke 10:25–37), the road to Emmaus (Luke 24:13–35), and Paul's vision on the Damascus road (Acts 9:17, 27; 26:13), and the narrative as a whole is full of references to "the way." Luke expands Mark's Isaiah quotation, "Prepare the way of the Lord" (Ἑτοιμάσατε τὴν ὁδὸν κυρίου, Mark 1:3; Luke 3:4; paralleled in John 1:23), to make it clear that this leads to "all flesh" seeing "the salvation of God" (Luke 3:5). The gospel goes on to stress the importance of the motif, from Jesus "speaking about his exodus" (ἔλεγον τὴν ἔξοδον αὐτοῦ, Luke 9:31) with Moses and Elijah, to Jesus "going on the way" (ἐν τῇ ὁδῷ, Luke 9:57), after he has set his face to Jerusalem (Luke 9:51). This

---

23. Marcus, *Way of the Lord*, 32, notes that of the usages of ὁδός in Mark's Gospel after 1:2–3, "the most significant are the seven references (8:27; 9:33–34; 10:17, 32, 46, 52—half of the Markan total) clustered in the Gospel's central section, 8:22–10:52, which describes Jesus' journey up to Jerusalem."

24. Figures for ὁδός are 22/16/20/4+20. Of John's four occurrences, three occur in this passage, and the other is in John 1:23, Εὐθύνατε τὴν ὁδὸν Κυρίου ("Make straight the way of the Lord"), parallel to Matt 3:3 // Mark 1:3 // Luke 3:4.

25. I argued in Mark Goodacre, "Re-walking the 'Way of the Lord': Luke's Use of Mark and His Reaction to Matthew," in *Luke's Literary Creativity*, ed. Jesper Tang Nielsen and Mogens Müller, LNTS 550 (London: Bloomsbury, 2016), 26–43, that Luke underlines, adapts, and transforms Mark's "Way of the Lord" motif in his gospel and Acts.

CHAPTER 7

same phrase, "on the way" (ἐν τῇ ὁδῷ), key in Mark's Gospel, is key in Luke too (Luke 10:31; 12:58; 19:36; 24:32, 35).

Much more could be said, and has been said, on this major Synoptic motif, but what is so interesting with respect to the Fourth Gospel is that it finds its way into one of John's "I am" sayings, and in a context that draws out the full sense that this is about a pathway to salvation. Given the different way that the Fourth Gospel structures Jesus's visits to Jerusalem, the kind of big road trip that we see in the Synoptics was clearly not an option, yet it seems that the Fourth Evangelist finds this way to incorporate the motif, in what became his most famous "I am" saying.

"I Am the True Vine" (John 15:1) and "I Am the Vine" (John 15:5)

The final "I am" saying comes in 15:1: Ἐγώ εἰμι ἡ ἄμπελος ἡ ἀληθινή, καὶ ὁ πατήρ μου ὁ γεωργός ἐστιν, "I am the true vine, and my Father is the vinegrower," repeated in a slightly different form a few verses later, 15:5: ἐγώ εἰμι ἡ ἄμπελος, ὑμεῖς τὰ κλήματα, "I am the vine; you are the branches." As with every other "I am" saying, the imagery is familiar from the Synoptics, all three of which use this classic symbol. The most famous example of vineyard imagery is the parable of the tenants in the vineyard (Matt 21:33–46 // Mark 12:1–12 // Luke 20:9–19), which itself quotes Isa 5, most clearly in Matthew's and Mark's versions, but Matthew's Gospel has two further parables that take in a vineyard setting, Matt 20:1–16, the parable of the laborers in the vineyard, and Matt 21:28–32, the parable of the two sons. Luke has one too, Luke 13:6–9, the parable of the barren fig tree.

Nevertheless, perhaps the most striking parallel to John's "I am the true vine" occurs in what is the same context in the Synoptics, the evening of Jesus's Last Supper with his disciples. The saying comes in all three Synoptics:

MATT 26:29	MARK 14:25	LUKE 22:18
λέγω δὲ ὑμῖν, οὐ μὴ πίω ἀπ' ἄρτι ἐκ τούτου τοῦ γενήματος <u>τῆς ἀμπέλου</u> ἕως τῆς ἡμέρας ἐκείνης ὅταν αὐτὸ πίνω μεθ' ὑμῶν καινὸν ἐν τῇ βασιλείᾳ <u>τοῦ πατρός μου</u>.	ἀμὴν λέγω ὑμῖν ὅτι οὐκέτι οὐ μὴ πίω ἐκ τοῦ γενήματος <u>τῆς ἀμπέλου</u> ἕως τῆς ἡμέρας ἐκείνης ὅταν αὐτὸ πίνω καινὸν ἐν τῇ βασιλείᾳ τοῦ θεοῦ.	λέγω γὰρ ὑμῖν, οὐ μὴ πίω ἀπὸ τοῦ νῦν ἀπὸ τοῦ γενήματος <u>τῆς ἀμπέλου</u> ἕως οὗ ἡ βασιλεία τοῦ θεοῦ ἔλθῃ.

MATT 26:29	MARK 14:25	LUKE 22:18
"And[26] I tell you, I will not drink from now[27] of this fruit of <u>the vine</u> until that day when I drink it new with you in the kingdom of <u>my Father</u>."[28]	"Amen[29] I tell you that[30] I will not any longer[31] drink of the fruit of <u>the vine</u> until that day when I drink it new in the kingdom of God."	"For I tell you,[32] I will not drink from now on of the fruit of <u>the vine</u> until the kingdom of God comes."

Alongside John 15, these are the only references to "the vine" (ἡ ἄμπελος) in the Gospels, so it is certainly worth reflecting on the fact that it occurs in the same setting in all four, against the background of Jesus offering wine to his disciples, perhaps another element that John is here presupposing from the Synoptic narratives (see further above, chapter 4). Just as Jesus had said, "This is my body," when he offers them bread, providing a pathway to "I am the bread of life" in John, so too here, having offered them the cup, Jesus says, "This is my blood" (Matt 26:28 // Mark 14:24; cf. Luke 22:17, 20), providing a pathway to "I am the true vine" in John. Moreover, like John, Matthew here has a reference to "my Father" in the phrase "in the kingdom of my Father" (ἐν τῇ βασιλείᾳ τοῦ πατρός μου, Matt 26:29).

John's secondary nature may be apparent here when one reflects on the author's use of the image. In the Synoptics, "the vineyard" provides a backdrop to the action, thus in the allegory Jesus is the "beloved son" (Mark 12:6), "my son" (Matt 21:37), "my beloved son" (Luke 20:13), who is sent by the landowner. And at the Last Supper, Jesus and the disciples drink from "the fruit of the vine" (Matt 26:29 // Mark 14:25 // Luke 22:18) when Jesus offers them the cup, which is the blood of the covenant, poured out for many. This is coherent. But John's use of the image, where Jesus himself becomes the "true vine," introduces some anomalies. If "my Father is the vinegrower," the logic of the image is that the Father also planted the vine, which is somewhat at odds with John's Christology elsewhere, the word made flesh (John 1:14), who ex-

---

26. NRSVue omits "And."
27. NRSVue, "I will never again drink."
28. NRSVue, "my Father's," adjusted here to draw attention to "my Father" in John 15:1.
29. NRSVue, "Truly."
30. NRSVue omits "that," creating an agreement with Luke (see note 32 below).
31. NRSVue, "never again."
32. NRSVue, "I tell you that," which creates an agreement with Mark against Matthew, whereas this is actually an agreement with Matthew against Mark.

CHAPTER 7

isted before Abraham (John 8:58). We should, of course, never push analogies too far, but this one is much less congenial to Johannine Christology in the round, and it may be because, as in all of the "I am" sayings, John is drawing on Synoptic imagery.

Why Synoptic Influence?

What this survey has shown is that the imagery deployed in all of John's "I am" sayings is very much at home in the Synoptic Gospels, so much so that it could have been derived from them. Some will say, of course, that the imagery comes not from the Synoptics but from our old friend, the pool of oral tradition. On this model, John's use of Synoptic imagery is simply the mutual usage of imagery picked up independently from oral tradition. It might also be said that a lot of the imagery comes from the Hebrew Bible, an agreed mutual source of the Synoptics and John, where it does not take long to find bread, shepherds, and vines.

To press this point, though, would be to miss several features of the "I am" sayings that suggest Synoptic influence. "The light of the world" (τὸ φῶς τοῦ κόσμου, Matt 5:14; John 8:12; 9:5) is not found in the Old Testament, nor is it found in any extant literature to this point. Matthew and John share a unique new expression. In this context, John's "I am the light of the world" invites us to take seriously the possible source in Matthew's "You are the light of the world."

Moreover, if "shepherd" imagery in John 10 seems very natural in the light of its frequent use in the Old Testament, the imagery of "a door" in the same context (θύρα, Luke 13:24; John 10:7, 9) seems less natural. There is also the question of context. John's "I am the bread of life" (John 6:35, 48) and "I am the bread that came down from heaven" (John 6:41; cf. 6:51) are featured just after the iconic story about the multiplication of the loaves, which appears in all four canonical Gospels (Matt 14:13–21 // Mark 6:32–44 // Luke 9:10–17 // John 6:1–15), just as the only references in all four gospels to the "vine" (ἄμπελος) appear in the eucharistic setting of the night before Jesus's crucifixion (Matt 26:29 // Mark 14:25 // Luke 22:18). These things could, of course, be coincidences, but appeals to coincidence become increasingly less convincing the more often they are made.

However, the most striking use of imagery that is also found in the Synoptics has to be in John 14:6, "I am the way, the truth, and the life." The image of "the way" has not, to this point in the narrative, been a major one in John. Outside of John 14, the imagery of "the way" occurs only in John in 1:23 ("Make straight the way of the Lord"), a quotation from Isa 40:1, which is itself prominent in the Synoptics in exactly the same context (Matt 3:3 // Mark 1:3 // Luke 3:4, "Prepare the way of the Lord"). In the Synoptics, the motif of "the way" is dominant, and it is arguably the key redactional motif not only in Mark but also in Luke. Furthermore, Matthew has a saying in which the Christian life is explicitly linked to "the way" that leads to "life" (Matt 7:13–14).

The point about John's commonalities with Synoptic imagery is a difficult one to grasp because of our familiarity with the Synoptics and John. The familiarity makes the imagery feel normative and inevitable—bread, light, shepherd, resurrection, road, and vine—especially when these images also have Old Testament roots. Yet if John were independent of the Synoptics, surely we might have expected some other, non-Synoptic images. Did that vast pool of oral tradition feature only images that also appear in the Synoptics? It is surprising, on the model of John's independence, that the tradition pool featured only Synoptic imagery. John's Jesus is like the Synoptic Jesus. He talks about "the light of the world," he makes himself a shepherd, he finds "the way" central to his mission, and he speaks about "the bread of life" in the context of the feeding of the five thousand, and "the vine" while he is sitting at the Last Supper with his disciples.

If John were independent of the Synoptics, we might have expected "I am" sayings that did not appear to share the narrow range of Synoptic imagery. Of course, we do not have access to the oral tradition, but we do have Paul, and in his version of the institution of the Eucharist he does not use the image of "the vine" that is common to the Synoptics and John. He repeatedly uses the term "the cup" (1 Cor 11:25, 26, 27, 28) but never "the vine." Furthermore, it does not take a lot of imagination to realize that there are hundreds of other images that John's Jesus could have used. He does not say, "I am a dyer, and you are the cloth," in spite of the fact that the "dyer" imagery is used for God and for Jesus in the Gospel of Philip (Gos. Phil. 61, 63). And he does not say "I am the lion, and they are the prey," in spite of the fact that the "lion" image appears in the Gospel of Thomas (Gos. Thom. 7). Nor does he say, "I am the potter, and you are the clay," an image that could have been straightforwardly adapted from Jer 18. Every Johannine "I am" saying utilizes imagery that we also find in the Synoptics, and this seems important.

CHAPTER 7

"I Am"

For readers of the Synoptics, the imagery in John's "I am" sayings is familiar. Jesus is the bread of life, the door, the good shepherd, the resurrection and the life, the way, the truth and the life, and the vine—all of these images are very much at home in the Synoptics. Yet there is a difficulty that should be addressed. It might be argued that even if the imagery in these "I am" sayings shows a surprising confluence with similar Synoptic imagery, this still does not address the fundamental difference between the Christology of the Synoptics and John, which is that John is so much more direct and unequivocal. This is the question of the "I am" characterization itself. Surely this does not come from the Synoptics? Here, at last, there must be some clear blue water between the lower Christology of the Synoptics and the higher Christology of John.

Things are not so straightforward. As so often, the firewall between the Synoptics and John disappears when we take a closer look. It is true that the Synoptics do not feature "I am" language with predicates, like "I am the door," but Jesus does say "I am" without further qualification in two key contexts. One occurs at the christological climax of Mark's Gospel, when Jesus's confession of his identity before the high priest leads directly to his death:

> Mark 14:61b–62: Again the high priest asked him, "Are you the Messiah, the Son of the Blessed One?" Jesus said, "*I am* ['Εγώ εἰμι], and 'you will see the Son of Man seated at the right hand of the Power' and 'coming with the clouds of heaven.'"

The confession features all three key elements of Mark's Christology, Jesus as Messiah, Son of God, and Son of Man, but in a saying that begins with "I am." John does not have a precise parallel to Mark's trial before the high priest (see above, pp. 86–88), but in the adjacent passage, the arrest, Jesus boldly says "I am" ('Εγώ εἰμι, 18:5, 6, 8), often translated "I am he," and the reaction of those who came to arrest him, that of stepping back and falling to the ground (John 18:6), is similar to the high priest's reaction in Mark, who tears his clothes and proclaims "blasphemy" (Mark 14:63–64).

The other occurrence of "I am" in Mark is even more interesting because it comes in exactly the same context in John. Back in chapter 1 (p. 8), we saw how close John is to Mark in the walking on the sea (Matt 14:22–33 // Mark 6:53–56 // John 6:22–25). Let us take a look at this parallel again, and this time add Matthew too. This is one of those places where John is Synoptic. John is closer to Matthew and Mark than is Luke, in which the passage does not appear.

John's Christological Transformation of the Synoptics

MATT 14:26–27	MARK 6:49–50	JOHN 6:19–20
οἱ δὲ μαθηταὶ ἰδόντες αὐτὸν <u>ἐπὶ τῆς θαλάσσης περιπατοῦντα</u> ἐταράχθησαν λέγοντες ὅτι Φάντασμά ἐστιν, καὶ ἀπὸ τοῦ <u>φόβου</u> ἔκραξαν.	οἱ δὲ ἰδόντες αὐτὸν <u>ἐπὶ τῆς θαλάσσης περιπατοῦντα</u> ἔδοξαν ὅτι φάντασμά ἐστιν καὶ ἀνέκραξαν, πάντες γὰρ αὐτὸν εἶδον καὶ ἐταράχθησαν.	ἐληλακότες οὖν ὡς σταδίους εἴκοσι πέντε ἢ τριάκοντα θεωροῦσιν τὸν Ἰησοῦν <u>περιπατοῦντα ἐπὶ τῆς θαλάσσης</u> καὶ ἐγγὺς τοῦ πλοίου γινόμενον, καὶ <u>ἐφοβήθησαν</u>.
εὐθὺς <u>δὲ</u> ἐλάλησεν αὐτοῖς ὁ Ἰησοῦς λέγων· Θαρσεῖτε, <u>ἐγώ εἰμι· μὴ φοβεῖσθε</u>.	<u>ὁ δὲ</u> εὐθὺς ἐλάλησεν μετ' αὐτῶν, καὶ <u>λέγει αὐτοῖς</u>· Θαρσεῖτε, <u>ἐγώ εἰμι, μὴ φοβεῖσθε</u>.	<u>ὁ δὲ</u> <u>λέγει αὐτοῖς</u>· <u>ἐγώ εἰμι· μὴ φοβεῖσθε</u>.
But when the disciples saw him <u>walking on the sea</u>, they were terrified, saying,	But when they saw him <u>walking on the sea</u>, they thought	When they had rowed about three or four miles, they saw Jesus <u>walking on the sea</u> and coming near the boat,
"It is a ghost!" And they cried out in <u>fear</u>.	it was a ghost and cried out, for they all saw him and were terrified.	and they had <u>fear</u>.[33]
<u>But</u> immediately Jesus spoke to them and said, "Take heart, <u>I am</u>,[34] <u>do not fear!</u>"[35]	<u>But</u> immediately he spoke with them, and <u>he says to them</u>:[36] "Take heart, <u>I am, do not fear!</u>"	<u>But</u> <u>he says to them</u>: "<u>I am, do not fear!</u>"

    The striking christological parallel can get buried because most English versions translate ἐγώ εἰμι as "It is I" and not "I am." The NRSVue adds a note that the Greek here is "I am," but only in John and not in Matthew or Mark. So here,

---

33. NRSVue, "were terrified," adjusted here to draw attention to the parallel with Matthew.
34. NRSVue, "it is I," also in Mark 14:50 and John 6:20.
35. NRSVue, "do not be afraid," also in Mark 14:50 and John 6:20.
36. NRSVue, "and said," adjusted here to draw attention to the parallel with John.

CHAPTER 7

at exactly the same point as in Matthew and Mark, and in the same wording, we have Jesus making the pronouncement, "I am."

John's first "I am" saying occurs just a few verses later, "I am the bread of life" (John 6:35). This is unlikely to be a coincidence. I would like to suggest that John adopts and adapts the walking on the sea from Matthew and Mark, in which Jesus says, "I am," as a means of introducing his new usage of "I am" with the predicate. Readers of the Synoptics have been prepared for John's "I am" sayings.

This process of providing material that is familiar to readers of the Synoptics before introducing something fresh is found elsewhere in John. The concept of "eternal life" (αἰώνιος ζωή) is a famous feature of his gospel, yet just before the first occurrence of the phrase, in John 3:15, the author twice uses terminology that is much more familiar to readers of the Synoptics, "the kingdom of God" (βασιλεία τοῦ θεοῦ), when Jesus tells Nicodemus that he needs to be "born from above" if he is "to see the kingdom of God" (John 3:3) or "to enter into the kingdom of God" (John 3:5). These are the only times that the "kingdom of God" features in John. Once "eternal life" has been introduced, just a few verses later, this becomes staple language in John, occurring seventeen times (John 3:15, 16, 36; 4:14, 36; 5:24, 39; 6:27, 40, 47, 54, 68; 10:28; 12:25, 50; 17:2, 3). Something similar happens with the Johannine language of "the Father" and "the Son," and we will explore this next.

"The Father" and "the Son"

One of the reasons that John's Christology sounds so distinctive is that the gospel speaks repeatedly of "the Father" and "the Son" in an absolute sense, whereas in the Synoptics, "Father" language is usually qualified, in phrases like "my heavenly Father," or "your Father who is in heaven." As with "eternal life," however, the absolute use occurs only after the identity of the Son has been established. Jesus's identity as "a father's only son" (John 1:14) and "God the only Son" (John 1:18) is clear from the prologue, and he is called "Son of God" by John the Baptist (1:34) and Nathanael (1:49), but the absolute language of "the Son" and "the Father" is established only after the iconic statement that "God gave his only Son" (τὸν υἱὸν τὸν μονογενῆ ἔδωκεν) in John 3:16. The next verse (John 3:17) is the first to use "the Son" without qualification, "God did not send the Son into the world to condemn the world" (οὐ γὰρ ἀπέστειλεν ὁ θεὸς τὸν υἱὸν εἰς τὸν κόσμον ἵνα κρίνῃ τὸν κόσμον). After this, the "Father" and "Son" language is pervasive.

Nevertheless, even the absolute use of "the Father" and "the Son" has its roots in the Synoptics, in a passage that sounds remarkably Johannine. Here is the relevant passage in full:

MATT 11:25-27	LUKE 10:21-22
Ἐν ἐκείνῳ τῷ καιρῷ ἀποκριθεὶς ὁ Ἰησοῦς εἶπεν· Ἐξομολογοῦμαί σοι, πάτερ κύριε τοῦ οὐρανοῦ καὶ τῆς γῆς, ὅτι ἔκρυψας ταῦτα ἀπὸ σοφῶν καὶ συνετῶν, καὶ ἀπεκάλυψας αὐτὰ νηπίοις· ναί, ὁ πατήρ, ὅτι οὕτως εὐδοκία ἐγένετο ἔμπροσθέν σου. Πάντα μοι παρεδόθη ὑπὸ τοῦ πατρός μου, καὶ οὐδεὶς ἐπιγινώσκει τὸν υἱὸν εἰ μὴ ὁ πατήρ, οὐδὲ τὸν πατέρα τις ἐπιγινώσκει εἰ μὴ ὁ υἱὸς καὶ ᾧ ἐὰν βούληται ὁ υἱὸς ἀποκαλύψαι.	Ἐν αὐτῇ τῇ ὥρᾳ ἠγαλλιάσατο τῷ πνεύματι τῷ ἁγίῳ καὶ εἶπεν· Ἐξομολογοῦμαί σοι, πάτερ κύριε τοῦ οὐρανοῦ καὶ τῆς γῆς, ὅτι ἀπέκρυψας ταῦτα ἀπὸ σοφῶν καὶ συνετῶν, καὶ ἀπεκάλυψας αὐτὰ νηπίοις· ναί, ὁ πατήρ, ὅτι οὕτως εὐδοκία ἐγένετο ἔμπροσθέν σου. Πάντα μοι παρεδόθη ὑπὸ τοῦ πατρός μου, καὶ οὐδεὶς γινώσκει τίς ἐστιν ὁ υἱὸς εἰ μὴ ὁ πατήρ, καὶ τίς ἐστιν ὁ πατὴρ εἰ μὴ ὁ υἱὸς καὶ ᾧ ἐὰν βούληται ὁ υἱὸς ἀποκαλύψαι.
At that time Jesus said, "I thank you, Father, Lord of heaven and earth, because you have hidden these things from the wise and the intelligent and have revealed them to infants; yes, Father, for such was your gracious will. All things have been handed over to me by my Father; and no one knows the Son except the Father, and no one knows the Father except the Son and anyone to whom the Son chooses to reveal him."	At that same hour Jesus rejoiced in the Holy Spirit and said, "I thank you, Father, Lord of heaven and earth, because you have hidden these things from the wise and the intelligent and have revealed them to infants; yes, Father, for such was your gracious will. All things have been handed over to me by my Father; and no one knows who the Son is except the Father, or who the Father is except the Son and anyone to whom the Son chooses to reveal him."

The passage has such a clear Johannine ring that it has been characterized as a "bolt out of the Johannine blue," or "the Johannine thunderbolt." It is worth pausing to reflect on how it could be that something that sounds so Johannine could appear in the Synoptics, and how this impacts the thesis of this book. Although this "Johannine thunderbolt" is frequently treated as a bizarre Johannine anomaly that invades the normative Synoptic Christology, I would like to suggest that we should invert this perspective. It is more plausible to see the author of the Fourth Gospel being inspired by this saying and developing it in his own Christology rather than seeing it as some kind of alien entity in Matthew and Luke. Let's take a closer look.

CHAPTER 7

The "Johannine Thunderbolt"

It is relatively rare for the image of the "Johannine thunderbolt" to be credited, but its origin appears to have been in the work of Karl von Hase in 1876, where it is not a "thunderbolt" but an "Aerolith," a meteorite, that has fallen from the Johannine sky.[37] The image is memorable and appealing, but the jarring nature of what it is attempting to illustrate ought to alert us to the possibility that all is not well. A bolt out of the blue is something alien, unexpected, and disruptive. But this is not a good way of characterizing Matt 11:27 // Luke 10:22, and the violence of the imagery signals a problem with our perspective.

One of the difficulties here relates to the Q hypothesis. The passage is attributed to Q because of the extraordinarily close agreement here between Matthew and Luke. This is arguably the most impressive piece of agreement between Matthew and Luke anywhere in the Synoptic tradition. The twenty-seven-word verbatim string is the longest anywhere in the double tradition.[38] In another context, I have argued that close verbatim agreement like this is far more likely to occur when one writer is copying directly from a source, as when Luke is copying from Matthew. It is rare to find such close agreement where two writers are copying from a third source, as when Matthew and Luke are both working from Mark. In other words, this kind of agreement is simply too good to be Q.

On the two-source theory, the effect of the close verbatim agreement is to project this content unambiguously onto Q. Since, on this theory, Matthew and Luke are only minimally intervening here in the wording of Q, the question of the origins and composition of the passage is a question to ask of Q rather than of Matthew. If, however, the first known literary occurrence of this passage is not in Q but in Matthew, our perspective on the problem shifts. It is no longer an issue that can be usefully explored by discussing its place in the composition of the sayings gospel. Instead, it invites us to ask about its genesis in Matthew.

Given the attribution of the "Johannine thunderbolt" to Q, the Matthean nature of its language and theology is often overlooked. Matthew 11:27 // Luke 10:22 begins with the statement that "all things have been given to me by my Father." Matthew's

---

37. Karl von Hase, *Geschichte Jesu, nach akademischen Vorlesungen* (Leipzig: Breitkopf & Härtel, 1876), 422 [527 in second edition of 1891], "Die einzige synoptische Stelle, darnach 'Niemand den Sohn erkennt ausser der Vater, und Niemand den Vater erkennt ausser der Sohn und wem irgend der Sohn es offenbaren wolle,' macht den Eindruck wie ein Aerolith aus dem johanneischen Himmel gefallen, allenfalls auch aus dem Gesichtskreise des Paulus." The fact that von Hase also links the thought with Paul is seldom remarked upon in the literature.

38. Mark Goodacre, "Too Good to Be Q: High Verbatim Agreement in the Double Tradition," in *Marcan Priority Without Q: Explorations in the Farrer Hypothesis*, ed. John C. Poirier and Jeffrey Peterson, LNTS 455 (London: T&T Clark, 2015), 82–100, at 85.

Jesus speaks with authority, an authority that he derives from the Father. In the Great Commission, he will similarly announce that "all authority in heaven and on earth has been given to me" (Matt 28:19). The parallels with this passage are clear:

MATT 11:25, 27	MATT 28:19
Ἐξομολογοῦμαί σοι, πάτερ κύριε τοῦ οὐρανοῦ καὶ τῆς γῆς. . . . Πάντα μοι παρεδόθη ὑπὸ τοῦ πατρός μου.	Ἐδόθη μοι πᾶσα ἐξουσία ἐν οὐρανῷ καὶ ἐπὶ τῆς γῆς.
I thank you, Father, Lord of heaven and earth. . . . All things have been handed over to me by my Father.	All authority in heaven and on earth has been given to me.

Like the Markan Jesus (Mark 1:27), Matthew's Jesus teaches with authority (Matt 7:29, ἦν γὰρ διδάσκων αὐτοὺς ὡς ἐξουσίαν ἔχων), but in Matthew the Son's authority is explicitly derived from his Father. The concluding temptation in Matthew focuses on a challenge to this most important tenet—the devil will give "all things" to this "Son of God" if he worships him (Ταῦτά σοι πάντα δώσω, ἐὰν πεσὼν προσκυνήσῃς μοι, Matt 4:9; cf. Luke 4:6). The implication in Matthew is that Jesus triumphs in this temptation and is instead given all these things by his Father.

The saying continues with the statement that "no one knows the Son except the Father, and no one knows the Father except the Son and those to whom the Son chooses to reveal him" (Matt 11:27). This kind of construction is found elsewhere in Matthew. Michael Goulder calls it a "repetitive converse logion":[39]

Matt 5:19: "Therefore, whoever breaks one of the least of these commandments, and teaches others to do the same, will be called least in the kingdom of heaven; but whoever does them and teaches them will be called great in the kingdom of heaven."

Matt 6:14–15: "For if you forgive others their trespasses, your heavenly Father will also forgive you; but if you do not forgive others, neither will your Father forgive your trespasses."

Matt 16:19: "Whatever you bind on earth will be bound in heaven, and whatever you loose on earth will be loosed in heaven."

Moreover, as we saw above, Son of God Christology is central to Matthew. While Mark sees Jesus as God's Son (Mark 1:11; 9:7; 12:6; 15:39), Matthew underlines and expands this element in his source, retaining all of Mark's references to the

---

39. Michael D. Goulder, *Midrash and Lection in Matthew* (London: SPCK, 1974), 298.

"Son" (Matt 3:17; 17:5; 21:37; 27:54) but adding several more (Matt 4:1–11, "If you are God's Son. . . ."; 14:33 R, "And those in the boat worshiped him, saying, 'Truly you are the Son of God'"; 16:16 R, "You are the Messiah, the Son of the Living God").

Similarly, the language of God as "Father" is Matthean. On one occasion Mark's Jesus speaks of "your Father in heaven" (Mark 11:25) and on another Jesus prays "Abba, Father" (Mark 14:36), but in Matthew, "Father" language is frequent and emphatic. Where Mark speaks of "the will of God" (Mark 3:35), Matthew speaks of "the will of my Father in heaven" (Matt 12:50). "Your heavenly Father," "my heavenly Father," "our Father who is in heaven"—all of these are mainstays of Matthean redaction.[40] Of the four gospels, it is Matthew and John who most frequently use "my Father" language, fourteen times and twenty-five times, respectively.[41] The phrase never comes in Mark, and it comes only four times in Luke (Luke 2:49; 10:22; 22:29; 24:49),[42] one of which is the parallel with the Matthean passage under discussion (Matt 11:27 // Luke 10:22).

The curiosity of this passage, though, and the element that most clearly gives it its Johannine ring is the absolute use of "the Father" and "the Son" rather than "my Father," which is much more common in Matthew, and "my Son." The Father-Son Christology itself is Matthean, but this specific way of talking about the Father and the Son does sound Johannine. The issue is actually an accident of context. Matthew's Jesus has been praying to his Father (11:25) and goes on to talk typically of "my Father" (11:27). But now he is setting up the repetitive converse statement, which requires a rhythm that does not use the possessive that he usually uses. Jesus is speaking, and so he cannot say "my Son." In order to make the poetry work, the pair "the Son" and "the Father" is required. Matthew's Jesus is simply referring back to these possessives established previously and balancing the clauses of the repetitive converse statement.

When viewed as an element in Matthew's Gospel, the so-called Johannine thunderbolt looks quite at home. It is driven through with language and theology that is typical of Matthew. The verses also work well in their Lukan context, and when Luke copies Matthew as closely as he does here, we have reason to imagine that the material was highly congenial. It is worth noting that the context for the saying segues in Luke into a series of passages, some from Matthew, some new, which further explore the themes related to the fatherhood of God.[43]

---

40. "Heavenly Father" has figures of 7/0/0/0; "Father who is in heaven" has figures of 13/1/0/0.

41. Matt 7:21; 10:32, 33; 11:27; 12:50; 16:17; 18:10, 19; 20:23; 25:34; 26:29, 39, 42, 53 (this excludes Matt 8:21, which references a human father); John 2:16; 5:17, 43; 6:32, 40; 8:19 (twice), 49, 54; 10:18, 25, 29, 37; 14:2, 7, 20, 21, 23; 15:1, 8, 10, 15, 23, 24; 20:17.

42. This excludes references like Luke 9:59, Luke's parallel to Matt 8:21 (previous note).

43. This is especially clear in relation to Luke 11:1–13, which deals with father-son relationships and prayer. Cf. Goodacre, *Case Against Q*, 111–12.

John's Christological Transformation of the Synoptics

While the wording in Matt 11:27 // Luke 10:22 does not occur verbatim in John, there are multiple parallels in the gospel.[44] The idea that "all things have been given to me by my Father" is a clear emphasis in John, perhaps most explicitly in John 13:3, "Jesus, knowing that the Father had given all things into his hands" (εἰδὼς ὅτι πάντα ἔδωκεν αὐτῷ ὁ πατὴρ εἰς τὰς χεῖρας), but often elsewhere (e.g., 5:19–20, 22; 10:29; 12:49; 17:2–5). Similarly, the idea of mutual knowledge of the Father and the Son recurs in John, perhaps most explicitly in John 10:14–15, where the knowledge is similarly extended to Jesus's own, "I am the good shepherd, and I know my own and my own know me, just as the Father knows me and I know the Father" (ἐγώ εἰμι ὁ ποιμὴν ὁ καλός, καὶ γινώσκω τὰ ἐμὰ καὶ γινώσκουσί με τὰ ἐμά, καθὼς γινώσκει με ὁ πατὴρ κἀγὼ γινώσκω τὸν πατέρα), but again, these kinds of thoughts are pervasive in John (e.g., 7:27–29; cf. 17:20–23, 25–26).

My suggestion is that the saying in Matt 11:27 // Luke 10:22 is among the most important sources for the Fourth Evangelist's thinking. It is key for the development of his Christology. So much of what he finds in the Synoptics is oblique, subtle, suggestive. But here is a clear statement of Jesus's relationship to the Father, not expressed in kingdom imagery, not expressed in parables, not expressed through "Son of Man" language. It is an unambiguous christological claim that coheres with the evangelist's thinking, and it becomes a central source of his theological reflection. It gives birth to his favorite language, first of "my Father," which is also some of Matthew's favorite language, and then to "the Father" and "the Son," and the intimacy of their relationship. John's knowledge of the Synoptics differs here from Matthew's and Luke's use of Mark. It is not so much source utilization as source inspiration. This passage and others like it inspire John's Christology.

In other words, we may have got the image the wrong way round. The direction of influence is from the Synoptics to John, and not the reverse. The enjoyable absurdity of the metaphor of a "Johannine thunderbolt," a "bolt from the blue," or an "Aerolith" should have alerted us that something was wrong. We have been misreading the Synoptics in light of our familiarity with John. The language and theology of the thunderbolt, with its underlining of Jesus's divine authority, and its stress on the Father and the Son, is at home in Matthew where it had its genesis. As Benedict Viviano says, "So far from being a bolt from the Johannine sky, Matt 11:27 is a/the germ from which all later Christology, including and especially the Johannine, develops."[45] Or, in other words, this is not so much a bolt from the Johannine blue as it is the Synoptic platform from which John launched his christological rocket.

---

44. See A. Denaux, "The Q-Logion Mt 11,27 / Lk 10,22 and the Gospel of John," in *John and the Synoptics*, ed. A. Denaux, BETL 101 (Leuven: Peeters, 1992), 113–47, at 141–47, for an exhaustive list of parallels.

45. Benedict Viviano, "John's Use of Matthew: Beyond Tweaking," *RB* 111 (2004): 209–37, at 232.

CHAPTER 7

I have argued in this chapter that John effects a christological transformation of the Synoptics. His core christological language derives from the Synoptic Gospels, and he is inspired by them, but he develops them in directions that make his Christology markedly distinct. The idea that Jesus is "the Messiah, the Son of God" is carried forward from the Synoptic Gospels, especially Matthew, and John makes belief in him his reason for writing (John 20:30–31). He also shares a remarkable fourteen different Synoptic terms for Jesus, not only regular ones like Messiah, Son of God, Son of Man, Lord, Teacher, Prophet, Jesus of Nazareth, and King of the Jews, but also less common ones like Rabbi, Rabbouni, King of Israel, Holy One of God, the coming one, and the Savior.

John's "I am" sayings, in spite of being so recognizably and distinctively Johannine, all feature imagery found in the Synoptics, developing Jesus's identification with bread, light, vine, shepherd, door, way, and resurrection. There are no "I am" sayings that feature non-Synoptic imagery. Moreover, the very concept of Jesus saying "I am" finds a close parallel in the walking on the sea (Matt 14:27 // Mark 6:50 // John 6:20), which occurs just before the first of John's "I am" sayings with the predicate, "I am the bread of life" (John 6:35).

Alongside the "I am" sayings, the most noticeable element in John's Christology is his frequent use of "the Father" and "the Son," and the mutual and intimate relationship between them. This, too, appears to be developed from the Synoptics, and especially Matthew, whose gospel has Jesus speaking of "my Father" almost as often as John's. Perhaps the most striking Synoptic passage in this context, though, is Matt 11:27 // Luke 10:22, in which Matthew and Luke speak about "the Father" and "the Son" in a way that sounds Johannine because it inspired his Christology.

So much of John's Christology is in continuity with Synoptic Christology. The key language and the key concepts all find parallels there. What John's Gospel does is to underline, emphasize, and center Jesus language so that it becomes simpler and more direct. The disciples, who so often fail to understand in the Synoptics, hear Jesus clearly in John. "Yes, now you are speaking plainly, not in any figure of speech!"

Conclusion

The Fourth Gospel

One of the oldest examination questions in the field of New Testament studies is "Why was John's Gospel written?" If, as I have been arguing in this book, John knew and used the Synoptics, the question can be focused more specifically: Why did John write this particular gospel, and why is this gospel so different from the others? It is a question that the canon of the New Testament, with its fourfold gospel, itself encourages us to ask. By the time that John says, "In the beginning was the Word," we have already read three gospels in which the focus is on the kingdom of God, the parables, and the Son of Man, in contrast to the Fourth Gospel with its focus on eternal life, the "I am" sayings, and "the Father," and "the Son." Nevertheless, the answer is in part that we tend to overestimate the extent of John's differences from the Synoptics, which in turn lead us to play down how far John was influenced by them. Although it is customary to make dramatic distinctions between the Synoptics and John, there are several ways in which John behaves like a fourth Synoptic Gospel, from similar words and phrases, to parallel passages, to similar sequences of passages, to the structure of the whole gospel, and the work's basic literary conceit—the story of a hidden Messiah who is properly understood only by insiders, and only retrospectively after the experience of the resurrection (see especially chapter 2).

For many, though, the similarities between John and the Synoptics are dwarfed by the differences, and John's distinctive profile makes mutual, independent knowledge of similar oral traditions the preferred model. The model has obvious advantages—it can project some of the most striking Johannine features, like realized eschatology, or John's high Christology, onto the earliest period, and it can make John's Gospel a major player in discussions of the historical Jesus. But for all its attractiveness, the model has serious shortcomings. I have attempted to argue in this book that John's Gospel does not know "Synoptic-like traditions" but the Synoptic Gospels themselves. The gospel is surprisingly similar to Mark in its structure, its conception, and sometimes even its details, right down to "two hundred denarii," "three hundred denarii," and "pistic nard," but it also has close ties with Matthew and Luke in the ways that they reinterpret Mark. In chapter 3, we saw five examples of Matthew's redaction of Mark showing up in John, and five examples of Luke's redaction of Mark similarly showing up in John. The Fourth Gospel is at a unique point in history, still inspired by Mark's Gospel yet influenced by the ways that Matthew and Luke retell its stories.

One of the difficulties with the way that many scholars have read John's Gospel is that they have not really embraced it as "Fourth Gospel," as a literary work that is engaging with Matthew, Mark, and Luke. We have become so enamored with its distinctive take on the Jesus tradition that we have isolated it from any influence from them, at the same time as finding a unique Johannine community that produced it, a community that had itself had no engagement with the Synoptics. Yet so much that we find in John is enriched if we see it in dialogue with them. There are multiple points at which John simply presupposes the narratives of the Synoptics (chapter 4) and appears not only to imagine the readers' knowledge of these events but to build on them to tell its story.

Yet if John knew the Synoptics, it raises the question of how the author engaged with them. I suggested in chapter 5 that John often effected a dramatic transformation of the Synoptics in taking the narrator's words and moving them into direct discourse, as the best dramatists will do, an insight that opens up the possibility that there is also an intertextual dramatic irony in John, where the book takes for granted Synoptic narration in order to give its own stories an added frisson. The difficulty with any view in which John is writing in the dramatic mode, however, is that John has such a prominent and vocal narrator, a point that is largely mitigated by the fact that the book makes its narrator a character in the drama, the legendary Beloved Disciple (chapter 6).

The difficulty with so many scholarly discussions of the Beloved Disciple is that they do not see the character as someone that early readers would have looked for in the works that were most familiar to them, the Synoptic Gospels. Any reader of John who was also a reader of the Synoptics would have had little difficulty in identifying this character as one of the twelve, one of the inner circle, John himself. He self-identifies by declaring, "We have seen his glory" (John 1:14). But if reading John in the light of the Synoptics sheds light on the identity of the Beloved Disciple, reading Jesus in the same way is also illuminating.

John effects a christological transformation of the Synoptics (chapter 7) by using their own familiar imagery, bread and vine, shepherd and sheep, door, way, light of the world, resurrection and life, but making it more direct and unambiguously Jesus centered, the "I am" language itself inspired by the Markan Jesus's absolute uses of "I am" before the high priest, and especially at the walking on the sea, closely paralleled in John, and introduced just before Jesus says, "I am the bread of life." But John draws inspiration also from the mislabeled "Johannine thunderbolt," in which the language of "the Father" and "the Son" develops into a major aspect of early Christian thinking.

To return to where we began this ending, every student of this topic wants to know why John wrote this gospel. We are lucky. Just as Paul told us why he wrote his Epistle to the Romans (Rom 15:15), and Luke told us why he wrote for Theophilus (Luke 1:1–4), so too John tells us why he wrote this gospel. In John 20:30–31, the narrator tells us, "Now Jesus did many other signs in the presence of his disciples that are not written in this book. But these are written so that you may believe that Jesus is the Messiah, the Son of God, and that through believing you may have life in his name." This is a christological reason for composition, with a soteriological application. The one who believes that Jesus is the Messiah, the Son of God, will have "life in his name," itself as Johannine a theme as you can find, which echoes John 3:16, where the one who believes in Jesus will have "eternal life." This life is characteristic of Jesus's own identity, who is "the way, the truth, and the life" (John 14:6). Yet although we hear the distinctive tones of the Fourth Evangelist's theology, it is striking that in the end, the most important confession is something that is already deeply embedded in the Synoptic Gospels, from which John drew his inspiration, that Jesus is "the Messiah, the Son of God." The Fourth Gospel might begin with the Johannine Word made flesh, but it ends by bringing us back to Jesus, Mark's Messiah, the Synoptic Son of God.

There are many Johannine riddles, and the question of the gospel's source material is only one of them. But if John was in relation with Matthew, Mark, and Luke, closer to the heart of the Synoptics than we had previously realized, then we know much more about the book's author, and its first readers, than we do if it emerged in isolation. No one has ever seen the signs source, and we cannot bathe in the pools of oral tradition, but when we read John alongside the Synoptics, we can fully appreciate it as the Fourth Gospel.

Works Cited

Aland, Kurt. *Synopsis of the Four Gospels—English.* Revised printing, Stuttgart: Deutsche Bibelgesellschaft, 1985.

———. *Synopsis of the Four Gospels—Greek/English.* 10th edition. Stuttgart: Deutsche Bibelgesellschaft, 1994.

———. *Synopsis Quattuor Evangeliorum.* 15th rev. ed. Stuttgart: Deutsche Bibelgesellschaft, 1996.

Allison, Dale. "'Jesus Did Not Say to Him That He Would Not Die': John 21:20–23 and Mark 9:1." Paper presented at the Annual Meeting of the Society of Biblical Literature. Baltimore, MD, 2013.

Anderson, Paul N. "The Origin and Development of the Johannine *Egō Eimi* Sayings in Cognitive-Critical Perspective." *JSHJ* 9 (2011): 139–206.

———. *The Riddles of the Fourth Gospel: An Introduction to John.* Minneapolis: Fortress, 2011.

———. "Why This Study Is Needed, and Why It Is Needed Now." Pages 13–74 in *Critical Appraisals of Critical Views.* Vol. 1 of *John, Jesus, and History.* Edited by Paul N. Anderson, Felix Just, SJ, and Tom Thatcher. SymS. Atlanta: Society of Biblical Literature, 2007.

Ashton, John. *Understanding the Fourth Gospel.* 2nd ed. Oxford: Oxford University Press, 2007.

Attridge, Harold W. "John and Other Gospels." Pages 44–62 in *The Oxford Handbook of Johannine Studies.* Edited by Judith M. Lieu and Martinus C. de Boer. Oxford: Oxford University Press, 2018.

Barker, James W. *John's Use of Matthew.* Minneapolis: Fortress, 2015.

Barrett, C. K. *The Gospel According to St. John: An Introduction with Commentary and Notes on the Greek Text.* 2nd ed. Philadelphia: Westminster, 1978.

———. "John and the Synoptic Gospels." *ExpTim* 85 (1974): 228–33.

Bauckham, Richard. "The Beloved Disciple as Ideal Author." *JSNT* 49 (1993): 21–44.

———. "John for Readers of Mark." Pages 147–71 in *The Gospels for All Christians: Rethinking the Gospel Audiences*. Edited by Richard Bauckham. Grand Rapids: Eerdmans, 1998.

———. *The Testimony of the Beloved Disciple*. Grand Rapids: Baker, 2007.

Becker, Eve-Marie, Helen Bond, and Catrin Williams, eds. *John's Transformation of Mark*. London: T&T Clark, 2021.

Blaine, Brad. *Peter in the Gospel of John: The Making of an Authentic Disciple*. Atlanta: Society of Biblical Literature, 2007.

Blinzler, J. *Johannes und die Synoptiker: Ein Forschungsbericht*. SBS 5. Stuttgart: Katholisches Bibelwerk, 1965.

Boer, Esther de. *The Gospel of Mary: Listening to the Beloved Disciple*. London: T&T Clark, 2005.

Bond, Helen. *Caiaphas: Friend of Rome and Judge of Jesus?* Louisville: Westminster John Knox, 2004.

Boomershine, Thomas E. "The Medium and Message of John: Audience Address and Audience Identity in the Fourth Gospel." Pages 92–120 in *The Fourth Gospel in First-Century Media Culture*. Edited by Anthony Le Donne and Tom Thatcher. New York: T&T Clark, 2011.

Borchert, G. L. *John 1–11*. NAC 25A. Nashville: Broadman & Holman, 1996.

Boring, Eugene. *An Introduction to the New Testament: History, Literature, Theology*. Louisville: Westminster John Knox, 2012.

Bowen, C. R. "The Fourth Gospel as Dramatic Material." *JBL* 49 (1930): 292–305.

Brant, Jo-Ann. *Dialogue and Drama: Elements of Greek Tragedy in the Fourth Gospel*. Peabody, MA: Hendrickson, 2004.

———. *John*. PCNT. Grand Rapids: Baker, 2011.

Bultmann, Rudolf. *History of the Synoptic Tradition*. Translated by John Marsh. Oxford: Blackwell, 1963.

Cadbury, H. J. *The Style and Literary Method of Luke*. Cambridge: Harvard University Press, 1920.

Caird, George B. "Charles Harold Dodd, 1884–1973." *Proceedings of the British Academy* 60 (1974): 497–510.

Chancey, Mark. *Greco-Roman Culture and the Galilee of Jesus*. SNTSMS 134. Cambridge: Cambridge University Press, 2011.

Charlesworth, James H. *The Beloved Disciple: Whose Witness Validates the Gospel of John?* Valley Forge, PA: Trinity International, 1995.

Connick, C. M. "The Dramatic Character of the Fourth Gospel." *JBL* 67 (1948): 159–69.

Conzelmann, Hans. "Present and Future in the Synoptic Tradition." *JTC* 5 (1968): 26–44.

Crossan, John Dominic. *The Birth of Christianity: Discovering What Happened in the*

Years Immediately After the Execution of Jesus. San Francisco: HarperSanFrancisco, 1998.

Davies, Margaret. *Rhetoric and Reference in the Fourth Gospel*. JSNTSup 69. Sheffield: Sheffield Academic, 1992.

Denaux, A., ed. *John and the Synoptics*. BETL 101. Leuven: Peeters, 1992.

———. "The Q-Logion Mt 11,27 / Lk 10,22 and the Gospel of John." Pages 113–47 in *John and the Synoptics*. Edited by A. Denaux. BETL 101. Leuven: Peeters, 1992.

Dodd, C. H. *Historical Tradition in the Fourth Gospel*. Cambridge: Cambridge University Press, 1963.

———. *The Interpretation of the Fourth Gospel*. Cambridge: Cambridge University Press, 1953.

Duke, Paul D. *Irony in the Fourth Gospel*. Atlanta: John Knox, 1985.

Engberg-Pedersen, Troels. *John and Philosophy: A New Reading of the Fourth Gospel*. Oxford: Oxford University Press, 2017.

Gardner-Smith, Percival. *St. John and the Synoptic Gospels*. Cambridge: Cambridge University Press, 1938.

Goodacre, Mark. *The Case Against Q: Studies in Marcan Priority and the Synoptic Problem*. Harrisburg, PA: Trinity International, 2002.

———. "The Evangelists' Use of the Old Testament and the Synoptic Problem." Pages 281–98 in *New Studies in the Synoptic Problem: Oxford Conference, April 2008; Essays in Honour of Christopher M. Tuckett*. Edited by Paul Foster, Andrew Gregory, John S. Kloppenborg, and Joseph Verheyden. BETL 239. Leuven: Peeters, 2011.

———. "The Farrer Hypothesis." Pages 47–66 in *The Synoptic Problem: Four Views*. Edited by Stanley E. Porter and Bryan R. Dyer. Grand Rapids: Baker, 2016.

———. "Fatigue in the Synoptics." *NTS* 44 (1998): 45–58.

———. "How Empty Was the Tomb?" *JSNT* 44 (2021): 134–48.

———. "Parallel Traditions or Parallel Gospels? John's Gospel as a Re-imagining of Mark." Pages 77–90 in *John's Transformation of Mark*. Edited by Eve-Marie Becker, Helen Bond, and Catrin Williams. London: T&T Clark, 2021.

———. "The Protevangelium of James and the Creative Rewriting of Matthew and Luke." Pages 57–76 in *Connecting Gospels: Beyond the Canonical/Noncanonical Divide*. Edited by Francis Watson and Sarah Parkhouse. Oxford: Oxford University Press, 2018.

———. "Re-walking the 'Way of the Lord': Luke's Use of Mark and His Reaction to Matthew." Pages 26–43 in *Luke's Literary Creativity*. Edited by Jesper Tang Nielsen and Mogens Müller. LNTS 550. London: Bloomsbury, 2016.

———. "Taking Our Leave of Mark-Q Overlaps: Major Agreements and the Farrer

Theory." Pages 201–22 in *Gospel Interpretation and the Q Hypothesis*. Edited by Mogens Müller and Heike Omerzu. LNTS 573. London: Bloomsbury, 2018.

———. *Thomas and the Gospels: The Case for Thomas's Familiarity with the Synoptics*. Grand Rapids: Eerdmans, 2012.

———. "Too Good to Be Q: High Verbatim Agreement in the Double Tradition." Pages 82–100 in *Marcan Priority Without Q: Explorations in the Farrer Hypothesis*. Edited by John C. Poirier and Jeffrey Peterson. LNTS 455. London: T&T Clark, 2015.

Goodwin, Charles. "How Did John Treat His Sources?" *JBL* 73 (1954): 61–75.

Goulder, Michael D. *Luke: A New Paradigm*. JSNTSup 20. Sheffield: Sheffield Academic, 1989.

———. *Midrash and Lection in Matthew*. London: SPCK, 1974.

Harnack, Adolf von. *Luke the Physician: The Author of the Third Gospel and the Acts of the Apostles*. London: Williams & Norgate, 1907.

Hase, Karl von. *Geschichte Jesu, nach akademischen Vorlesungen*. Leipzig: Breitkopf & Härtel, 1876; 2nd ed., 1891.

Hengel, Martin. *The Johannine Question*. London: SCM, 1989.

Hitchcock, F. R. M. "Is the Fourth Gospel a Drama?" *Theology* 7 (1923): 307–17.

Hobart, William K. *The Medical Language of St. Luke*. Grand Rapids: Baker, 1954.

Jeremias, Joachim. *The Parables of Jesus*. Rev. ed. Translated by S. H. Hooke. London: SCM, 1963.

Kähler, Martin. *The So-Called Historical Jesus and the Historic Biblical Christ*. Translated by Carl E. Braaten. Philadelphia: Fortress, 1964.

Kümmel, W. G. *Introduction to the New Testament*. Rev. ed. Nashville: Abingdon, 1975.

Lincoln, Andrew. *The Gospel According to St. John*. BNTC. London: Continuum, 2005.

Marcus, Joel. *John the Baptist in History and Theology*. SPNT. Columbia: University of South Carolina Press, 2018.

———. *The Way of the Lord: Christological Exegesis of the Old Testament in the Gospel of Mark*. Louisville: Westminster John Knox, 1992.

Martyn, J. Louis. *History and Theology in the Fourth Gospel*. 3rd ed. Louisville: Westminster John Knox, 2003.

Méndez, Hugo. "Did the Johannine Community Exist?" *JSNT* 42 (2020): 350–74.

———. *The Gospel of John: A New History*. Oxford: Oxford University Press, 2025.

Miller, Susan. "'Among You Stands One Whom You Do Not Know' (John 1:26): The Use of the Tradition of the Hidden Messiah in John's Gospel." Pages 243–63 in *The Ways That Often Parted: Essays in Honor of Joel Marcus*. Edited by Lori Baron, Jill Hicks-Keeton, and Matthew Thiessen. Atlanta: SBL Press, 2018.

Morris, Leon. *The Gospel According to John*. Rev. ed. NICNT. Grand Rapids: Eerdmans, 1995.

———. "John, Gospel According to." *ISBE* 2:1098–1107.

Muddiman, John. "John's Use of Matthew: A British Exponent of the Theory." *ETL* 59 (1983): 333–37.

Myers, Alicia D., and Bruce G. Schuchard, eds. *Abiding Words: The Use of Scripture in the Gospel of John*. Atlanta: SBL Press, 2015.

Neirynck, F. "The Anonymous Disciple in John 1." *ETL* 66 (1990): 5–37. Reproduced on pages 617–50 in *Evangelica II: 1982–1991; Collected Essays by Frans Neirynck*. Edited by F. Van Segbroeck. Leuven: Leuven University Press, 1991.

———. "John 4,46–54: Signs Source and/or Synoptic Gospels." *ETL* 60 (1984): 367–75.

———. "John and the Synoptics: The Empty Tomb Stories." Pages 571–99 in *Evangelica II: 1982–1991; Collected Essays by Frans Neirynck*. Edited by F. Van Segbroeck. Leuven: Leuven University Press, 1991.

The New English Bible: New Testament. Oxford: Oxford University Press; Cambridge: Cambridge University Press, 1961.

North, Wendy E. S. *What John Knew and What John Wrote: A Study in John and the Synoptics*. Lanham: Lexington, 2020.

O'Day, Gail R. "The Johannine Literature." Pages 70–85 in *The New Testament Today*. Edited by Mark Allan Powell. Louisville: Westminster John Knox, 1999.

Painter, J. "The Johannine Literature." Pages 555–90 in *Handbook to Exegesis of the New Testament*. Edited by Stanley E. Porter. NTTS 25. Leiden: Brill, 1997.

Parker, Pierson. "John the Son of Zebedee and the Fourth Gospel." *JBL* 81 (1962): 35–43.

Parsenios, George L. *Rhetoric and Drama in the Johannine Lawsuit Motif*. WUNT 258. Tübingen: Mohr Siebeck, 2010.

Peterson, Jeffrey. "Matthew's Ending and the Genesis of Luke-Acts: The Farrer Hypothesis and the Birth of Christian History." Pages 140–59 in *Marcan Priority Without Q: Explorations in the Farrer Hypothesis*. Edited by John C. Poirier and Jeffrey Peterson. LNTS 455. London: T&T Clark, 2015.

Poirier, John C., and Jeffrey Peterson, eds. *Marcan Priority Without Q: Explorations in the Farrer Hypothesis*. LNTS 455. London: T&T Clark, 2015.

Reynolds, Barbara, ed. *1937–1943: From Novelist to Playwright*. Vol. 2 of *The Letters of Dorothy L. Sayers*. New York: St. Martin's, 1998.

Rothschild, Clare. *Hebrews as Pseudepigraphon: The History and Significance of the Pauline Attribution of Hebrews*. WUNT 235. Tübingen: Mohr Siebeck, 2009.

Sanders, E. P. *The Tendencies of the Synoptic Tradition*. SNTSMS 9. Cambridge: Cambridge University Press, 1969.

Sayers, Dorothy L. *The Man Born to Be King: A Play-Cycle on the Life of Our Lord and Saviour Jesus Christ*. London: Gollancz, 1943.

Schneiders, Sandra. "'Because of the Woman's Testimony...': Reexamining the Issue of Authorship in the Fourth Gospel." *NTS* 44 (1998): 513–35.

Shepherd, Tom. "The Narrative Function of Marcan Intercalation." *NTS* 41 (1995): 522–40.

Smith, D. Moody. *John Among the Gospels*. 2nd ed. Columbia: University of South Carolina Press, 2001.

Stein, Robert H. "The Matthew-Luke Agreements Against Mark: Insight from John." *CBQ* 54 (1992): 482–502.

Stibbe, M. W. G. "The Elusive Christ: A New Reading of the Fourth Gospel." *JSNT* 44 (1991): 19–37.

Streeter, B. H. *The Four Gospels: A Study of Origins*. London: Macmillan, 1924.

Tripp, Jeffrey. *Direct Internal Quotation in the Gospel of John*. WUNT 493. Tübingen: Mohr Siebeck, 2019.

Van Segbroeck, F., ed. *Evangelica II: 1982–1991; Collected Essays by Frans Neirynck*. Leuven: Leuven University Press, 1991.

Viviano, Benedict. "John's Use of Matthew: Beyond Tweaking." *RB* 111 (2004): 209–37.

Watson, Francis, and Sarah Parkhouse, eds. *Telling the Christian Story Differently: Counter-narratives from Nag Hammadi and Beyond*. London: T&T Clark, 2020.

Watts, Rikki E. *Isaiah's New Exodus in Mark*. Grand Rapids: Baker, 2000.

Westcott, Brooke Foss. *The Gospel According to John: The Authorised Version with Introduction and Notes*. London: Murray, 1894.

Windisch, Hans. "John's Narrative Style." Translated by David Orton. Pages 25–64 in *The Gospel of John as Literature: An Anthology of Twentieth-Century Perspectives*. Edited by Mark Stibbe. NTTS 17. Leiden: Brill, 1993.

Witherington, Ben, III. "What's in a Name? Rethinking the Historical Figure of the Beloved Disciple in the Fourth Gospel." Pages 203–12 in *Aspects of Historicity in the Fourth Gospel*. Vol. 2 of *John, Jesus, and History*. Edited by Paul N. Anderson, Felix Just, SJ, and Tom Thatcher. SymS. Atlanta: Society of Biblical Literature, 2009.

Wrede, D. W. *The Messianic Secret*. Translated by William Wrede. Cambridge: Clarke, 1971. Translation of *Das Messiasgeheimnis in den Evangelien: Zugleich ein Beitrag zum Verständnis des Markusevangeliums*. Göttingen: Vandenhoeck & Ruprecht, 1901.

Index of Authors

Aland, Kurt, 31
Allison, Dale, 126n25, 127, 131n31
Anderson, Paul, 15–16, 141n17
Ashton, John, 39n29
Attridge, Harold W., 62n40

Barker, James W., 45n3, 46n4
Barrett, C. K., 1n1, 34, 46, 58n31, 97n11
Bauckham, Richard, 76n7, 113
Becker, Eve-Marie, 9n20, 45n1
Blaine, Brad, 107n1
Blinzler, J., 76n6
Boer, Esther de, 111n8
Bond, Helen, 9n20, 45n1, 87n18, 88n20
Boomershine, Thomas E., 106n20
Borchert, G. L., 3
Boring, Eugene, 80n12
Bowen, C. R., 94n6
Brant, Jo-Ann, 94n6, 106n21
Bultmann, Rudolf, 74, 99n13

Cadbury, H. J., 61n36
Caird, George B., 2n2
Calvin, John, 1
Chancey, Mark, 29n18
Charlesworth, James H., 108n2
Clement of Alexandria, 1, 131
Connick, C. M., 94n6

Conzelmann, Hans, 43
Crossan, John Dominic, 35n24

Davies, Margaret, 76n7, 83n14, 146n20
Denaux, A., 1n1, 159n44
Dodd, C. H., 2–6
Duke, Paul D., 102n18

Engberg-Pedersen, Troels, 39n29, 43n36

Farrer, Austin, 47n9

Gardner-Smith, Percival, 4–5, 6, 14–15, 22
Goodacre, Mark, 17n40, 22n2, 30n19, 36n26, 45n2, 50n17, 53n21, 55n22, 96n8, 100n14, 133n36, 156, 158n43
Goodwin, Charles, 12
Goulder, Michael D., 47n9, 58n32, 157

Harnack, Adolf von, 61n36
Hase, Karl von, 156n37
Hengel, Martin, 110n7, 113, 132
Hitchcock, F. R. M., 94n6
Hobart, William K., 61n36

Jeremias, Joachim, 2

Kähler, Martin, 36–37, 39
Kümmel, W. G., 1n1

INDEX OF AUTHORS

Leonardo da Vinci, 131
Lincoln, Andrew, 38–39n28, 47n9, 144n19

Marcus, Joel, 104n19, 146n22, 147n23
Martyn, J. Louis, 94
Méndez, Hugo, 125n23, 132n35
Miller, Susan, 40–41n31
Morris, Leon, 14, 16
Muddiman, John, 47n9
Myers, Alicia D., 12n29

Neirynck, Frans, 1n1, 47n9, 101n16, 120n16
North, Wendy E. S., 12n30

O'Day, Gail R., 1n1

Painter, J., 33n21
Parker, Pierson, 132
Parkhouse, Sarah, 38n27
Parsenios, George L., 94n6
Peterson, Jeffrey, 102n17

Reynolds, Barbara, 93n2
Rothschild, Clare, 125n23

Sanders, E. P., 98–99n13
Sayers, Dorothy L., 93–95
Schneiders, Sandra, 111n8
Schuchard, Bruce G., 12n29
Shepherd, Tom, 35n23
Smith, D. Moody, 4n12
Stein, Robert H., 50n15
Stibbe, M. W. G., 41n33
Streeter, B. H., 7, 46, 83

Thackeray, W. M., 106
Tripp, Jeffrey, 12n30

Viviano, Benedict, 159

Watson, Francis, 38n27
Watts, Rikki E., 146n22
Westcott, Brooke Foss, 74n4, 76n6
Williams, Catrin, 9n20, 45n1
Windisch, Hans, 94n6
Witherington, Ben, III, 111n9
Wrede, William, 39

Zeffirelli, Franco, 93, 131

Index of Subjects

Acts of the Apostles, 40, 63–64, 69, 70, 75, 112, 114, 133, 147
Apocryphon of John, 133

Beloved Disciple
  death of, 6, 125–27
  faithfulness of, 40
  as a Galilean disciple, 115–25
  identity of, 107–33
  as a Jerusalem disciple, 113–15
  as narrator, 106, 128–31
  one of the twelve, 108–10
  readers of the Synoptics' attitude toward, 18, 107–33
Bethlehem, 103, 140n16

canonical bias, 12, 38
Christology, John's
  agreement with Matthew, 18, 135–37, 154–59
  coming one, the, 139
  Father and son language, 130–31, 135, 154–59
  from above, 103
  Holy One of God, 139–40
  "I am" sayings, 134, 137, 140–54
  Jesus of Nazareth, 139
  King of Israel, 139–40
  King of the Jews, 139
  Lord, 139–40
  Messiah, 38–44, 45, 73, 103, 119, 126, 135–37, 140, 152, 158, 160, 161, 163
  Prophet, 139
  Rabbi, 139–40
  Rabbouni, 139–40
  Savior, 139–40
  Son of David, 103, 139–40
  Son of God, 14, 18, 73, 135–37, 140, 152, 154, 157–58, 159, 160, 161, 163
  Son of Man, 42, 98, 99, 126, 138, 152
  Teacher, 138
  thunderbolt, Johannine, 154–59, 160, 163
  transformation of Synoptics (*see* Synoptic Gospels: John's dramatic transformation of)
  Word made flesh, 19, 106, 128, 130, 135, 137, 149–50, 163
community, Johannine, 94, 162
consensus, 1

denarii, 15, 28–29, 30, 162
dependence, language of, 15, 17–18
diagnostic shards, 14–17, 72
Dialogue of the Savior, 16, 137

173

differences, appeal to, 1, 5, 6, 8, 14–16, 17, 20, 43, 58, 131, 134, 152, 161
disciples
  Andrew, 19, 25, 32, 79, 82, 84, 102, 111, 112n10, 116, 117, 118, 119, 124
  Bartholomew, 112n10
  as "the chosen," 40, 82–83, 91, 109–10, 113n11, 115, 123
  James, son of Alphaeus, 112n10, 114n13
  James and John, sons of Zebedee, 111–12, 117–25
  Judas Iscariot, 9, 25, 27, 30, 35, 40, 58–60, 72, 82, 83, 101, 109, 112, 114
  Judas not Iscariot, 102, 109, 111, 112n10
  Lebbaeus, 112n10
  Martha and Mary, 26–27, 29, 30, 56, 57, 69, 83–84, 90, 93, 101–2, 123–24, 135–36, 145
  Mary Magdalene, 33, 40, 52, 54, 55, 88, 89, 101, 102, 106, 107, 108, 111, 113
  Mary wife of Clopas, 40, 106
  Matthew, 112n10
  mother of Jesus, 40, 55, 101, 106
  mother of the sons of Zebedee, 112n10, 114
  Nathanael, 19, 82, 102, 107, 111, 112n10, 116, 123, 154
  Peter, 15, 19, 24, 25, 31, 32, 34, 35, 47, 59, 60, 70, 79, 82, 84, 85, 87, 88, 91, 98, 101, 105, 107, 109, 111–29, 135–36, 145
  Philip, 25, 82, 102, 109, 110, 111, 112n10, 116
  Simon the Cananaean (Zealot), 112n10
  Thaddaeus, double-checking, 112n10
  Thomas, doubting, 25, 102, 107, 108n2, 109, 111, 112n10, 113, 123, 146
drama and dramatic mode, 93–106

direct speech, Johannine, 94–97, 128
direct speech, Lucan, 99n13, 102
direct speech, Matthean, 98–100
dramatic irony, intertextual, 86, 102–3
dramatis personae, altering, 25, 101–2
revision, dramatic, 104–5

eschatology
  eternal life, 3, 19, 154, 161, 163
  kingdom of God, 2–3, 19, 51, 126–27, 134, 149, 154, 157, 161
  realized, 2–4, 19, 161
E. T. (film), 107

family, metaphorical, 55–56
fatigue, editorial, 30, 56
form criticism, 5

Gospel of Mary, 16, 111n8, 137
Gospel of Peter, 110, 124, 133
Gospel of Philip, 111n8, 151
Gospel of Thomas, 1–2, 17, 38, 132–33, 137, 151

Hebrews, Epistle to the, 125n23
hidden Messiah, 38–44, 45, 161
historical Jesus, 2, 3, 5, 161

interpolations and jumbled sheets, 81, 91
introductory classes, 5, 20, 25, 39, 91, 113, 131
Jesus. See Christology, John's; historical Jesus
John the Elder, 107, 108, 109, 123, 132n34

Lazarus, 19, 26, 29, 56–57, 83–84, 90, 93, 107, 108, 111, 123, 142, 145, 146
literary conceit, 18, 38–44, 72, 161
locusts, fried, 95
Luke's Gospel

knowledge of Matthew, 1, 2, 53–54, 58n33, 96, 102
Lucan redaction in John, 18, 30, 45, 56–70, 71–72, 106, 162
medical language in, 60–61
narrator in, 71–72, 102

Mark-Q overlaps, 22n2
Mark's Gospel
disciples in, 40, 42, 82, 84, 85, 109, 111–12, 114, 116–21, 125–27, 160
"I am" sayings in, 152–54, 160, 162–63
intercalation, 34–35
John's agreements with, 6–9, 36–44, 152–54
narrator in, 66, 78, 94–100, 104, 105
Mary, Gospel of. *See* Gospel of Mary
Matthew's Gospel
Matthean redaction in John, 10, 18, 30, 45–55, 71–72, 162
minor agreements with Luke, 53–54, 96n10
narrator in, 71–72, 100–101, 102
poetry in, 25, 157–58
messianic secret. *See* hidden Messiah
mother of Jesus, 40, 106

narrator, Johannine, 41, 75, 79, 82, 104–6, 115, 119, 120, 128–31, 133, 162
Nature of the Rulers (Hypostasis of the Archons), 16, 72
New English Bible, 3

Old Testament, John's use of, 12, 96n9
omission of material, John's, 16–17, 85, 96
oral tradition
access to, 14, 16
appeal of, 3–6, 161
contrasted with links, 71–72

difficulties with, 28–29, 33–34, 37, 43–44, 47–48, 50, 58, 60, 71–72, 89–91, 150–51, 161–62
evangelists' skepticism about, 6
"Synoptic-like," 17, 39, 89, 161
watery imagery for, 5, 16, 71, 150, 151, 163
orders, parallel, 31–38, 44, 161

Paul, 2, 38, 69, 70, 73–74n1, 75, 107, 112, 114, 136, 147, 151, 156n37, 163
Peter, Gospel of. *See* Gospel of Peter
Philip, Gospel of. *See* Gospel of Philip
Protevangelium of James, 16, 30, 100–101, 124, 133
pseudepigraphic hesitation, 124
pseudepigraphon, John's Gospel as, 132–33

Q hypothesis, 1, 5, 31, 38, 156

redaction criticism, 25
replacing the Synoptics, 92
resurrection
as hermeneutical key, 42–43
in John, 10–11, 15, 31, 34, 36, 39, 42–43, 88–89, 102, 113, 116, 120–23, 133, 134, 141–42, 145–46, 151, 152, 160, 161, 162
in Luke, 10–11, 42, 89, 102
in Mark, 42–43, 88–89
in Matthew, 6, 88–89, 102
in Paul, 2

Satan, 58–60
selectivity
in John, 16–17, 73, 74–75
in Luke, 74
in Mark, 73–74
in Paul, 73n1
self-representation, authorial, 132–33
signs, 16–17, 163

signs source, 5, 47n9, 81, 89, 90–91, 163
structures, literary, 1, 17, 18, 19, 20, 25–28, 34–35, 36–38, 43–44, 148, 161–62
synopsis, Gospels in, 20–31, 43
Synoptic Gospels
  definition of, 20–30
  firewall between John and, 19–20, 152
  John's christological transformation of, 18, 134–60, 162–63
  John's dramatic transformation of, 18, 85–86, 92, 93–106, 162
  as John's intertexts, 92
  John's presupposition of, 18, 55n23, 58n31, 73–92, 95–96, 102–3, 162
synoptic problem, 1, 20, 43, 96n8

tadpoles, 95
Thomas, Gospel of. *See* Gospel of Thomas
two-source theory, 1

verbal agreement, extent of, 6–18
virginal conception, 103

Index of Scripture and Other Ancient Texts

Old Testament

Genesis
1:1 — 19
2–4 — 72

Exodus
23:20 — 96n8

1 Kings
17:18 — 12

Psalms
22:19 — 12
82:6 — 12

Qoheleth (Ecclesiastes)
1:1 — 124
12:9 — 124

Isaiah
5 — 148
6:9–10 — 40
6:10 — 41
7:14 — 140
40:1 — 96, 151
53:1 — 12, 41

Jeremiah
18 — 151

Micah
5:4 — 145

Zechariah
13:7 — 145

Malachi
3:1 — 96n8

Deuterocanonical Books

Wisdom of Solomon
9:7–8 — 125

Ancient Jewish Writers

Josephus

Antiquities
18.5.2 — 104n19

New Testament

Matthew
1–2 — 37
1:1 — 137
1:1–17 — 103
1:1–18 — 19, 118n15
1:16 — 137
1:17 — 137
1:18 — 137
1:18–25 — 103
1:19 — 100
1:23 — 139–40
2:1–12 — 103
2:2 — 139
2:4 — 100–101, 137
2:6 — 145
2:20 — 103
2:23 — 139
3:1 — 60, 104
3:1–6 — 32
3:1–12 — 118
3:1–17 — 37, 118
3:2 — 98n13
3:3 — 96n8, 138, 147, 151
3:5–6 — 78
3:6 — 104

3:7	78–79	6:14–15	157	10:5–15	82
3:11	21–22, 139	7:3	55	10:9–10	98n13
3:11–12	32	7:4	55	10:23	138
3:13–17	32, 78, 118	7:5	55	10:32	158n41
3:16	78, 96n10	7:9	143n18	10:33	158n41
3:17	137, 158	7:13–14	142, 144, 147, 151	11:2	137
4:1–11	118, 158	7:14	146	11:3	139
4:3	137	7:21	69n48, 138, 158n41	11:4–6	74n2
4:3–4	143n18	7:22	69n48, 138	11:5	142, 145
4:6	137	7:29	157	11:10	96n8
4:9	157	8:1–4	47	11:19	138
4:12	77	8:2	138	11:23	79
4:12–17	118	8:5	79	11:25	158
4:13	80	8:5–13	32, 47	11:25–27	154–59
4:18	112n10, 117, 118	8:6	138	11:27	158, 160
4:18–22	32, 47, 79, 82, 111, 116, 118	8:8	138	12:8	138
		8:14–15	47	12:9	69
4:20	117	8:15	46–48	12:10	98n13
4:21	112n10, 117, 119	8:16–17	74n2	12:15	74n2
4:21–22	117	8:19	138	12:32	138
4:22	121	8:20	138	12:38	138
4:23	86	8:21	138, 158n41	12:40	138
4:23–25	47, 74n2	8:25	138	12:46–50	55
5–7	47	8:29	137	12:48	55
5:2	50	8:32	98n13	12:49	55
5:13	144	9:1–8	7	12:50	158
5:14	141, 144, 150	9:6	138	13:10	98
5:18	78n8	9:9–10	82	13:10–17	40
5:19	157	9:11	138	13:13–15	40
5:22	55	9:18–26	142, 145	13:14–16	40
5:23	55	9:28	138	13:37	138
5:24	55	9:35	86	13:41	138
5:29	61n37	9:36	145	13:54	86
5:30	61n37	9:38	138	13:54–58	118n15
5:37	69n48	10:1–4	82	13:57	139
5:39	61n37	10:2	111, 112n10	14:1–12	77
5:47	55	10:2–4	112n10	14:13–21	25, 32, 97, 141, 143, 150
6:3	61n37	10:3	114		
6:11	141, 143	10:4	59n34	14:14	74n2

14:20	97n11	17:22	138	22:24	138
14:22–33	8n17, 32, 152	17:22–23	145	22:32	145
14:26–27	153–54	17:24	79, 138	22:36	138
14:27	160	17:24–27	112n10	23:8	55, 138
14:28	138	18:1	98n13	23:10	137
14:28–33	112n10	18:10	158n41	23:37	69n48
14:30	138	18:10–14	142, 145	23:39	139
14:33	137, 158	18:15	55	24:17	62
14:34–36	74n2	18:19	158n41	24:27	138
15:10–11	50	18:21	55, 138	24:30	138
15:15	98, 101	18:21–22	112n10	24:37	138
15:22	98, 138	18:35	55	24:42	138
15:25	138	19:16	138	24:44	138
15:27	138	19:27–30	112n10	25:11	69n48, 138
15:29–31	72n4	19:28	138	25:31	138
15:32–39	33, 141, 143	20:1–16	143, 148	25:31–46	142, 145, 146
16:5–12	141, 143	20:17–19	145	25:32	145
16:13	138	20:18	138	25:34	158n41
16:13–20	32, 112n10	20:20–28	112	25:37	138
16:13–27	126	20:22	114n12	25:40	55
16:14	139	20:22–23	85	25:44	138
16:16	137, 158	20:23	158n41	25:46	146
16:17	158n41	20:28	138	26:1–2	99
16:19	157	20:30	138	26:2	138
16:21–23	112n10, 145	20:31	138	26:3	87
16:22	138	20:33	50, 138	26:6	26
16:27	138	21:1–9	32	26:6–13	25–30, 32, 58, 84, 101
16:28	126, 138	21:3	138		
17:1	111, 126	21:9	139	26:7	57n27
17:1–8	112n10, 128	21:11	139	26:7–11	26–28
17:1–13	126	21:12–13	31, 32	26:9	57n27
17:4	128–29, 138	21:14	74n2	26:12	25, 57n27
17:5	130, 137, 158	21:16	8	26:14	59n34, 83
17:8	50	21:28–32	143, 148	26:14–15	98n13
17:9	98, 138	21:33–46	143, 148	26:17–19	112
17:12	138	21:37	149, 158	26:18	138
17:15	130, 138	21:46	63, 139	26:20	108–9
17:16	135–36	22:16	138, 147	26:21	9, 109
17:20	8	22:23–33	142, 145	26:21–25	32

INDEX OF SCRIPTURE AND OTHER ANCIENT TEXTS

26:22	138	27:15	66	1:2	96n8
26:23	109	27:17	137	1:2–3	95, 146, 147
26:24	138	27:22	137	1:2–4	94
26:25	139	27:27–29	48–50	1:2–6	32
26:26	141, 143	27:28–29	9–10	1:2–8	118
26:27	99	27:29	139	1:2–11	118
26:28	149	27:30	50n16	1:3	19, 142, 147, 151
26:29	143, 148–49, 150, 158n41	27:32–56	33	1:4	96, 98n13, 104
		27:37	139	1:4–5	94
26:30–35	32	27:40	137	1:5	78, 104
26:31	84, 142, 145	27:42	139	1:6	94
26:31–35	112n10	27:43	137	1:7–8	21–22, 32
26:36–46	16, 85, 112n10, 114	27:46	16	1:9	139
		27:48	100n14	1:9–11	32, 78, 118
26:37	111	27:54	137, 158	1:10	78, 96
26:39	85, 158n41	27:56	112n10, 114	1:11	137, 157
26:42	158n41	27:57–58	51–52	1:12–13	118
26:45	138	27:57–61	33	1:14	76
26:47	83	27:59–60	52–54	1:14–15	118
26:47–56	32	27:60	88	1:15	3
26:49	139	27:61	52, 89	1:16	117, 118
26:50	62	27:62–66	53	1:16–20	32, 47, 79, 82, 111, 112n10, 116, 118
26:51	50	27:65–66	88		
26:51–52	22–25	28	142, 145	1:18	117
26:53	24n6, 158n41	28:1	89, 101	1:19	117, 119
26:56	84	28:1–2	89	1:20	117, 121
26:57	87	28:1–8	33	1:21	79, 86
26:57–68	32, 34	28:9–10	33, 54–56	1:21–39	118n15
26:58	112n10, 115	28:10	54–56	1:24	15, 135, 139
26:63	136, 137	28:11–15	6, 53	1:27	157
26:64	138	28:16–20	33	1:29	111
26:65–66	98n13	28:17	25, 102	1:29–31	47, 112n10
26:68	137	28:19	157	1:31	46–48
26:69	101n15			1:32–34	74n2
26:69–75	32, 34, 112n10	**Mark**		1:35	40
26:71	139	1:1	137	1:36	112n10
27:1–2	33	1:1–8	37	1:39	47, 86
27:11	69, 139	1:1–10:52	36	1:40–45	47
27:11–26	33	1:1–14:43	37	2:1	79

Index of Scripture and Other Ancient Texts

2:1–12	6–8	5:7	137	7:28	138
2:1–3:6	36	5:13	98n13	7:33	40
2:9	7	5:19	138	8	15
2:9–12	7–8	5:21	80	8:1–10	33, 141, 143
2:10	7, 138	5:21–43	35, 142, 145	8:4	97
2:10–12	47	5:25–34	35	8:8	97
2:13	79	5:35	138	8:9–10	40
2:13–14	82	5:35–43	35	8:13	40, 81
2:28	138	5:37	111, 112n10	8:14–21	141, 143
3:2	69, 98n13	6	15	8:17	40
3:6	78n8	6:1–6	118n15	8:22–10:52	147n23
3:7	40, 79	6:2	86	8:23	40
3:7–8	47	6:4	139	8:27	142, 147n23
3:10	74n2	6:6b–32	35	8:27–30	32
3:11	137	6:7–13	82	8:27–38	126
3:13	40	6:8–9	98n13	8:28	139
3:13–19	82, 112n10	6:13	74n2	8:29	135–36, 137
3:16	112n10	6:14–29	35, 77	8:31	138
3:16–18	111	6:15	139	8:31–33	112n10, 142, 145
3:17	112n10	6:30–32	35	8:38	138
3:18	114n13	6:30–44	25, 97	9:1	126, 127
3:19	59n34	6:31–32	40	9:2	40, 111, 126
3:20–35	35	6:32–44	32, 141, 143, 150	9:2–8	112n10, 128
3:22–30	35	6:34	145	9:2–13	126
3:31–35	35, 55	6:37	15, 29	9:5	128, 139
3:33	55n25	6:38	8	9:5–6	129
3:34	55n25	6:42	97	9:7	130, 137, 157
3:35	158	6:45	80	9:8	50
4:1	79	6:45–52	32	9:9	98, 138
4:2	74	6:46	40, 69n48	9:9–10	42
4:10	40, 98	6:49–50	153–54	9:12	138
4:10–12	40	6:50	8, 160	9:17	138
4:12	40	6:52	40	9:19	8
4:33	74	6:53–56	74n2, 152	9:30–32	142, 145
4:34	40	7:14–15	50	9:31	138
4:35	80	7:17	98, 101	9:32	40
4:36	40	7:24	40	9:33	79
4:38	138, 139n15	7:26	98	9:33–34	142, 147n23
5:1	80	7:27	96n8, 97	9:34	98n13

INDEX OF SCRIPTURE AND OTHER ANCIENT TEXTS

9:38	138, 139n15	12:6	149, 157	14:27	40, 84, 142, 145
9:38–41	112	12:12	63	14:32–33	40
9:41	137	12:14	138, 147	14:32–42	16, 85, 105, 112n10, 114
9:43	61n37	12:18–27	142, 145		
10:17	138, 142, 147n23	12:19	138	14:33	111
10:20	138	12:27	145	14:35	105
10:24	8	12:32	138	14:36	85, 158
10:28–31	112n10	13:1	138	14:41	138
10:30	55n25	13:3	40, 111, 112n10, 114	14:43	83
10:32	142, 147n23	13:6–9	148	14:43–52	32, 37
10:32–34	142, 145	13:10	98	14:43–16:8	37
10:33	138	13:21–22	137n3	14:45	69n48, 139
10:35	138	13:26	138	14:46	62
10:35–45	112	14:1	99	14:47	22–25, 60–61, 101
10:38–39	85	14:1–2	35	14:48–49	61–64
10:45	138	14:1–11	35	14:49	74
10:46	142, 147n23	14:3	14, 26, 57n27	14:50	84
10:47	139	14:3–7	26–28	14:50–52	40
10:48	138	14:3–9	25–30, 32, 35, 58, 84, 101	14:53–65	32, 87
10:51	50, 139			14:53–72	35
10:52	142, 147n23	14:4	30, 57n27	14:54	34, 112n10, 115
11:1–10	32	14:5	30, 57n27	14:55	69n50
11:1–11	37	14:6	30	14:55–65	34, 35
11:1–16:8	37	14:8	25	14:61	136–37
11:3	138, 143	14:9	62	14:61–62	152
11:5–8	143	14:10	83, 98n13	14:62	138
11:9	139	14:10–11	35, 58–60	14:63–64	152
11:12–14	35	14:12–16	112	14:64	98n13
11:12–25	35	14:14	138	14:66	101n15
11:15–17	31, 32	14:17	108	14:66–72	32, 34, 35, 112n10
11:15–19	35	14:18	9, 109		
11:18	69	14:18–21	32	14:67	139
11:19	40	14:20	109	14:69	101n15
11:20–24	112n10	14:21	138	15:1–15	33
11:20–25	35	14:22	141, 143	15:2	69, 139
11:21	139	14:23	99	15:6	66
11:25	158	14:24	149	15:6–8	97
11:27–12:44	74	14:25	143, 148–49, 150	15:6–9	64–66
12:1–12	143, 148	14:26–31	32, 112n10	15:9	139

Index of Scripture and Other Ancient Texts

15:12	139	1:39–80	38	4:41	137
15:12–14	66–67	1:43	138	4:44	86
15:15	98	1:76	139	5:1	74n3, 81
15:16–18	48–50	2:1–20	103	5:1–10	122
15:17–18	9–10	2:4	103	5:1–11	31, 32, 33, 82, 111, 112n10, 116–17, 122–25
15:18	139	2:11	103, 137, 138, 139		
15:19	50n16	2:26	137		
15:21–41	33	2:49	158	5:2	81, 117, 118
15:26	139	3:1–6	32	5:3	118
15:32	137, 139	3:1–20	37	5:8	117, 118–19, 138
15:36	100n14	3:1–22	118	5:10	112n10, 119
15:39	157	3:2	87	5:11	117, 121
15:42–43	51–52	3:3	78n9, 104	5:12	74n3, 138
15:42–47	33	3:4	96n8, 147, 151	5:15	74n2
15:22	98	3:5	147	5:17	74n3
15:24	97	3:7	79	5:17–26	7
15:34	16	3:15	137n3	5:24	138
15:39	137	3:15–18	32	5:27–28	82
15:46	52–54, 88	3:16	21–22, 96n10	6:5	138
15:47	50, 52, 89	3:19–20	77	6:6	60, 86
16	142, 145	3:21	74n3	6:7	69
16:1	89, 101	3:21–22	32, 78	6:12–16	82, 112n10
16:1–4	89	3:22	78, 96n10, 137	6:13	108n4, 109n6
16:1–8	33	3:23–38	118n15	6:14	111, 112n10, 119
16:6	139	3:38	137	6:15	114n13
16:7	112n10	4:3	137	6:16	59n34
16:8	40, 55	4:3–4	143n18	6:17–19	74n2
		4:6	157	6:22	138
Luke		4:9	137	6:29	61n37
1–2	37	4:15	86	6:41	55n25
1:1–4	163	4:16	86	6:42	55n25
1:2	110n7	4:16–30	118	6:46	138
1:5	74n3	4:24	139	7:1–10	32
1:5–25	19, 38	4:31–33	86	7:6	138
1:8	74n3	4:31–44	118	7:11–17	142, 145
1:26–38	103	4:34	139	7:13	138
1:27	103	4:38–39	47, 112n10	7:16	139
1:32	103, 137	4:39	46, 48	7:19	138, 139
1:35	137	4:40–41	74n2	7:20	139

183

7:21–23	74n2	9:27	126	11:45	138
7:22	142, 145	9:28	111, 126	12:8	138
7:27	96n8	9:28–36	112n10, 126, 128	12:10	138
7:34	138	9:31	147	12:13	138
7:36–50	25, 29, 32, 33, 56, 58, 84, 113	9:32	106, 130	12:40	138
7:37–38	56–58	9:32–33	129	12:41	112n10, 138
7:39	139	9:33	128, 139n15	12:42	138
7:40	138	9:35	130, 137	12:58	142, 148
7:41–43	29n17	9:38	138	13:6–9	143
7:44–45	29	9:43–45	145	13:10	86
8:2	74n2	9:44	138	13:15	138
8:10	40	9:49	139n15	13:23	138
8:19–21	55	9:49–50	112n10	13:23–25	144
8:21	55n25	9:51	74n3, 84, 147	13:24	142, 144, 147, 150
8:22	74n3, 81	9:51–56	112	13:33	139
8:23	81	9:54	138	13:34	69n48
8:24	69, 139n15	9:57	147	13:35	139
8:28	137	9:58	138	14:1	74n3
8:33	81	9:59	138, 158n42	15:3–7	142, 145
8:40–56	35, 142, 145	9:61	138	16:19–31	142, 146
8:45	112n10	10:1	138	16:31	146
8:49	138	10:17	74n2, 138	17:3	55n25
8:51	112n10	10:21–22	154–59	17:5	108n4, 138
9:1–6	82	10:22	158, 160	17:11	74n3
9:6	74n2	10:24–27	39–40	17:22	138
9:8	139	10:25	138	17:24	138
9:10	108n4	10:25–37	142, 147	17:26	138
9:10–17	25, 32, 97, 141, 143, 150	10:31	142, 148	17:30	138
		10:38	84	17:37	138
		10:38–39	83n14	18:6	138
9:17	97n11	10:38–42	56, 83–84, 90	18:8	138
9:18	74n3	10:39	138	18:18	138
9:18–20	112n10	10:40	138	18:28–30	112n10
9:18–21	32	10:41	69, 138	18:31	138
9:18–26	126	11:1	74n3, 138	18:31–34	145
9:19	139	11:1–13	158n43	18:35	74n3
9:20	135, 137	11:3	141	18:37	139
9:22	126, 138, 145	11:30	138	18:41	138
9:26	138	11:39	138	19:8	138

Index of Scripture and Other Ancient Texts

19:10	138	22:32	55n25	23:55	89n21
19:28–40	32	22:33	138	24	19, 142, 145
19:31	138	22:38	138	24:1	89n21
19:34	138	22:39–46	16, 85	24:1–12	33
19:36	142, 148	22:42	85	24:2	89n21
19:37	74n2	22:47	83	24:3	138
19:38	139	22:47–53	32	24:5–8	42
19:39	138	22:48	138	24:7	138
19:45–46	31, 32	22:49	138	24:10	89, 101, 108n4
19:47–48	69	22:49–51	22–25	24:12	112n10
20:1	74n3	22:50	50, 60–61	24:13–35	142, 144, 147
20:9–19	143, 148	22:52–53	61–64	24:19	139
20:13	149	22:53	47, 62, 64	24:26	137
20:19	62, 63, 64	22:54–55	115	24:30–31	144
20:21	138, 147	22:54–62	32, 34, 112n10	24:32	142, 148
20:27–40	142, 145	22:54–71	32	24:34	112n10, 138
20:28	138	22:56	101n15	24:35	142, 144, 148
20:38	145	22:61	138	24:36	10–11
20:39	138	22:66–71	34, 87	24:36–49	33
21:7	138	22:67	137	24:38	25, 102
21:12	62	22:69	138	24:40–41	10–11
21:27	138	22:70	137	24:41	102
21:36	138	23:1–5	33	24:46	137
22:3–6	58–60	23:2	69, 137	24:49	158
22:7–13	112, 114	23:3	139		
22:8	112	23:4	66–70	**John**	
22:11	138	23:13–25	33	1	19, 116
22:14	108	23:14	66–70	1–2	75
22:17	149	23:18–19	64–66	1:1	19
22:18	143, 148–49, 150	23:20–22	66–70	1:1–12:11	35
22:19	141, 143	23:22	66–70	1:1–17:26	37
22:20	149	23:26–49	33	1:6–8	37
22:21	109	23:35	137	1:14	41, 106, 116, 128–31, 133, 137, 149, 154, 162
22:21–23	32	23:36	100n14		
22:22	138	23:37	139		
22:23	83	23:38	139	1:15	14n31, 37, 139
22:29	158	23:39	137	1:17	137
22:31	59, 69	23:50–56	33, 89n21	1:18	108n3, 137, 154
22:31–34	32, 112n10	23:53	53	1:19	79

185

1:19–23	32	2:1–11	77, 116	4:23	4
1:19–28	118	2:1–12	36	4:25	137
1:19–36	37	2:2	82	4:27	82
1:20	14n31, 137n3	2:4	12	4:29	14n31, 137
1:22–23	95	2:11	82, 116	4:31	82, 139
1:23	147, 151	2:12	77, 82, 116	4:33	82
1:24	79	2:13–22	32, 36	4:36	154
1:24–28	32	2:13–25	31	4:39	14n31
1:26	40–41n31	2:13–3:21	75	4:42	139
1:26–27	21–22	2:16	158n41	4:43	116
1:27	139	2:17	82	4:43–54	81, 116
1:29	104	2:19–22	36	4:44	139
1:29–34	32, 118	2:22	42, 82	4:45	116
1:30	14n31	3	105	4:45–54	47
1:32	78, 96	3–10	75	4:46	81, 116
1:34	154	3:1	123	4:46–54	32
1:35	118, 120	3:2	138, 139	4:50	14n31
1:35–42	32, 47, 84, 116, 118, 121, 133	3:3	13, 69n48, 154	4:52	46–48
		3:5	69n48, 154	4:53	14n31
1:35–51	77	3:7	13	5	81
1:36	104, 117	3:11	69n48	5:1	75
1:37	117, 118–19, 120	3:13	138	5:1–15	6–8
1:38	117, 121, 138, 139	3:14	138	5:5	7
1:39	117	3:15	154	5:8	7
1:40	117, 119	3:16	3, 137, 154, 163	5:8–9	7–8, 47
1:40–41	119	3:17	137, 154	5:14	75
1:40–42	102	3:18	137	5:15–18	78
1:41	137	3:22	75, 82	5:16	78n8
1:42	117, 119	3:22–24	76	5:17	158n41
1:43	110, 116	3:24	76–77, 89–90	5:18	78n8
1:43–45	110	3:26	139	5:19	69n48, 137
1:43–51	82, 102, 116	3:28	14n31	5:19–20	159
1:44	84, 116	3:31	139	5:20	137
1:45	139	3:35	137	5:21	137
1:45–46	116	3:36	154	5:22	137, 159
1:49	137, 139, 154	4:8	82	5:23	137
1:51	69n48, 138	4:14	154	5:24	69n48, 154
2	82	4:17–18	14n31	5:25	4, 69n48, 137
2:1	116	4:19	139	5:26	137

5:27	138	6:50–58	144	8:1–10	113
5:33	79	6:51	141, 143, 150	8:12	140, 141, 144, 150
5:33–35	77–79	6:53	69n48, 138	8:19	158n41
5:35	77–79	6:54	154	8:20	86
5:39	154	6:59	82, 86, 116	8:28	138
5:43	158n41	6:60	82	8:31–33	13
6	15, 81, 82	6:61	82	8:34	69n48
6:1	75, 79–81, 90, 91, 116	6:62	138	8:36	137
6:1–15	32, 97, 143, 150	6:64	110n7	8:41	103
6:1–71	116	6:65	14n31	8:44	59
6:3	82	6:66	82	8:49	158n41
6:5	102	6:66–71	81–82	8:51	14n31, 69n48, 127
6:5–9	25	6:67–71	32	8:52	3, 14n31, 127
6:7	15, 29, 69, 102	6:68	138, 154	8:54	158n41
6:8	82, 102	6:69	15, 135, 139	8:58	69n48, 150
6:9	101n15	6:70	59, 81–83, 91, 110	8:59	41
6:12	97	6:71	59n34, 109	9:1–41	94
6:14	139	7	62, 103	9:2	139
6:16–21	32	7:1	75, 116	9:5	140, 141, 144, 150
6:17	116	7:1–13	116	9:7	14n31
6:19	82	7:3	116	9:11	14n31
6:19–20	153–54	7:9	116	9:17	139
6:20	8, 160	7:10–11	41	9:21	14n31
6:22–25	152	7:14	86	9:22	137
6:23	116, 138	7:25–29	103	9:23	14n31
6:24	82, 116	7:26	137	9:35	138
6:25	139	7:27	137	9:38	138
6:25–60	143	7:27–29	159	9:39	40
6:26	69n48, 97	7:28	86	9:40	14n31
6:27	138, 154	7:30	47, 61–64	9:41	14n31
6:32	69n48, 158n41	7:31	137	10	150
6:35	14n31, 140, 141, 143, 150, 154, 160	7:37–38	12	10:1	69n48, 144
		7:40	139	10:1–21	144
6:40	137, 154, 158n41	7:41	137	10:2	144
6:41	14n31, 140, 141, 143, 150	7:41–42	102–3	10:7	69n48, 140, 142, 144, 150
		7:42	137		
6:44	14n31	7:44	62, 64	10:9	140, 142, 144, 150
6:47	69n48, 154	7:50	115	10:10	3
6:48	140, 141, 143, 150	7:52	139	10:11	140, 142, 144, 145

INDEX OF SCRIPTURE AND OTHER ANCIENT TEXTS

10:14	140, 142, 144, 145	12:1–2	29	13:7	75n5
10:14–15	159	12:1–8	25–30, 32, 84, 101	13:9	138
10:18	158n41	12:3	14, 56–58	13:10	14n31
10:23	86	12:3–8	26–28	13:11	14n31
10:24	137	12:4	59n34	13:13	138
10:25	158n41	12:6	30	13:14	138
10:28	154	12:7	25, 30	13:16	69n48
10:29	158n41, 159	12:12–19	32, 37	13:18	40, 82, 110, 115
10:30	14	12:12–21:25	37	13:20	69n48
10:31–39	13	12:13	139	13:21	9, 69n48, 109
10:33	14	12:16	42	13:21–30	32, 109, 133
10:34	12	12:21–22	102	13:23	108
10:36	13, 137	12:22	102	13:25	14n31, 138
10:37	158n41	12:23	138	13:26	59n34
11	56, 101	12:24	69n48	13:26–27	58–60
11–12	56	12:25	154	13:26–30	109
11–21	75	12:27	105	13:30	109
11:1	83–84, 123	12:27–30	104–5	13:31	138
11:1–2	90	12:27–33	85	13:32	137
11:1–12:8	102	12:34	137, 138	13:33	40
11:2	56–58, 84, 138	12:36	41	13:36	138
11:3	111n9, 138	12:36–37	41	13:36–38	32
11:4	137	12:37–43	41	13:37	138
11:8	139	12:38	12	13:38	69n48
11:12	138	12:40	40	14:2	158n41
11:16	102	12:41	41	14:4	146
11:21	138	12:47	16	14:5	102, 138, 146
11:25	141, 142, 145	12:49	159	14:5–7	109
11:27	135–36, 137, 138, 139, 145	12:50	154	14:6	134, 141, 142, 146–48, 150–51, 163
11:28	138	13	113		
11:32	138	13–14	109		
11:34	138	13–17	36, 111, 115	14:7	158n41
11:36	111n9	13–20	113	14:8	138
11:38–44	145	13:1	40	14:8–9	102
11:39	138	13:2	59	14:8–14	109
11:46–53	88	13:3	159	14:9	110, 115
11:54	41	13:4–5	29–30	14:12	14, 69n48
12:1	26, 84	13:6	138	14:13	137
		13:6–9	109	14:18	40, 55

14:20	158n41	18:1–12	32	19:3	139
14:21	158n41	18:1–14	37	19:4	66–70
14:22	59n34, 102, 138	18:1–21:25	37	19:5	49
14:22–23	109	18:5	139	19:6	66–70
14:23	158n41	18:6	152	19:7	137
14:28	14	18:7	139	19:19	139
15:1	141, 143, 146, 148–50, 158n41	18:8–9	84n15	19:21	139
		18:10	50, 60–61	19:23	97
15:5	141, 143, 148–50	18:10–11	22–25, 101	19:24	12, 97
15:8	109, 158n41	18:11	24n6, 85–86, 91–92	19:25–27	40, 84, 114n12, 121, 133
15:9	40				
15:10	158n41	18:12–14	87	19:26	111n8
15:12–13	40	18:13	87	19:26–27	111
15:13	56	18:13–24	32	19:28	100n14
15:13–15	40, 56	18:14	115	19:30	16
15:14	56	18:15	34, 115	19:35	84, 121, 133
15:15	56, 158n41	18:15–16	101n15, 113, 114–15	19:38	51–52
15:16	82, 110, 115			19:38–42	88
15:19	82, 110, 115	18:15–18	87	19:39	115
15:23	158n41	18:15–27	35	19:39–42	52
15:24	158n41	18:16	115	19:41	52–54
15:27	110, 115	18:17	101n15	20	113
16:14	14n31	18:18	34	20:1	88
16:15	14n31	18:19	87	20:1–2	88–89
16:16–18	14n31	18:19–23	87	20:1–10	133
16:17	109	18:19–24	34	20:1–18	89, 102
16:20	69n48	18:20	86	20:2	52, 88–89, 101, 138
16:23	69n48	18:22	87	20:2–12	111
16:29	109	18:24	86–88	20:8	40, 121
16:32	4, 84	18:25–27	32, 34, 87	20:13	138
17:1	137	18:28	87	20:16	138, 139
17:2	154	18:33	139	20:17	54–56, 158n41
17:2–5	159	18:38	66–70	20:17–18	54–56
17:3	137, 154	18:39	66, 97, 139	20:18	40, 138
17:12	84n15	18:39–40	64–66	20:19–20	10–11
17:20–23	159	19	113	20:20	40, 138
17:25–26	159	19:1–3	48–50	20:24–29	25, 102
18	113	19:2	49	20:25	40, 138
18:1	109	19:2–3	9–10, 49	20:28	138

20:28–29	40	9:2	147	**Romans**	
20:30–31	135, 160, 162	9:4	69	1:3	38
20:31	136, 137	9:17	147	15:15	163
21	116, 118, 123n21	9:27	147		
21:1	75, 80, 116, 123	12:1	63	**1 Corinthians**	
21:1–14	31, 122–25	12:2	112	7:10–11	74n1
21:1–24	116	12:19	75	7:12–16	74n1
21:1–25	120, 133	13:28	69, 70	11:25	151
21:2	55n23, 88–89, 123	14:3	75	11:26	151
21:3–11	122	14:28	75	11:27	151
21:5	55n26	15:35	75	11:28	151
21:7	111, 138	16:7	147		
21:12	138	16:10–17	133	**Galatians**	
21:15	138	16:12	75	1:18	114
21:15–19	121	18:25	147	1:19	112, 114
21:16	138	18:26	147	2:9	112, 114
21:17	138	19:9	147		
21:18	69n48	19:23	147	**2 Peter**	
21:19	121	20:5–15	133	1:16–18	130n30
21:20	14n31, 108, 121, 138	20:6	75		
21:20–22	121	21:1–8	133	**1 John**	
21:20–23	111, 125, 126	21:27	64	1:1–4	110n7
21:21	138	22:4	147		
21:22	121	22:7	69	**Revelation**	
21:22–23	6	23:9	70	18:13	57n27
21:23	55n25	23:28–29	70		
21:24	125, 128, 133	24:5	70	**Early Christian Writings**	
21:25	17	24:14	147		
		24:20	70	**Acts of John**	
Acts		24:22	147	90	130n30
1:13	112	25:6	75		
1:21	110n7	25:14	75	**Gospel of Peter**	
3:1–11	112, 114	26:13	147	16	100n14
3:7	60	26:14	69	59–60	124
4:1–31	112, 114	27:1–28:16	133		
4:3	63	28:8	48	**Gospel of Philip**	
4:21	70	28:25–27	40	61	151
5:18	63			63	151
8:14–25	112, 114				

Gospel of Thomas		Protevangelium of James		GRECO-ROMAN LITERATURE	
Incipit	38, 133	14:4	100		
1	38	21:4	100–101	Theocritus	
7	151	25:1	124	*Epigrams*	
13	133			16	127n28